This book shows Black wo
interracial relationships and deal with the social pressures that such relationships inevitably attract. It shows how you can clear out your old social conditioning and inhibitions about interracial relationships, tune out the expectations that you should date only Blacks and clarify your reasons for romantic and sexual attraction to White men. This book shows where and how you can go about meeting White men, how to make yourself more interracially approachable, offers guidelines for screening mature and emotionally available White males into your social life and helps you move beyond the shortage of Black men. This book clears away the misconceptions that all too many Black women have about White men and explains what really goes on inside the minds of White men who seek out and date Black women. Women often see men as foreign psychological territory, and racial differences can accentuate such misperceptions and misunderstandings. Black women who have considered the possibilities that interracial relationships offer are all too familiar with the broad spectrum of unspoken taboos and social pressures often serve to block Black women from getting involved in interracial relationships. This book explains the psychosexual origins of the various forms of social opposition to those wearing "the scarlet letter of interracial dating," from the stares interracial couples encounter almost everywhere they go, to why parents work so hard at breaking up the interracial relationships of their offspring to why certain types of disturbed individuals become enraged at the sight of total strangers who happen to be in interracial relationships. Find out how you can best understand, cope with, and tune out, the variety of social pressures that often inhibit Black women from getting, and staying, involved with White men and initiate unembarrassed interracial relationships.

The Interracial Dating Book For Black Women Who Want To Date White Men

Second Edition

Adam White

The Interracial Dating Book For Black Women Who Want To Date White Men
Second Edition
Adam White

ISBN-13:
978-1463678302

ISBN-10:
1463678304

https://www.Createspace.com/3644866

By The Same Author:
The White Man's Guide To Dating Black Women

Table Of Contents

Chapter One
Why Black Women Should
Consider Dating Interracially

"We must not be timid from a fear of committing faults; the greatest fault of all is to deprive oneself of experience."
Vauvenargues
Reflections and Maxims

Your Solution To The Shortage of Black Men

Millions of White men are interested in dating Black women, and outnumber the Black women available for interracial dating several to one. 57% of single White men are open to dating interracially, compared to 51% of single Black women.[1] White men who have never married, or are divorced, widowed or separated outnumber similarly-disposed adult Black women more than three-to-one: 29.2 million White men, compared to 8.4 million Black women. There's plenty to go around.

The odds are even better for single Black women with associate's, bachelor's or advanced degrees. Single White men with such degrees outnumber similarly-disposed Black women more than five-to-one: 7.2 million White men, compared to 1.3 million Black women. There's even more to go around for Black women with degrees. Remember, 57% of them are open to dating interracially.

Why Black Women Date White Men

While individual Black women have very personal reasons for dating interracially, should you speak with a number of Black women who have done so, the reasons they most often mention for dating White men usually include:
*they are emotionally available
*they are open to long-term relationships
*they don't dominate every aspect of the relationship
*they don't play endless games
*they don't act like little boys
*they respect you

1

*they really know how to treat Black women
* they know how to be romantic
*they don't abuse you
*they have fewer hangups about oral sex and foreplay
*they tell you what's on their minds
*they act relaxed and secure about themselves
*they compliment you and make you feel appreciated
*they had fathers at home who were role models
*we have a lot of interests in common
*the physical differences between the races are exciting

Black women say these things because the necessity of coping with the social pressures the interracial relationships attract tends to screen immature White men and Black women alike away from interracial relationships in the first place. Not very surprisingly, if the mature constitute most of those who get screened into interracial relationships, most of the White men you hear about being involved with Black women will be a notch or two better than average. You hear about the success stories, but not the more numerous might-have-beens and false starts that fall by the wayside. Not all White men are mature, and not all White men who become involved with Black women treat them right. On average, however, the odds are that an adult White man who can handle being in an interracial relationship is likely to be mature along other dimensions as well, including the way he treats women.

Interracial Romantic And Sexual Curiosity

"I don't regret for a single moment having lived for pleasure."
De Profundis
Oscar Wilde

Sexual curiosity about White men is a good reason for Black women to explore interracial dating. Sexual curiosity should be satisfied, not locked up, squelched, left unspoken and unexplored. If so, to what end, for what purpose? Sexual desires and yearnings are an intrinsic part of being human, an inescapable part of every adult's daily stream of consciousness. Who among us does not think about sex at some point every day? You are free to pursue your tastes wherever they may lead. Should this lead to Black women enjoying themselves in bed with White men, the consenting

2

adults involved are the only parties with any say in the matter. Don't be ashamed or apologetic about being interested in interracial sex. Catering to others' expectations will not make you happy in bed.

Do you daydream about White hands roaming all over your body and stirring cream into your coffee? Should your fantasies involve White men, those fantasies merit further introspection. If thoughts of White men give rise to strange, forbidden urges and feelings you half-heartedly try to push from your mind, your heart skipping a beat all the while, that is likely to be the right way for you to go. Those urges and feelings that bubble up from within your heart of hearts are what you really want, however publicly unacceptable to embrace or admit. Interracial relationships and sex should not be held up as a forbidden, impossible dream allowed to come to mind only in guarded moments before an iron curtain censor of the mind drops down. Probe into the matter and question yourself about just why it draws you on. If you can admit to being willingly and helplessly tantalized by the allure of interracial relationships and sex, you will find obliging, like-minded White male company abounding to help you sail those seas of supposedly forbidden pleasures.

"Forbidden fruit a flavor has that lawful orchards mocks"
Emily Dickinson
"Forbidden Fruit"

Interracial relationships are surrounded by an aura of unspoken taboos that enhance their exotic reputation, making them appear excitingly forbidden, mysterious, and "different." Interracial relationships are less common than same-race relationships, and by virtue of having had fewer opportunities to wear grooves in the minds of the many, generates considerable friction in scraping against the uninformed neurons of the uninformed multitude. Fantasies and speculation rush in to fill the informational vacuum.

Curiosity about interracial relationships and sex can be rooted in an interest in physical novelty. Some Black women have an esthetically-based sexual curiosity about men of another color, often intermingled with an interest in the comparative novelty of White male physiology and psychology. They like the way White skin and other physical features differ from the darker male physical features to which they are more accustomed. Such women often mention their esthetic delight in such

3

things as the color contrast between Black and White hands when clasped together, the differences between White and Black hair, skin, noses, lips, and related matters.

Physical appearance is a common motive for sexual attraction. Such looks as you may care for are purely a matter of taste, and as many different tastes exist as there are people to hold them. There is no accounting for taste, and no need to account for them to anybody. Taste is its own end and needs no justification. Who you find attractive is exclusively your own concern. Those whose tastes run against finding racial differences a source of interest should have little problem avoiding interracial entanglements of their own, given the extra effort interracial relationships often require. Others have no right to limit your fields of play or foreplay.

"We can love nothing except with reference to ourselves; and we are merely following our own taste and pleasure."
La Rochefoucauld
Maxims

White male attitudes about intercourse and foreplay are another source of sexual curiosity. Men are not all the same after the lights go out. White men as a group generally have fewer inhibitions about giving oral sex and engaging in extended foreplay. A Black woman who hears this would naturally be curious about an interracial relationship's potential for increasing her sexual pleasure. A single Black woman who doesn't get what she wants from her Black sexual partner is fully justified in looking around for a White partner who can meet her sexual needs. Her curiosity might be intertwined with another factor, such as an interest in the esthetics of color differences.

Some Black women think interracial relationships and marriages offer more romantic and emotional pluses than same-race marriages. They are attracted to White men as boyfriends and potential husbands with whom they can have enjoyable marriages and make biracial babies, for intertwined romantic, emotional, sexual, psychological and esthetic factors that come with the desire to make such commitments. Some Black women are very comfortable with Whites, possibly due to having grown up in integrated neighborhoods. They see interracial marriage as a natural next step, and not much of a big deal. Since Black men have long felt free to

4

enter into interracial marriages in considerably larger numbers than Black women, Black women increasingly see no good reason not to do exactly the same should the right White male walk into their lives. There's no good reason for a Black woman to not get into an interracial marriage that meets her definition of her needs. While not all interracial marriages make it, neither do all same-race marriages. There's no reason to hold interracial relationships to a higher standard if such interferes with meeting your needs.

While admittedly a touchy subject in some quarters, some Black women see interracial relationships as a way to have light-skinned children. Race mixing, whether inside or outside a marriage, has a reputation as a minefield-laden issue, though the explosions and shock waves reverberate exclusively inside the idle minds of spectators not themselves involved in interracial relationships.

What looks like a sociological battlefield from the outside differs little from a same-race relationship on the inside. For the two people most directly concerned in such interracial relationships, it is the personal issue of "us and our baby," and not a red-hot sociological issue that concerns others any more than a same-race marriage with children concerns third parties.

A responsible, adult Black woman's reproductive melanin-mixing choices and selection of the brand of cream of her choice for stirring into her coffee are matters of individual choice of no concern to melanin-dilution hall monitors. Marriage and reproduction are private matters, and an adult Black woman is free to paint her children the color of her choice with the white-handled brush of her choice. Your freedom of choice, freedom of association, freedom of reproduction and freedom of taste always take precedence over others' tastes and ideologies. Racial ideology is just one of many tiresome pretexts of convenience for external control and manipulation of private relationships.

"The only way to get rid of a temptation is to yield to it. Resist it, and your soul grows sick with longing for the things it has forbidden to itself."
Oscar Wilde
The Picture Of Dorian Gray

Some Black women make no bones about wanting affluent husbands and boyfriends, and see numerous White males offering that characteristic, to say nothing of other qualities of interest. While money is hardly the best of reasons for a relationship or marriage, once again it is always the exclusive right of the two individuals concerned to decide how to arrange their lives for their mutual satisfaction. After all, it's common knowledge that some same-race marriages are entered into for reasons that are primarily financial. Interracial relationships should not be held to a higher standard than same-race relationships if such interferes with enjoying your life. If the only thing that makes you happy is money, you might as well find an obliging White male instead of wasting away on the vine.

"You'll find there are many who'll wed for a penny."
William Schwenck Gilbert
The Mikado

Some Black women are romantically and sexually attracted to White men for a smorgasbord of hard-to-express, subconscious, taste-related reasons they can't begin to articulate or understand. They know what they like, and that's it. This is common. Interracial relationships and marriage open up subtle psychological entrances to fulfillment that would otherwise remain closed for some women. For whatever reasons might lie buried in the depths of their subconscious minds, they best reach their sexual and emotional peaks with White men.

Should a Black woman not be really sure just why she prefers to go the interracial route, as long as she feels it's right for her, it's okay, regardless of whether it leave others wondering. After all, few people in same-race marriages and relationships are asked to justify why they married or got involved with the person they did, beyond saying it felt right. For that matter, feeling a need to justify a private relationship to a third party is proof that the person feeling that need is on the wrong track. Interracial dating and marriage should not be held to a higher standard, unless such a higher standard fills some sort of identifiable need that benefits the two people most directly concerned. Other people's opinions don't count.

Why Black Women Date Interracially Less Often Than Black Men

"Why should there be one law for men, and another for women?"
Oscar Wilde
The Importance of Being Earnest

Look around at the odds for Black female/White male relationships during your lunch hour or weekend. You'll see more Black women visibly involved with White men would have been the case a decade or two ago. However, while the odds have improved, they are still nowhere near the visibly better odds for Black male/White female relationships that you also see very much in evidence. Interracial marriage statistics reveal a similar pattern. Black men marry interracially more than twice as often as Black women.

One school of thought holds that, for any large group of men, the odds are you will be compatible with a few of them. Were the development of interracial relationships a statistically predictable matter of relationships developing out of chance encounters with large numbers of compatible others of various races, you would expect to see roughly equal percentages of Black women and Black men paired off with companions of other races were you to observe a large enough group over the course of time. But, despite the increased opportunities for contacts with members of other races in schools, workplaces and neighborhoods, this has not happened.

In fact, given that there are millions more single Black women than single Black men, and that those Black women have a greater workforce presence than Black men, which brings them into contact with large numbers of potentially compatible White males, you would expect the numbers to be the other way around. But still you see disproportionately more Black men paired off with White women. Obviously, something is interfering with the development of Black female/White male relationships.

What keeps Black women out of interracial relationships? Social and psychological pressures directed against Black women are the primary culprits. Many Black women have subconscious negative attitudes about White men. Lack of opportunities to meet men of other races is another factor, especially for Black women who live and work in single-race neighborhoods. Lack of knowledge or misinformation about how to attract and meet White men is another problem. The inability to get motivated enough to get started keeps many Black women from even getting into the running.

Black Women Are Not Standby Equipment

There are millions more unattached Black women than unattached Black men. Deducting from that total those Black men unavailable due to substance abuse, unemployment, incarceration, involvement with White women and homosexuality results in a bleak demographic landscape for Black women. The situation is quite the opposite for Black men, rare commodities fully aware of the extent to which they are in short supply. As long as Black women outnumber Black men, certain types of Black men will play their demographic advantage to the hilt by treating many Black women as standby equipment. They play the system for what it's worth, and the pool of unattached Black women is the system they play. All too many Black men choose to take on the role of sultans on the Black social stage, the privileged few among the unattached many. Black women are their standby-equipment harem girls, from whom they expect appropriate tributes.

Being put on standby status means that the polygamous sultan deems you to be a harem girl whose services are not required for the moment. The sultan picks the harem girl whose tributes of the flesh he desires for the evening, and the unchosen wait on the shelf until his whim deems otherwise. Should the sultan tire of one harem girl's charms, there's plenty more where she came from, and not all are Black. Sultans can not understand why any harem girl would find fault with this system, their viewpoint being that the privilege of harem membership is ample reward for any harem girl. You have no leverage over these sultans, because they have no incentive to change. There's nothing to be gained, and much to be lost, should the winds of change blow through their private harems in the Black social desert. Don't be fooled by the fictitious carrots they dangle to induce Black women to pull their social lives along. They offer nothing of substance. Should you limit your socializing to certain types of Black sultans, your only rewards will be empty promises and endless reassurances, as far into the future as the eye can see.

Black women who make the mistake of taking on the role of standby equipment status leave themselves no choice but to contort their lives to fill the role expectations that go with being a spare tire. Standby equipment is a role with no room for emotional growth. The degree to which you trim yourself down to suit a sultan's lowly role expectations is also the degree to which you stunt your personality to play that role. The longer you accept relegation to standby status, the more your self-regard and social reality suffer. Standby status is a game you are predestined to lose. Don't settle for being a pawn on a sultan's chessboard. Closing your mind to the reality in front of you blocks you from moving beyond standby status. Recognizing it as a no-win game is the first step to better things, but the only real way to win at no-win games is to walk out and find a game with better odds. The emotional isolation of standby equipment status is a good reason to seek out interracial relationships.

"True ideas.....lead us into flowing human intercourse. They lead away from eccentricity and isolation."
William James
Pragmatism

College-Educated Black Women

The lack of a sufficient number of college-educated Black men is yet another good reason for Black women to date interracially. There's no shortage of anecdotal evidence about how tough it is for college-educated Black women to meet good men. Black female college graduates often bemoan their inability to find single Black men on their own educational level. As you ascend the educational ladder, you see increasingly more Black women than Black men, both in school and afterwards. The thin ranks of college-educated Black males are further depleted by interracial dating and marriage by educated Black men.

Many college-educated Black men feel free to date "down" with women of various races who, however physically attractive or emotionally complementary, are nevertheless less educated than the Black men in such relationships, further reducing the pool of Black men available to college-educated Black women.

"College was their idea of social self-respect."
Henry Adams
The Education Of Henry Adams

Being well-educated is a problem only if your tastes in men are racially monodimensional. Interracial dating opens the door to a pool of interracially-receptive White male college graduates receptive to interracial dating several times larger than the pool of Black female college graduates. College graduates as a group tend to be more liberal and open-minded on social issues and in their personal lives than the general population, making them a group of particular interest to single, college-educated Black women.

While everyone knows of exceptions to the rule, people with similar educational backgrounds are generally more likely to be compatible than people with very different educational backgrounds. They tend to have had similar experiences, think about similar things, have similar jobs, have similar interests, live in similar neighborhoods, and as a result have more to talk about and do together. A college professor with a doctorate lives in a different mental world than does a high school graduate working as a sales clerk. The odds are that the professor and sales clerk will hook up with someone like themselves, and not with each other. Should you be a college graduate looking for White men with whom you are likely to have some basis for potential compatibility, one place to start is with the educated White males. There are exceptions. But, be aware that exceptions tend to be people who, however outwardly dissimilar in terms of race or education, have compensating psychological characteristics not readily apparent to casual observers, such as very similar personalities and outlooks on life.

Black women looking for compatible White men should not begin and end their search with the pool of college graduates. Education is not the sole factor in determining compatibility, and not all intelligent White men choose go to college. Characteristics such as appearance, personality, emotional maturity and general intelligence can also be major factors in determining compatibility. Consider the emotional maturity factor. The one White guy you really connect with might be a blue-collar worker or technician. Think long and hard before you pass him by. Keep in mind that the debate about whether white-collar Black women should get involved with blue-collar men of whatever race can hit home in the most unpleasant way when you are alone at home on Saturday night to mull it over. If two people are emotionally compatible, the opinions of those outside the relationship don't count, and count least of all when the two of you are together. Should the opinions of others regarding your private life really matter to you, you have a lot of growing up to do. Dating and mating are the most personal of concerns, not matters for public debate. Every Black woman must make her own decisions about a number of tradeoffs in seeking a White male: emotional, educational, psychological, economic and the like. Dating "down" the educational ladder might lead to meeting some "up" White men and experiences, depending on what you enjoy in a man. Remember, you're looking for a man, not a resume.

Your Social Vacation

When on a tropical-island vacation, you're not just visiting another country. You're also on vacation from the nest of old psychological associations you've built up over the years in your everyday life. Being on vacation lets you shed the old and try out the new. You've heard about people who take on new personalities while on vacation far away from home. A vacation is both an opportunity to give yourself permission to try being different, and to become the person you really are underneath, the part of you that never came out because your environment, and the people in it, discouraged expressing that side of yourself. You may be too good at being the kind of social animal that others expect you to be. Should you have spent most of your life around people of one race, you probably have an excess of practice at taking on certain social roles for Black audiences. Your social environment doesn't allow you to take a vacation from those ingrained role expectations.

Interracial dating lets you fly off on vacation from the world of Black relationships and social expectations, set down in a new port of call and make a fresh start in a place where fundamentally different types of relationships are the norm. The old social cues and expectations are not there to lead you on. White men look and act differently than Black men. The greater their physical, psychological and cultural differences, the easier it is for you to make a break with the past due to the absence of old associations and cues that once led you on. You don't feel the need to act the same old way with new types of men, and their expectations differ

11

from those of Black men. You can give yourself permission to become a different, less inhibited person in the context of a new psychological landscape peopled with different types of men. Being on a psychological vacation lets you shed your old habits, modes of thought and associations, and try your hand at being someone new among new types of people.

"What makes us like new acquaintances is not being sufficiently admired by those who know us too well."
La Rochefoucauld
Maxims

Have you ever seen what happens when you transplant a small indoor potted plant to a more spacious outdoor garden? You might not have thought it possible for a small plant to change in character so much just by being transplanted to a bigger garden with more fertile soil. You might be surprised at the alacrity with which it spreads out new roots and blossoms in the sunshine. Things you didn't know you had in you will show themselves as you distance yourself from the old and become progressively more immersed in the new. You may be predisposed to become a different type of person, needing only the right circumstances, events or people to trigger what has always quietly been waiting to go off inside you. You'll find many White male fellow travelers along the interracial dating road whose predispositions complement your own, and you can be sure that somewhere out there are one or more men who can light up your life.

"I, who thought to sink, was caught up into love, and taught the whole of life in a new rhythm." Elizabeth Barrett Browning
Sonnets From The Portugese

[1] Sources: *Washington Post,* September 10, 1995, page C5; *Jet,* October 2, 1995, page 22

Chapter Two
Reprogramming Yourself
For Interracial Dating, Part I

"Our beliefs are really rules for action."
William James
Pragmatism

Value Your Tastes

"Happiness lies in the taste, and not in the things; and it is from having what we desire that we are happy -not from having what others think desirable."
La Rochefoucauld
Maxims

Deep within your mind is a labyrinth of tastes with a million hidden corridors chiseled out of your life's experiences. This labyrinth of tastes is the end result of endless interactions among your inborn propensities and inclinations, the opportunities for expression life gives you and the outcomes of your many good and bad choices. The more twists of taste your experiences reveal mortared together within the caverns of your being, the more intimately have your experiences connected to the latent tastes within your inner depths. This labyrinth leads nowhere in particular. Tastes have no destination or purpose other than to point you back at yourself. They reflect and echo what awaits expression from the pool of personality within you. Your tastes are ultimately highly individualized matters of psychological biochemistry.

This labyrinth of tastes grew in part out of the opportunities for expression you encountered every day, and is your mind's accumulation of reactions to finding what suited your tastes. Your tastes have always been present within you, awaiting only opportunities for expression. Your experiences bring to light latent tastes from within you. Tastes being mental guideposts indicating where you found experiences worth remembering and seeking again, good and bad experiences alike left guide markers to direct your future choices, good ones leaving visible guideposts for attraction, bad ones leaving shadowy guideposts for avoidance. New experiences constitute experimental attempts to find what might suit you in new contexts and situations, and each day exposes you to new opportunities to reveal ever more of the taste potentials within you. Interracial relationships are one of many ways to learn new things about yourself.

Only you know what satisfies your tastes. You distilled your tastes from the thousands of choices made in choosing and having experiences. You just make such informed judgments as you can, drawing on past experiences for guidance in evolving new expressions of taste. Others can not look within you to feel as you feel. It is impossible to formulate any single equation of individual taste that will fit all occasions and all people.

"Few.....would be happy if others had the determining of their occupations and pleasures."
Vauvenargues
Reflections And Maxims

No two people have quite the same tastes because no two people are born with the same makeup and inclinations, and no two people have had the same life experiences or identical everyday choices that would lead to them having identical tastes. While people from similar backgrounds can be expected to have much in common, being similar does not mean being identical. Even twins can be radically different by reason of leading lives with numerous unshared details, such as movies seen, people encountered at work, and even newspaper headlines glanced at in passing.

Parents often try to pass on their own tastes to their offspring as a means of validating their life experiences and tastes as being universal truths, but the reality is that any one person's tastes have no validity or meaning beyond suiting that one individual's tastes. Demands for uniformity of tastes say more about the mental limitations of the person making the demand than the human potential for variability. Life is too bewilderingly complex for any one standard to encompass all experiences and situations for billions of people with endless differences of taste. Only bullies demand that all should have the same tastes.

"Different things delight different people."
Marcus Aurelius
The Meditations Of Marcus Aurelius

Cast your net of tastes for men as broadly as for other tastes. Liking chocolate does not preclude appreciating vanilla, either sequentially or simultaneously. As you experience more, your tastes refine and expand as you encounter more of what life offers. Discovering what you really prefer in men, and finding such men, can take years. Given the effort required for self-discovery, it's the height of presumption for third parties to pretend to know what makes you happy. Yet some do just that. The louder their volume, the less their relevance. Listen to the inner voice of your tastes, not the rude voices huffing and puffing outside. Your tastes are sacred values by virtue of being reflections from your pool of personality, and are to be savored like fine wine. There is never any need to account to others for your tastes.

Developing Individual Standards Of Taste

"Enjoy pleasures, but let them be your own, and then you will taste them; but adopt none; trust to nature for genuine ones."
Philip Stanhope, Earl of Chesterfield
Letters To His Son

Given the inherent differences between individuals, each of us must develop our own standards of taste and opinion. Accepting another person's standards of opinion about interracial relationships or other topic is often a sign that you have yet to develop standards of your own for particular areas of interest. Should you lack sufficient information to evaluate new psychological territory such as interracial dating, you might be tempted to pursue the supposed shortcut of taking on another person's opinions and tastes as a surefire road to instant practical wisdom. Imitation is rarely a shortcut to anything worthwhile. Imitation means taking a piece from somebody else's mental jigsaw puzzle and try to force it into a puzzle where only a puzzle piece of your own making could possibly fit. In some cases, third parties with an axes to grind will spare no effort to push themselves and their tastes on you. Parasites have a knack for sensing where the easy pickings are to be found, and those with as-yet unformed tastes can be the easiest of cherries to pick. Ill-fitting, second-

15

hand, substitute opinions and tastes will rush in to fill your mental vacuum of undeveloped tastes and opinions, should you make the mistake of allowing them in in the first place. Some things you must do yourself, and defining your personal tastes is one such thing. No other person can possibly pretend to know or define what makes you happy, though many will pretend that they do know. Letting group expectations define your tastes is even worse, because all they will do is tell you that they expect you to live up to their expectations, without reference to your needs. A camel is a horse designed by a committee, and committees refuse to sweat out riding the emotional camels they design or pick out for the discomfort of people like you.

Meeting your personal needs should be your sole standard of reference for evaluating potential relationships. This standard also applies to supposedly frivolous relationships. There is nothing frivolous about meeting your legitimate needs. A relationship that meets your needs is not frivolous, however short-term, transitional or ill-defined both those needs and the relationship might be. Frivolous is simply a psychological parasite's term for you doing what doesn't meet their personal need to control you, despite it meeting your needs perfectly. Such people are often jealous or envious of those in real relationships, and your ability to get into any sort of relationship makes those unable to get into happy relationships burn with envy. The perceived novelty of interracial relationships makes the fires of their envy burn even hotter.

"The best thing in him is his complexion."
William Shakespeare
As You Like It

Dating a White guy whose primary asset is his height is not frivolous. Should height or skin color turn you on, there's no reason to pass up a potentially positive experience, even if you know it is predestined to be short-term. Even a short-term, frivolous relationship can add positive value to your life in the short run. Only control junkies would say that you should avoid short-term, frivolous relationships because they are of the opinion that you should engage only in relationships guaranteed to turn out perfectly. All this means is that they don't like the idea of interracial relationships and they like the idea of you getting into one even less. Saying that you should be really careful about getting into an interracial

16

relationship and the like are just softball propaganda techniques designed to keep you away from whatever it is the jealous and envious don't want you enjoying. Check it out yourself instead of letting someone else's opinion or propaganda substitute for your own judgment and experience.

"Untrue beliefs work as perniciously in the long run as true beliefs work beneficially."
William James
Pragmatism

Holding interracial relationships to a higher standard for some unstated reason triggers off a negative, implosive chain reaction that imposes more cumulative hardships on you than you might expect at first glance. Holding to a higher standard diverts you away from not just one potentially positive experience, but also away from a long chain of positive experiences that might have been, but which never will be. For example, being diverted away from becoming involved with someone interesting makes you miss out on more than what the two of you might have done your first time together. You also miss out on a lot of unexpected, unpredictable other things the two of you might have done down the road, but which you will never wind up doing together because catering to a third party's higher standard kept you from meeting or going out in the first place. Instead of having learned about someone you might have gotten something going with, all you have to show in its place is a third party's satisfaction with your ascetic behavior. Living up to a parasite's expectations leads nowhere. Since their goal is to keep you out of interracial relationships, the more you miss out on, the better they feel. Your loss is their gain. Taking on third parties' ill-fitting higher standards for interracial relationships is a mistake that generates the worst sort of negative compound interest for your interpersonal satisfaction account, and could even become a one-way ticket to emotional bankruptcy. Letting someone else control any part of your life starts off a chain reaction that ripples through your life like an expanding cloud of radioactive waste. Think for yourself and choose for yourself. The burden of proof is always on the person who wants interracial relationships to be held to a higher standard. Higher standards mean you lose out on opportunities that never return.

17

"Be upon your guard against those who upon very slight acquaintance, obtrude their unasked and unmerited friendship upon you; for they probably cram you with them only for their own eating." Philip Stanhope, Earl of Chesterfield
Letters To His Son

Don't Hold Interracial Relationships To A Higher Standard

"In our most private choices we are swerved from our orbit by the solar attraction - or repulsion -of the conventional"
Edward Alsworth Ross
Social Control

Should you never have been in an interracial relationship, it might look like a chancier matter than getting involved with a Black man, and appear surrounded by so many unknowns that it's easy to be tempted into thinking that only daredevils could possibly think about getting into interracial relationships. A host of shadowy, nameless things seem to be lurking around the campfire of interracial relationships, lying in wait to pull you into their lair with their pincers. Should you choose to become involved interracially, you might be tempted to "play it safe," seeking out only White men whom your friends would probably put their seal of approval as a "safe" bet, someone who looks good, at least on paper, to others in terms of occupation, income and education, someone who seems "safe" and marriageable and is generally the sort of guy mommy wants you to find (except that he's White). Don't do this. What little supposed satisfaction you get from catering to others' expectations and preconceptions is far outweighed by your reduced satisfaction with your life as a whole.

Catering to others' tastes and expectations in interracial relationships automatically and inevitably means scaling back on catering to your own tastes and needs. Taking on an anti-interracial role to suits others' expectations precludes taking on interracial dating roles that suit your needs and expectations. Holding prospective interracial relationships to higher standard, better known as a double standard, than a same-race relationship provides you with no benefits, but does generate endless complications as part of a bad bargain. A higher standard means nothing more or less than missing out on what's available because you take on another's tastes as your own and try to conform to their ill-fitting expectations. A given White guy may not meet a third party's needs, but you are the person looking for someone who suits you, not that third party. The only way to learn what is right for you is through experience or judgments based on comparisons with your past experiences. A copycat who takes on other's opinions as their own walks on a dead end street. A conformist copycat's life is a nobody's life. Should you think you have good reason for holding interracial relationships to a higher standard, identify just what supposed benefits you get from holding to this higher standard. The burden of proof is on the person proposing the double standard. Such proof will never come, because it does not exist. You will find no pluses in catering to others' expectations, only endless minuses. The sad truth is, such higher standards are never bring anything beyond gratifying psychological parasites who want company in their misery. There's nothing to be gained by catering to the expectations of those who want to abuse and control you.

"True ideas are those we can assimilate, validate, corroborate and verify, false ideas are those we cannot."
William James
Pragmatism

New things admittedly can look risky when seen from a distance, and it's natural to want to reduce the risks assumed to be inherent in trying to get a new type of relationship going. However, these supposed "risks" exist primarily in the minds of third parties, not in the minds of those actually in interracial relationships. Interracial relationships are no different than other relationships for those on the inside. Two people on the same wavelength see endless things in each other not readily apparent to uninformed third parties
Some who see physical differences automatically project and interpolate other differences with no basis in reality. This is a mistake. Visual differences do not automatically translate into riskiness or danger. Such people simply hold the mistaken assumption that one unfamiliar element, skin color, automatically means that everything else is unfamiliar to the point of being dangerous or evil. This is quite wrong, and provides supporting evidence that second-rate minds are the devil's playground. Passing judgment on interracial relationships on the superficial basis of visual contrasts highlights the superficiality of their thought processes

19

more than anything else. Their lack of understanding does not obligate you to share in their problems or slow your life down to their level of expectations. Don't put your life on hold waiting for other people to understand and agree with you. You do not need the understanding, agreement or consent of others to go about getting on with your life.

Holding interracial relationships to a higher standard than a same-race relationship means having a double standard for interracial relationships, as if they were somehow a thing apart from other types of human relationships. Double standards are plausible-sounding pretexts of convenience for racial biases, envy and jealousy. The ultimate aim of a double standard is to prevent you from dating interracially. It is simply a covert method of controlling you. Double standards exist for the sole purpose of providing hidden benefits to those trying to get others to accept them. Double standards are voodoo standards: prohibitions on interracial dating only work if you believe in them in the first place. If you don't believe in them, it's just another fraud that rolls off your back. The request that you adhere to a double standard is a pretext of convenience for someone who wants to make interracial relationships hard, or impossible to get into. Set the standards for anybody or anything high enough and nothing will ever get started. Whatever the reason for a double standard or a higher standard, get it out in the open in broad daylight and see it for what it is, just another fraudulent inducement to control people.

"Minds of moderate caliber ordinarily condemn every thing which is beyond their range."
La Rochefoucauld
Maxims

The burden of proof is always on the person espousing double standards, not the person on the receiving end. Those espousing double standards seek to manipulate you by getting you to let down your psychological guard to give them an opportunity to get control over you. Control does not usually mean minute-by-minute control in the sense pulling a puppet's strings, but rather subtle, indirect manipulation that quietly maneuvers you into accepting their double standard and results in you voluntarily restricting your possibilities for enjoyment of life. You wind up dancing alone for the puppet master's amusement when you could be out dancing a Black-and-White duet. Yes, this happens. There are all too many people out there whose sole excuse for living is diverting others away from enjoying their lives. The only way out of this is to develop and value your own tastes to the extent that others' tastes and expectations become no more relevant than background radiation.

"The sexual instinct being socially disruptive is habitually dismissed with slanting allusion and contempt."
Edward Alsworth Ross
Social Control

Since you know more about what goes on in your head than anyone else, the opinions of those who want you to take on double standards are strictly optional. Other people's expectations and opinions don't count unless you let them count. You can take them or leave them. Should you express tastes in men not to the liking of others, nothing will happen except that you will get on with your life in a world where some people will walk around not liking the way you arrange your life, and nothing more. You will not be struck by lightning.

Don't miss out on men who meet your needs because psychological parasites hold that your tastes do not meet their particular and demanding double standards of expectations of perfection. Their applause for you falling into line to salute their tastes will neither warm you up on cold winter mornings nor take you out on Saturday nights. Those who don't like a White male's height, resume, career prospects, marital history or skin color do not have to date him or even stay in the same room as him. Their right to babble on about double standards ends where your right to satisfy your tastes begin. Draw the line and push them out of your life, or at least out of hearing range. You have an unlimited right to your tastes and preferences, and your personal tastes in men not subject to anyone's approval. Keep the vampires at bay with your personal brand of verbal garlic.

"Expectation has always been used in managing people."
Edward Alsworth Ross
Social Control

There's never any advantage in catering to other's expectations for your personal life. If you think there is, get it out into the open for scrutiny and illumination. If it's not open for public inspection, it's guaranteed to be fraud or manipulation until proven otherwise. Such critics expect others to live up to their standards of taste and offer nothing in return, least of all proof that their off-the-cuff opinions are anything more than jealousy, envy and racial biases. Such are just attempts to manipulate you into wasting your time into trying to live up to their standards. What you may not be aware of is that many such critics don't actually care whether you live up to their standards, because that is not the real issue. The real issue is who decides whether you enjoy yourself by virtue of controlling access to your personal pleasure spigot. Maneuvering you into taking on their tastes, expectations and opinions as your own makes them the real power brokers behind your throne, and diverts you away from potentially enjoyable relationships. Psychological parasites feed on the unhappiness of others, and are happiest when feasting on the unhappiness they themselves create in unwitting puppets. Parasites need victims, but you don't need them for anything. Push them out of your life as fast as possible. Any time spent with them is wasted.

Satisfy Your Curiosity And Forget About Being Consistent

"There are various sorts of curiosity: one is from interest, which makes us desire to know what may be useful to us; another is from pride, and arises from a desire of knowing what others are ignorant of."
La Rochefoucauld
Maxims

It's okay to date Whites if you are "curious." Curiosity is a normal reaction to a world full of interesting things found in normal people, and is a distinguishing characteristic of being human. Indulge your curiosity. Such men as you may curious about might or might not turn out be right for you, but you'll never know unless you give it a try. Those who say that you shouldn't be curious about White men are best given a wide berth. They offer nothing but dead-end negativism. Life is too full of variety to scale yourself down to the expectations of mental midgets afraid of the great outdoors. You get nothing in return for taking on the limited horizons of the incurious to keep them company in their misery.

Your curiosity and tastes need not be consistent. Those who pound the table to demand that you show a pattern of consistency in your tastes in men just want to slow you down to catering to their expectations as a means of controlling you. Their aim is to limit your enjoyment of life's opportunities by manipulating you into taking on some measure of their tastes, opinions and expectations as your own, despite the endless and obvious potential for incongruencies and mismatches. You can no more take on another person's tastes as your own any more than you can take on their clothing as your own. Neither will fit. Consistency and conformity in patterns of tastes and behavior serve only the purposes of those making such demands, not those they expect to contort their lives in misguided efforts to make their unneeded and unworkable opinions work. Catering to others' expectations meets their needs, not yours, and leads nowhere.

A Black man might demand you confine yourself to Black men, for no reason beyond it being his expectation that Black women are "supposed" to associate only with Black men. Catering to his expectations brings you nothing. A Black woman, such as your mother, might hold up a higher standard for your edification to the effect that you should date only men who come up to her personal standards for marriageability. Their gods are not your gods. Staying home alone is your reward for making the mistake of taking on her opinions as your own, instead of going out and having real-life experiences you can use as the basis for developing your own judgments.

Whatever form others' demands take, it always comes down to them manipulating you into limiting your field of action. These can often be people you know well, and because you know them well, psychological alarms that would otherwise automatically spring into action with strangers remain untriggered. People you know well are often the ones who expect some measure of conformity of you in payment for their continued social acceptance of you. They don't want to see somebody who used to be very predictable go off and do unpredictable things that might make them jealous. They have no choice but to use covert, backdoor methods of manipulation to get you to conform to their expectations, since there's no way they can come out and tell you that they know best what you should do with your life without you laughing in their face. They also suspect that, should you follow your tastes where your nose leads you, you might wind up enjoying yourself with a White guy, and become completely distracted away from future contact with them. The world is

23

full of warped people who want you to keep them company in their misery.

"Ignorance is like a delicate exotic fruit; touch it and the bloom is gone."
Oscar Wilde
The Importance Of Being Earnest

Curiosity can lead to developing unexpected interests in types of men you never suspected existed. The more widely you cast your net, the more potentially interesting fish you might draw in. Should limited exposure to different types of men have made you uncertain about what your needs and interests might be, randomly indulging your curiosity, within rational constraints about personal safety, can help you to progressively approximate what sorts of men can best meet your needs.

There's no penalty for looking around, but the penalty for failing to satisfy your curiosity is joyless stagnation. You can and should date different types of White, and Black, men as you see fit. Be consistently inconsistent in your tastes in your tastes should you be so inclined. Life is an ice cream store with many flavors awaiting your discretion. Caring about what others think of your tastes is the road to ruin. Don't let others inflict their opinions about the propriety of your tastes on you. Their expectations don't count.

"Imagination cannot invent so many contrarieties as naturally exist in the heart of every individual."
La Rochefoucauld
Maxims

If you want to check out different types of men, don't be consistent. What for? What practical purpose of yours does it serve? What's in it for you? You can associate with outwardly different types of White guys should they meet some real or perceived need of yours, regardless of whether or not others see any connecting thread among the choices to which your tastes lead. You are not in the business of begging others for approval of your private life. Critics who demand conformity and consistency of you should be left stranded by the side of road with one less hypnosis candidate in their audience.

24

"Curiosity.....[is] the impulse toward better cognition."
William James
Talk To Teachers on Psychology

Clearing The Driftwood Out of Your Mind

"Every group of every kind whatsoever demands that each of its members shall help defend group interests. Every group stigmatizes anyone who fails in zeal, labor and sacrifices for group interests."
William Graham Sumner
Folkways

We pick up a lot of mental driftwood over the years. This is particularly true early in life, when our minds absorb information and attitudes from around us like sponges, with little critical reflection and analysis. Your head has thus become filled with a mixture of stuff that is true, untrue, partially true, unverifiable, irrelevant or meaningless. The racial attitudes you assimilated are part of this complex attitudinal package in your head. The undertow of early-life programming can strand you in the Sargasso Sea of conformity if you don't watch your step.

You're probably unaware of how unwittingly you picked up others' prepackaged attitudes and tucked them away in the back of your mind without examination. You picked up these attitudes at home, school, on vacation and from your friends. While many are perfectly okay to hold, certain attitudes and beliefs can drag down your interracial dating progress. Should you need to take actions to get an interracial relationship going that go against the grain of long-held attitudes and beliefs, the effect on you will be the same as trying to navigate a ship through a harbor filled with driftwood and seaweed: noise, bumps and friction. Steering your ship properly requires removing, or steering around, the driftwood blocking you from a smooth passage.

You're likely to have picked up a few negative beliefs and attitudes about White men somewhere along the way. Maybe you had an aunt who told you that any Black girl who gets involved with a White boy is headed for grief, as sometimes happens. Maybe a Black male relative who told you

25

that White men use Black women for a night, throw them away and then never talk to them again, not mentioning that certain types of Black men have been known to do exactly the same. You get the idea. Years of hearing talk where White men are always the bogeyman gives your subconscious mind numerous bits and pieces of raw material that it quietly pieced together into a generalized, subconscious picture of White men as bad news for Black women.

"In the present day, power holds a smoother language, and whomsoever it oppresses, always pretends to do so for their own good: accordingly, when anything is forbidden to women, it is always thought necessary to say.....that they depart from their real path of success and happiness when they aspire to it."
John Stuart Mill
The Subjection Of Women

Should you have had little social contact with real-life White men, the only things in your mental file cabinet when the subject of White men comes up will be images of White men as bad guys. If the only thing you know about Whites regards slavery and sharecropping, those few facts will expand like a hot-air balloon to fill all the mental space available. You may not be consciously aware that this conversational residue from the past is what makes you feel that dating Whites is somehow wrong. Having a mind full of such subterranean mental driftwood can make you feel cautious, inhibited and somewhat uneasy even thinking about interracial dating, and even more uneasy about taking the steps necessary to get involved interracially. Being aware that you have been involuntarily programmed in this manner is the first step in deprogramming yourself and putting attitudinal countermeasures into effect. Program yourself for your own purposes, rather than drift through life steered by programs written by others.

Pressures are intrinsically irrational and require some sort of expression of anger, psychological manipulation, veiled threat against you, or a suspension of critical analysis on your part to get you to against your rationally-determined best interests. You would never go along with such pressures otherwise. Note that you are rarely pressured by others to make changes that suit you, only to make changes that suit others. This is the pressure to conform to the groupthink, the lowest common denominator of thought that others have in common with you. Groupthink means you can only do what does not make others jealous or envious because they do not have it, or can not do it, themselves. You get no benefit from scaling yourself down to the lowest-common-denominator expectations of others. If you think you do, try to identify it. You have to pressure yourself to direct your thoughts and behavior in directions that enhance your life. If you don't, someone else or some group will do their best to get your life on the track they have decided to put you on.

If you think this is an exaggeration, think about how often parents try to steer the lives of their offspring into "acceptable" channels. For example, your mother might say that "everyone" knows that Black women are not supposed to like White men. This is an attempt at psychological manipulation. She sets up expectations that you turn off your mind and become an unthinking herd animal, for no reason beyond her expecting it of you. No reason is presented for imitating such behavior except that others act that way, conformity for the sake of conformity. However, should a million people do a stupid thing, it's still a stupid thing. Don't let yourself be manipulated into turning off your mind. Almost everybody wants to run your life, and fool you into turning off your critical judgment is usually the first step. Are You Already Interracial?

While interracial dating is a hot-button issue for some people, the reality is that interracial relationships are probably as old as the human race. Contacts between races often leads to interracial procreation, Blacks being a case in point. Eighty to ninety percent of American Blacks probably have White or Native American ancestry in their family trees, though their interracial ancestry is not always visually discernible to casual observers. As far back as the seventeenth century, there was intermarriage between Black slaves and White indentured servants.

After the Civil War, Blacks intermarried with Native Americans in Texas, Oklahoma and elsewhere, in addition to intermarriage between freed slaves and working-class Whites. There are a variety of other reasons, good and bad, why many Blacks are already interracial. Why bring this up? If you have a deep-down feeling that interracial dating and relationships are somehow weird, if it seems completely alien to even be thinking about dating a White, chances are you already part White or Native American, and wouldn't be around to think about the pros and cons of interracial dating were those interracial relationships not already in your family tree. If you need a precedent for interracial dating, you might find one in your family photo album. Interracial dating looks like less of a step into unknown territory if you have always been a part of that territory yourself.

"In history, as in traveling, men usually see only what they already had in their minds."
John Stuart Mill
The Subjection Of Women

Chapter Three
Reprogramming Yourself
For Interracial Dating, Part II

"The repeated statement is embedded in the long-run in those profound regions of our unconscious selves in which the motives of our actions are forged. At the end of a certain time we have forgotten who is the author of the repeated assertion, and we finish by believing it." Gustave Le Bon
The Crowd

Admitting Your Attraction

"A woman's thoughts run before her actions."
William Shakespeare
As You Like It

At some point you must admit, if only to yourself, that you are attracted to White men. Admitting it to others can come later. This does not mean making some sort of dramatic public statement or confession. After reflecting on, and probing into, the matter, your internal resistance will slowly fade, a little switch will click somewhere in your head and your life will start to move in a different direction. Getting to that point requires drilling through various mental roadblocks buried deep within the infrastructure of your personality.

You may have one of several common mental roadblocks against admitting your attraction. One is the belief that Black women are not "supposed" to like White men. This is simply the expectation of people who want you to take on their beliefs as your own without good cause. Should such beliefs have become lodged in your mind early in life, it, loosening the grip they develop over time also requires time.

The earlier in childhood such memories get tucked away upstairs, the tougher and more encrusted with age they become by virtue of remaining undisturbed. The more settled-in mental roadblocks become, the more it requires to dislodge them. The effort required will not leave you exhausted and gasping for breath, however. An ounce of thought will save you a ton of sweat.

29

"I am afraid that you have been listening to the conversation of someone older than yourself. That is always a dangerous thing to do, and if you allow it to degenerate into a habit, you will find it absolutely fatal to any intellectual development."
Oscar Wilde
The Critic As Artist

Black women are typically exposed to only one viewpoint regarding interracial relationships when growing up, and are hit with it from all sides. This is propaganda. Propaganda benefits those preaching it, not those on the receiving end. If it can't be explained in terms of direct benefits to you, it's propaganda designed to benefit others. The intent behind such propaganda is to nip in the bud the mutual attraction that springs up between women and men of all races in the absence of such propaganda by making Black women less likely to develop such attractions.

Certain types of Black men don't want Black women dating interracially, and prefer that Black women grow up thinking that Black men are the only way to go. Mental blocks like this crumble under their own weight after you drill into their weak points to probe their hold over you and find there is far less substance to them than meets the eye. Should anyone tell you that you are not supposed to discuss the matter, you can safely assume that it is a fraud or con game of some sort until proven otherwise. The only reason someone would want you to not examine something is if they have something to hide.

"An idea is true so long as it is profitable to our lives."
William James
Pragmatism

Filling your mind's garden with anti-interracial weeds leaves no room for interracial rose bushes to take root and bloom. Some who do this to you might do so because they don't know better than to pass along what they themselves picked up along the way, while others do it because they enjoy molding the minds of others and steering them wrong. Human beings have a need to pass on their beliefs, traditions and practices to those around them. An unexamined tradition taken on faith is suspicious material until checked out. Whatever the reason for passing along questionable customs, the aim is always to suspend or reduce your capacity for independent judgment about what's best for you, and substitute second-hand, second-rate opinions, beliefs and attitudes that benefit third parties. The more these suspicious customs and beliefs spread out within your mind, the more likely they are to become an entrenched substitute for a personal sense of independent judgment about your best interests.

Whatever the details of their excuses, propagandists seek to control you by inserting aims of their own choosing within you as a means towards that end. This is particularly easy to do to subjects too young to have yet developed their own opinions. They simply insert the recording of their choice into your mind as a means of making it your subconscious opinion as well.

Let the truth shine in on your life and watch the psychological weeds dry up and blow away. In some cases you may need to plant a preparatory belief within yourself before admitting your attraction, the belief that interracial dating itself is a good thing. Although related to beliefs about White men, this is actually a separate and distinct belief that underlies other beliefs. It's hard to get started thinking about the subject of White men in general should you be held back by the underlying belief that interracial dating is a bad thing itself.

"The common excuse of those who bring misfortune on others, is that they desire their good."
Vauvenargues
Reflections And Maxims

Admitting your attraction can be a positive outcome of developing your sense of independent judgment. Admitting your attraction is a psychological doorway on the path to validating that your tastes and desires, by virtue of being yours, take automatic priority over the limitations others pressure you to stay circumscribed within. Admitting what you like is the first step on the road to fulfillment and a better personal life. You must do this yourself, because nobody but you will look out for what makes you happy. Admitting your attraction gets the ball rolling and gathering momentum in pushing against the grain of old social conditioning and inhibitions.

31

Attraction And Avoidance

You might simultaneously feel both attraction and avoidance towards White men and not understand why two sets of conflicting motivations could both be at work in your mind. The attraction part is the real you, the avoidance part is the conditioned echo of anti-interracial propaganda. Consciously remembering the many negative comments heard over the years which have diffused their influence throughout your mind starts diluting their subconscious hold on you by virtue of identifying the true source of your inhibiting beliefs as influences external to yourself. Psychoanalyzing yourself in this manner to identify, and pick apart, memories of the external sources of negative beliefs is integral to eliminating your subconscious inhibitions about interracial dating. Self-psychoanalysis can start to uproot what's blocking your way.

You might feel inhibited about getting involved with White men due to attitudes picked up when growing up. Maybe relatives said you can't trust Whites because they cheated your uncle out of some money and mistreated Black women as a group during slavery. Were all Whites like that, you would have good cause to avoid them, but all Whites are no more like that any more than all Blacks act one way. Reaching into your mind to pick apart such memories lets you see that others held those beliefs, and they wanted you to validate their beliefs and outlook on life by getting you to take them on yourself. Should you have taken on others' beliefs in this unthinking, imitative manner, you would naturally have bad feelings about getting involved with Whites, since what little you know led to a generalized negative picture subconsciously assembled out of the many snippets of negativism to which you were exposed.

Conversely, you might have developed a generalized attraction to White men due to having heard things, saw things, read things, fantasized things, or had personal experiences that you associate with positive states of mind and experiences. You might have a thing for blue-eyed men because you idolized a blue-eyed rock star you saw on television back in grade school. You might have read about a Black female celebrity who had positive experiences with a White male companion. Reading romance novels might make you think of White men in terms of romantic fantasies. Some White men may have helped you or treated you properly somewhere along the line. A string of little positive things like this can have a cumulative impact resulting in positive feelings and associations regarding White men. Your subconscious mind looks for patterns in the stream of information to which you are exposed every day. You feel both attraction and avoidance because you heard and experienced both positive and negative things regarding White men over the years. Deciding whether to pick up and follow the positive or negative strand of experiences and follow it to wherever it may lead is your decision to make.

Beliefs of any kind, whether derived from experience or others' propaganda, spread throughout your mind by making repeated points of contact and association with your other thoughts. You can consciously reinforce and enhance positive beliefs by increasing the number of times those positive beliefs make contact within your mind through repetition. The more often you run an idea through your mind in different contexts or situations, the more mental associations and linkages it sets up within your mind as a whole. As time goes on, repeating and associating the idea that interracial dating is a good thing eventually establishes so many contact points within your mind such that it becomes your automatic response whenever the topic of interracial dating comes up. Your old, anti-interracial dating memories and beliefs fade into the woodwork as they get replaced by more positive beliefs. Associating a new belief with new people, situations and contexts slowly allows that belief to permeate the overall thought pattern of your life.

Start Mentally Screening In White Men

"It is never too late to give up our prejudices."
Henry David Thoreau
Walden

Even should you be pretty cautious about the whole idea of interracial dating, you can start to proactively lay the foundation for interracial relationships in small, but real, ways at almost any time. How to do this? Rewire your mind for interracial relationships. Start thinking about White men as real-life companionship possibilities instead of completely screening them out of your mental field of potential companions. Black women often tune out the White men with whom they come into contact in the course of a day. Stop filtering them out. Classify them as possibilities, and actively think about them as possibilities. Start building up positive mental associations regarding White men as possibilities for companionship. Thought will lay the foundation for action. Practicing such habits induces both thoughts and later actions to follow in the groove you lay down.

Start classifying the White men with whom you come into contact with each day as possibilities of direct potential interest to you. Most Black women have a variety of opportunities for casual contact with White men on buses, subways, elevators, hallways, lines in fast food restaurants and stores. Instead of tuning out the men you pass by in everyday situations, tune into them. Look at them and consciously think of them as real possibilities instead of just background. While you probably wouldn't be interested in most such men after learning more about them, you are not yet at that stage of the game. You can be more selective later on. The initial idea is to start rewiring your attitudes so that you start taking conscious notice of the possibilities that pass your way every day. Conscious means dwelling on the possibilities for a spell and letting those thoughts circulate through your mind. Unless you first rewire your attitudes, outwardly expressing an interest in White men is more likely cause a short circuit than get you humming.

Your interpersonal electricity will automatically flow into the same old circuits and do the same old things unless and until you go out of your way to take the time and trouble to reroute your attitudinal wiring. Rewiring your attitudes rechannels your interpersonal electricity into your new interracial dating circuit. Look at those White men with whom you have some sort of contact, even if your present interracially-neutral mindset blocks you from doing more than looking. Some Black women have subconscious qualms about looking at White men except in passing. Get into the habit of thinking of some of the specific White men you see every day as having the potential to bring positive experiences your way. Assign some positive values to them in thinking about them, even if it's sheer fantasy for the time being. This will start changing your attitudes about them, and will in turn also have the effect of starting to make you look like a possibility to them. Why? Men can tell what you think of them because it's written on the expression on your face. Men notice women who like men, and avoid women who look like they don't like men.

Absorb and sift information about White men for future reference. Create a personal database for possible future action. Information means general impressions, not written reports or memos. Someone who plans to buy a car a few months down the road takes note of cars in which she might have an interest, and you should do much the same with White men. Observe White men and take note of what you like about some of them, the way they look, the way they talk, the way they laugh and anything else about them that interests you. After a while, you'll start thinking of certain types of men as your "type."

Over the course of time, your thoughts and preferences will slowly become more focused, and your nonverbal reactions regarding White men will slowly change without you really being aware, at least on a day-by-day basis, of your gradual attitudinal shift. Things like the amount of eye contact you make will start changing. You won't really notice the imperceptible rate of change on a day-by-day basis, but you nevertheless will be changing, slowly but surely.

This does not mean taking steps to turn your thoughts into action at first. Your initial preoccupation should be rewiring your mental circuitry behind the scenes, one wire at a time. The reason for doing it this way is that taking action down the line will be less jarring if preceded by a period where new thoughts, plans and mental practice simulations slowly wear a groove in your mind. Your actions will follow in the groove of thought and mental practice you lay down beforehand.

Taking action comes more smoothly and less disconcertingly when it does not go completely against the grain of deep-set, long-held attitudes and experiences, and is anchored in the new mental bedrock you have laid down. The more positive associations you build up in your mind, the more allure and appeal your proposed actions exert over you, and the more ease and grace you will experience when you take action further down the interracial dating road. Thinking about White men in positive ways makes a Black woman look and sound more interesting than someone trying to look friendly while simultaneously trying to hack her way through a mental logjam of old negative attitudes and impressions about White men.

"Activity is contagious."
Ralph Waldo Emerson
"The Uses Of Great Men"

How You Can Develop Useful New Habits

"Habit is everything - even in love."
Vauvenargues
Reflections And Maxims

You develop both good and bad habits the same way: by practicing them. The more often you practice or repeat any sort of behavior, good, bad or indifferent, the deeper a groove it wears in your mind and the more likely it is to become automatic behavior. Attitudes and beliefs influence the development of habits by determining how much internal resistance your mind puts up against doing something new. Your attitudes about interracial dating determine whether or not the new habits you want to put into place have a fighting chance of getting established in the first place. You can program yourself to develop new habits by choosing new habits and then practicing them.

You build your house of habits brick by brick, a little bit each day. You can no more develop new habits overnight any more than you can build a house in one day. Consciously deciding to develop a new habit of thought or action is a good starting point, but just a starting point. Thought has to start getting translated into reality at some point or you are wasting your time doing intellectual gymnastics. You might start out practicing just a little bit of new behavior at a time until you feel comfortable with practicing more comprehensive forms of that behavior. Developing positive new habits is only one side of the coin. You also need to go out of your way to neutralize, or extinguish, piece by piece, old attitudes that obstruct the development of new habits and prevent you from having new types of experiences.

"Prolonged exposure to a circle or group that speaks always with the same decision and the same commands, benumbs the will over whole areas of thought."
Edward Alsworth Ross
Social Control

36

In the early phases of developing new habits, first focus on changing your attitudes and beliefs. Later on, focus on actual behavior. Attitudes and beliefs are the soil into which you attempt to plant new habits. The new attitudes you develop will determine, and modify, the new behaviors you seek to practice to the extent to which they promote or retard their introduction and acceptance. The more positive your attitude, the steadier the ground you stand on in trying out new behavior. Bad attitudes keep the soil fallow, because attitudes already in place will resist your attempts to plant discordant strains of contrary new behaviors. The shakier and more doubtful your underlying attitudes about interracial dating, the less firm the ground you stand on in trying out real-life interracial dating behavior. Your old attitudes need to be examined and replaced with attitudes that facilitate the introduction of new behaviors, or at least do not get in your way.

You need not do this entirely on your own. Human beings are social animals, and sometimes change can best be accomplished in a supportive, reassuring small group context, such as a few like-minded girlfriends at roughly the same stage of development as yourself regarding interracial dating. A group situation can help some types of people at certain stages of development by allowing members to share ideas and approaches with other group members and give some measure of social support to your intentions. Hearing outside viewpoints can shed light on obstructive beliefs and attitudes of which you may not have been consciously aware. Some people benefit from a supportive group environment, others do not. You can't generalize.

The down side is that the necessity for a mutually supportive group environment that supports all group members equally can sometimes slow high-octane individuals down to the crawling velocity of the group. Also, be sure to exclude from your group anyone with negative ideas about interracial dating, regardless of why they hold such attitudes. Such people will only slow you down and drain you of your enthusiasm should you give them the chance. You want to know more about how to get on with it, not why someone thinks it's not a good idea. You will find all the negativism regarding interracial relationships you can handle without inviting it into your living room.

Your first attempt to break down your long-held belief that Black women are not supposed to like White men might involve reaching into the depths of memory to uncover that your father told you that Black girls are not supposed to like White boys. He might have generalized his belief that you can't trust White men from negative experiences with particular White men on a particular job.

While your father told the truth as he knew it about his experiences, his limited personal experiences can not be generalized to include all White men as a group. After thinking this over, you might then decide that, being an adult, you are smart enough to seek out experiences on your own that will give you the raw material you need to distill your own customized guidelines. If your father is correct, your experiences will confirm his logic. If you are correct, you can go your own way. The most likely outcome is having a mixture of good and bad experiences you can use to synthesize rough guidelines to avoid certain types of White men, and conversely seek out other types. Clearing out the driftwood lets you sail on and form new habits.

"One generation abandons the enterprises of another like stranded vessels."
Henry David Thoreau
Walden

Try on for size the new attitudes you pick to make sure they feel right on you, or else you will continue to feel internal resistance to practicing new habits, because what you claim to want to do might sound superficially plausible, but lacks the depth of internal psychological support you need from the overall psychological infrastructure of your attitudes and beliefs. Your mind will reject what doesn't fit unless you persist in slowly sanding off the rough edges of the old inhibitions. After a while, the other parts of your mind will gradually fall into place. When you are really ready, you'll know it. Doubts will not spring to mind when you think of interracial dating. Should your attitudinal soil be particularly recalcitrant due to extensive permeation with fossilized attitudes, new attitudes will just take a bit more time to spread out roots and dissolve the old than expected. Tell the truth to yourself and a psychological infrastructure conducive to interracial relationships will start to take root.

38

It Takes Time

"Patience is the art of hoping."
Vauvenargues
Reflections And Maxims

You don't learn a foreign language overnight, and the same applies to your private collection of new attitudes and new behaviors about interracial dating. Since interracial dating probably goes against the grain of some long-held beliefs, clearing out long-neglected attitudinal underbrush will take months, and maybe longer. The pieces of your new attitudes and behavior will take a while to fall into place as they slowly but surely replace older attitudes and modes of behavior. Sometimes you might have to take a building block approach, putting certain things in place before putting certain other things into place. For example, you may like the idea of interracial dating as an abstract idea for improving your social life, but still act very cold when you actually get around White men. If the thought of being around a White man is still a bit too novel for you to relax around them, you still have a way to go. Pick apart your old attitudes, gradually insert new attitudes, and let them slowly permeate your consciousness. Program yourself to meet your needs.

There's no quick fix. You can't do it all in one day. Our minds are not computers into which we can insert a new attitude program and start running it immediately. Your new attitudes and behaviors will not be just isolated bits and pieces of you, separate and distinct from everything else about you, but are rather a complex psychological infrastructure of behaviors and attitudes that you will slowly integrate into your overall personality. As little things about you change, the pieces of the new you will fit better into the world of interracial relationships. As time goes on, you will feel both more comfortable about both the idea and practice of interracial dating because the idea and practice become integrated into your overall personality pattern.

"How poor are they that have not patience! What wound did ever heal but by degrees?"
William Shakespeare
Othello

Developing An Overlay Of Positive Experiences

Should your experiences with men to date all have been bad, you need to get off to a fresh start. This means looking to have some positive experiences with men as soon as is practical. These need not be major-league experiences, just positive experiences of any level of magnitude that start tilting you in a positive direction. The reason is that, should you have a huge backlog of bad experiences, you consequently have negative associations about men, and must start to overlay, and eventually replace, them with positive experiences that will eventually, by sheer force of volume, push the negative ones out of your mind as your primary reference points regarding men. The more positive experiences and associations you have regarding men, the less of a hold bad memories retain over you. This requires seeking out positive experiences, if you want to have any positive experiences to draw on. At some point you must start redecorating your room with pictures of happy scenes to cover up your old mural of the many sad tales of your life. It's hard to be happy when sad tales are all you have to draw on. No matter how many bad experiences you've had, you can eventually force them to recede from mind by piling up good experiences of every size and shape on top and bury the bad ones beneath.

"Pluck from the memory a rooted sorrow,
Raze out the written troubles of the brain."
William Shakespeare
Macbeth

Start out small in seeking positive experiences. Maybe say hello to someone interesting at work or someone new in your neighborhood, and see how things develop. As long as your experiences are of a positive nature, their exact magnitude is secondary in the short run. Seeking out positive experiences is only one side of the coin. An extremely important secondary consideration is to consciously avoid anyone like those guys with whom you've had bad experiences. Developing an overlay of good experiences requires avoiding whatever you know from experience is likely to lead to bad experiences. Should you have excessive experience dealing with the wrong types of men, you are likely to unconsciously and automatically revert to type and sniff out what you have the most experience dealing with: the bad news guys. If all of your bad experiences have been with men who have been tall, well-dressed, very good dancers and great conversationalists, stay away from White guys anything like that. Avoid abusive men regardless of the subconscious temptation to revert to type. If you act like a masochist, sadists will sniff you out wherever you go. No matter how comfortable you suppose you are with men of that type, do something new and see where it leads.

"Those who cannot remember the past are condemned to repeat it."
George Santayana
The Life Of Reason

Don't assume that White men will do something unpleasant until after they actually do it, and you'll will find it happens far less often than you'd think. Get a feel for the new psychological territory and you will be better equipped to meet the locals. You may or may not go anywhere in particular your first or second time out, but at least you will be on the inside and exploring new territory. Think about your past mistakes. Avoiding repeating them clears the stage for positive experiences. If you don't remember the mistakes of your past, you are sure to repeat them. Be sure to avoid locals who remind you in any way of men who gave you grief in the past. Avoiding certain types of bad-news men makes developing an overlay of positive new experiences come to you easier.

Desensitize Yourself To Short-Term Failure

Should you not have had any really positive relationships with men, you might overvalue the idea of getting into a good relationship to the point where the idea that it might "fail" scares you away from giving it a go. A particular relationship might or might not work out, but you'll never know how it might have turned out unless you give it a try. The real problem is not that it might "fail" or not work out (most relationships never hit the big time), but rather the negative connotations and associations tagged on supposed "failure" by third parties. Few things work perfectly the first time around, and normal people know this, while abnormal people harp on

41

their opinion of how they expect you to be perfect. They want you to feel bad about having given it a try because they demand perfection of anyone they can influence. Feeling bad on their say-so makes you likely to take counsel of their fears. This is a form of manipulation designed to limit your freedom of action and association, with nothing offered in return to compensate for that loss. People who do this to you are bad news, and should be excluded from every area of your life. Their standards of perfectionism add nothing to your life, and are actually thinly-disguised forms of jealousy, envy and the desire to control you. No blame or guilt should be felt due to a relationship not having worked out, because the alchemy of another person's reactions to you is not something anyone can control. It's okay to try and not make it, but it's not okay to be afraid to try. No benefits of any kind accrue to you for not trying. The only known benefits accrue to parasites who get a perverse form of pleasure from manipulating into a state where you can't enjoy yourself and lack the confidence to even try to get out of the box of expectations you allow them put you into. Don't let others monitor your social life or cross-examine you about your failure to live up to their standards. Seal such psychological parasites out of your private life. Tell them nothing. Don't overvalue others' opinions to the extent that you thereby wind up miss out exploring life's enjoyable possibilities, because you think it's better to do nothing than "fail" to live up to someone else's expectations.

You mentally devalue food and drink which do not appeal to your taste, and your choice of associates is also a matter of personal taste. Desensitize yourself to others' expectations and opinions. Many who try to stigmatize you for not running your life their way are often themselves too chicken to get into interracial relationships themselves, and making you feel guilty is part of an elaborate act to create props for their delusions of social grandeur. Misery loves company and will work at creating human puppets to keep them company.

"There is nothing either good or bad but thinking makes it so."
William Shakespeare
Hamlet

Chapter Four
White Male Emotional Availability
And Dating Interests

"When a girl finds a fellow's outside to her taste, she then sets about guessing the rest of his furniture."
Oliver Goldsmith
She Stoops To Conquer

Guidelines For Seeking Emotionally Available White Men

Emotional availability is a byproduct of psychological and economic adaptation to fulfill multiple adult social roles and responsibilities in the larger society, roles such as husband, father, employee, son, romantic companion and the like. Men who feel secure about these areas of their lives become receptive to opening up emotionally and to entering into adult relationships with women. Conversely, men who, for whatever reason, fail to take on the multiple social roles and responsibilities that come with achieving adulthood, tend to be emotionally unavailable.

Men who fail to learn to take on multiple social roles and responsibilities eventually become unable to fill those roles due to lack of practice and feel tensions from having this incapacity. They see others around them fulfilling those roles, and find themselves the odd men out, the ones who don't fit. Their refusal to take on multiple social roles and responsibilities deprives them of a variety of forms of psychological satisfaction derived from the status conferred by others as well as by their own psyches in fulfilling those roles. They react by becoming defensive and hostile to those around them. They don't open up because they are afraid they will suffer by comparison in the eyes of others, particularly women. They become increasingly emotionally unavailable over time because they spend all of their time and energy justifying what they already are instead of changing and adjusting to the demands of living in our society. They tend to associate with other emotionally unavailable men who also refuse to take on multiple social roles and responsibilities, reinforcing their existing tendencies by patting each other on the back about refusing to change. Such men are unlikely to change and become emotionally available because they block themselves off at every turn from absorbing

43

new information and copying other types of role models. They lock themselves into staying as they already are. Should they become locked into this mindset early in life, it becomes hard to shake off later on. It is the same as learning a foreign language: easy to learn when you are young and your mind is flexible, much more difficult as you become older and more set in your ways.

"It would seem that men do not find enough defects in themselves; they augment the number by certain singular qualities which they affect to put on, and these they cultivate with so much assiduity that they at length become natural defects which are no longer capable of correction."
La Rochefoucauld
Maxims

Emotionally available men are usually those men who have adjusted to the demands of living in our society. By contrast, emotionally unavailable men expect the world to adjust to them, not adjust themselves to the world. Such thinking often predestines them to fail to adjust to social life in the larger society. Failure to adjust results in lack of income and the trappings of status. Status is a byproduct of, and reward for, taking on multiple roles and responsibilities. Lack of status, and its attendant psychological tensions, is the result of the failure to take on multiple adult social roles and responsibilities. Low status means they wind up thinking less of themselves, knowing that others think less of them due to their having not taken on adult roles. Women seek men with status, and men who do not take on multiple roles have less to offer. When they think less of themselves, they are unable to become emotionally available because they do not have enough confidence about being accepted by others for what they are to open up to others.

Emotionally available White males become emotionally available because that is the logical outcome of the overall trend of their lives. Being nice to women is a personality trait consistent with feeling good about themselves. They can relax and become emotionally available because they feel secure about themselves because they have the psychological satisfaction and social status that derive from haven taken on multiple social roles and responsibilities. They have a sort of a psychological home base from which they can go out and explore. They are less likely to disrespect women because having control over their own lives means they have less frustration-derived need to seek status by controlling every part of a relationship.

Men who have "made it" feel free to let their hair down and open up to women. Men who feel they have an internal psychological deficit, as if they have not really made it, can't cut it in relationships. All they can think about is not having made it. They don't want others to find out that they are on thin ice and put them down. They work at taking control of relationships because only by assuming authority can they divert attention away from their personal deficits by talking tough, wearing an emotionless mask and grounding the relationship on authoritarianism.

"The inferior class of men always at heart feel [disrespect] towards those who are subject to their power."
John Stuart Mill
The Subjection Of Women

Taking on multiple social roles and responsibilities has no relationship whatsoever to income level. A minimum-wage factory worker who fulfills the roles of husband, father and employee is an adult. A high-income stock analyst who defines every part of his life in terms of his work and whose emotional development is frozen on the whining, self-centered adolescent little-boy level is not an adult. The key is to not let one's life become completely dependent on any one single role or set of responsibilities. Defining one's self in any one single way, regardless of the nature of that particular definition, necessarily means blocking off other avenues for potential development. Adult men must have more than one frame of reference for dealing with the rest of the world. No single role can possibly meet all of the demands that different social audiences, and one's own internal needs, require.

One-role men wind up treating everybody and everything in terms of living up to the demands of their single self-determined role. Men who define themselves solely in terms of their jobs relegate women to secondary roles in their lives, since such men refuse to broaden their mindset to include adapting themselves to take on other social roles beyond the monochromatic workplace role. Such men cannot move beyond the bounds of thinking of every part of life in terms of their particular single limited role. They lock themselves into playing one role in every possible part of life, as in the case a high pressure salesman who never stop selling himself twenty-four hours a day, regardless of how inappropriate that behavior is for non-workplace social contexts.

"Civility is a desire to receive it in turn, and to be accounted well bred."
La Rochefoucauld
Maxims

One common form of emotional unavailability is where men define themselves primarily in terms of their bond with a male social reference group. A good example is a fraternity member who bonds with other members of his fraternity. Bonding with other men automatically involves a particular form of conformity wherein men scale down expressing their individual preferences and interests to a level acceptable to other members of the group. Their bond is one of conformity around similar views and limitations on acceptable behavior. If the group deems that members shall act only in certain ways with women, that is how all shall act if they want to stay in the group. Such men are barred from becoming emotionally available because they are locked into the single role of bonded-male conformist, which prevents their personal interests and inclinations from flourishing in the face of actual or potential peer-group disapproval.

The internal standards of reference of the male peer group dictate that women are outsiders not to be trusted. It is as if an invisible advisor sits on their shoulders and whispers into their ears that they should always keep the opinions of the group in mind when in relationships with women, or even in considering relationships with women. For such men, the group consensus, not individual choice, determines the limits of their emotional availability. The bond such men share with their male peer groups is the determining factor in deliberately blocking them from psychological growth and maturity. The demands of taking on the peer group member role requires acting out role characteristics that block them from developing the capacity for taking on other roles for female audiences. Such emotional unavailability is not a minor personality trait. It is the logical outcome of a whole way of life organized around freezing themselves into the role of little boys who avoid taking on multiple social roles and responsibilities because their peer groups do not like the idea. Men who get no practice at taking on adult social roles do not become emotionally available adult men. They don't know how, and block off opportunities to learn how as a result of group conformist pressures.

The more entrenched the bond between the members of any male social reference group, the more the strength of that bond precludes a bond of intimacy from developing between such men and normal women. This applies to fraternities, street gangs, sports teams and any other male group. Bonds between men encourage conformity to the behavioral norms of that group, setting up another barrier to interracial relationships by projecting distrust onto outsiders with whom they do not share that bond. If you want to find a White male who is a good prospect for an interracial relationship by virtue of being emotionally available, the best place to start is with a man who thinks for himself and can use his mind to cut his way through the pressures to conform to which men are constantly subjected. White males with the mental flexibility to take on multiple social roles and responsibilities for different audiences must necessarily be good at tuning out irrelevant audiences in the process of taking on a role for any one particular audience, such as that of their female companion or their own inner needs and interests. Men who can't stop thinking about, and catering to, the expectations and opinions of third parties are not adults and can not be expected to behave or think as adults, a precondition for emotional availability. Their mindset precludes becoming multidimensional adults.

"A man who does not think for himself does not think at all."
Oscar Wilde
The Soul Of Man Under Socialism

Of course, having social status as a result of, and reward for, having taken on multiple social roles does not in and of itself ensure that a man will not have problems that make him unsuitable for interracial relationships. Taking on multiple roles is a precondition for becoming emotionally available, but does not in and of itself guarantee emotional availability. Plenty of such men have drinking problems, personality disorders and abusive tendencies that disqualify them. But, on average, men who take on multiple roles and responsibilities are less likely to have certain types of life-situation problems that create continual high anxiety. By contrast, men filled with rage about their low social status, which is in turn derived from their failure to take on multiple roles and responsibilities, are looking for targets onto which they can project their frustrations, not companions in intimacy. The higher your self-esteem, the better you feel about yourself. People who feel good about themselves can afford to be emotionally generous with others.

A Black woman seeking an emotionally available White male should be on the lookout for certain psychological characteristics. Compatible White males should not be locked into any one role as the center of their self-definition, be it their job, their male social reference group or the role they play for their parents. If all he can talk about is his job, his drinking buddies, or what his mother thinks, forget him. Men who feel the need to look to others for permission or approval to get into interracial relationships are bad news. Whatever a man's income level and educational level, his behavior should indicate he has enough satisfaction with his current level of social status, which is itself a byproduct of his having taken on, or not taken on, multiple social roles and responsibilities, to not walk around with a chip on the shoulder about how unhappy he is. Satisfaction with status relaxes, dissatisfaction makes men boil.

Living up to the demands of this self-imposed angry-male role makes such men unable to take on other social roles that go with being adults. The frustrations that arise from trimming down the other parts of their lives to fit into such a role makes them unsuitable for interracial relationships. Generalized frustrations about life as a whole are guaranteed to spill over into your relationship with him, and the last thing an interracial relationship that attracts external social pressures needs is self-induced pressures generated by those inside the relationship. You will find that men open to playing multiple roles and taking on multiple responsibilities are relaxed because taking on these roles and responsibilities acts as a sort of psychological stabilizer that keeps them relaxed about themselves and consequently open to adult relationships. Feeling good about themselves by virtue of having taken on multiple roles and responsibilities and the social and psychological satisfactions and status that go with such roles and responsibilities makes them susceptible to being emotionally available. By contrast, men who fail to take on multiple roles and responsibilities feel bad about themselves and can't get close to others because their lack of status makes them feel others will put them down once they learn about the truth about them. This explains why low-status men are often accused of wearing masks that hide what they really are. Don't get involved with men who carry around grudges or who want to "get even" with the rest of the world because they think they've gotten bad deals in life. You don't need men with problems for anything, and need to get on with your life.

Color Blind And Racially Preferential Dating

"If a man does not keep pace with his companions, perhaps it is because he hears a different drummer. Let him step to the music which he hears, however measured or far away."
Henry David Thoreau
Walden

Five types of White men have interracial dating potential. First is the "color blind" group. These White men had no special interest in Black women until a particular Black woman caught their eye. Their interest, at least initially, focuses on a particular Black woman, not Black women in general. Such men have typically lived in primarily-White areas most of their lives and probably attended primarily-White schools. They have had limited contact with Blacks in general, and Black women in particular. By whatever means, they came into contact with a particular Black woman who unlocked a door in the mind. The interpersonal chemistry clicked, and things took off. These White men have "color blind" dating preferences, in the sense of some nonracial characteristic about the individual Black woman being the determining factor of interest to him. Race is either a neutral or non-pivotal factor. These White men might or might not go on to date other Black women, depending on the degree to which those Black women embody those nonracial characteristics important to particular men.

The characteristics of interest to such men are matters of personal taste. Almost anything could be important to a particular man. It might be intellectual, psychological, physical, sociological, or even as quirky as her accent. For one White male, the deciding factor might be a consuming mutual interest in leisure time activities such as classical music or tennis. Another White man might have a decided preference for a certain type of figure. Yet another might have a thing for a Southern accent. Still another might just like her personality and the way she laughs. This type of White male will make a move on a Black woman only if he sees a matchup with the Black woman along a nonracial dimension such as lifestyle interests, education, social class, personality, and so on. Race is essentially a neutral factor, at least in the initial phases of the relationship. As time goes on, should he meet more Black women who suit his tastes, he might develop a generalized preference for Black women as a group and focus his interests on women within that group.

Some such men go on to develop an exclusive interest in Black women to the exclusion of other racial groups, and some will not. Should their first interracial relationship break up, they will retain their preference for Black women exhibiting that particular nonracial trait of interest. Some will go on to develop some degree of preference for women similar to Black women with whom they have had positive experiences. Some Black women are much the same way. For example, some Black women might say that a man, regardless of race, must exemplify one or more particular characteristics to be of interest, such as being over six feet tall or a devout Christian. As with color-blind White men, such Black women probably took little notice of White men in general until a particular White male who fit the bill caught their fancy, and such Black women went on to develop a preference for particular types of men with whom they have had positive experiences.

The second type of White male interested in Black women prefers Black women to White women. They date Black women because they are Black. They don't ignore race, say that they don't notice it or say that women of every race have their own sort of beauty. Race is the deciding, or primary, initial factor of esthetic, physical attraction in making their dating choices. Race is what attracts them initially, and they continue to date Black women because they enjoy their company as well as the way they look. Black hair, skin, figures, and other physical characteristics appeal to these men. The other side of the coin is, all other things being equal, they would probably not be interested in those same Black women were those women White. They seek compatible women exclusively within the pool of Black women. Some Black women have a similar taste for White male physical differences. They like the way White men look, but can not explain any further beyond stating that their personal tastes tend to the lighter side of the color line.

Men are highly reactive to visual stimuli, and some are initially attracted to Black women for purely physical reasons, just as some Black men are

50

attracted to blonde women for purely physical reasons, the reason being novel visual stimuli. Such White men often mention a preference for smooth, dark skin. Others say that Black women have different types of figures that they find more appealing than those of White women, or that their hair texture or facial features look better than those of White women. Their definition of "better" comes down to their personal tastes, and nothing more. The common theme is that they like certain physical features not found among White women, but common among Black women. Some racially preferential White men develop their interests in Black women as early as high school, while others slowly develop their tastes over the course of time based on a gradual, cumulative development of interest in certain things about Black women. They gradually tune out White women as they become more interested in Black women. Your competition for these men is other Black women.

Some words of caution are in order. While racially preferential White men prefer Black women, that does not mean that they will date the first Black woman with whom they come into contact, unless all they are looking for is a short-term relationship. You wouldn't date just any old White guy, would you? Men develop detailed personal preferences regarding women over the course of time. Most will look for Black women close to their own general level of education and intelligence, someone with whom they have common certain tastes, opinions, lifestyles, activities and attitudes. In brief, it should come as no surprise that they want someone compatible. Some like intellectuals, others prefer down-to-earth, pragmatic types. Some have a thing for full lips and natural hair, others go for various physical types. Some like thick figures, some like svelte figures. Some have a thing for giggly women, others prefer calm and sober types. If they've dated several Black women before meeting you, they probably have a general idea of the range of characteristics that their preferred physical/intellectual/emotional/social "type" should have, and will probably be unreceptive to other types. Most White men don't see the issue in such highly analytical terms, however. Men don't draw up checklists of must-have characteristics for women. If they analyze what they are looking for at all, they just say "I know what I like." When they run across someone who is their type, they recognize them, make a move and sort out the details later.

The third type of White male is in the early, experimental stages of interracial dating, and as yet doesn't know enough about Black women to decide how he wants to go over the long term. They are still in the process of gathering information. Dating Black women is something new for them, just as dating White men is something new for many Black women. Not yet knowing just what their Black female "type" is makes them fairly flexible about who they date, but they are unlikely to make long-term commitments until they know a lot more. After dating several Black women, such men gradually accumulate a critical mass of information about Black women that helps them develop fixed preferences regarding Black women. Such men can wind up going in almost any direction, from marrying a Black woman to dating both Blacks and Whites, to going back to dating only Whites, depending on how compatible they found themselves to be with those women they dated along the way. Some Black women go through a similar transitional or experimental phase, dating White to see how it turns out, how they like it and whether or not there are any White male types with whom they feel really comfortable.

The fourth type are those cosmopolitan White men who date women of several races. They'll date women of any race if they seem interesting. They are not color-blind. They just appreciate the differences that women of different races offer, and see no reason to restrict themselves to one flavor when they live in a store where many different flavors are available. There is no way to spot them in a crowd, but they do tend to be good at approaching women who catch their eye, and might also tend to have a few too many girlfriends for the comfort of many Black women for whom they might bring up memories of Black male players with similarly broad interests.

The fifth type of White male interested in Black women are those men who don't know as yet that they might like Black women. They are potentially receptive to Black women, but their interests remain buried inside their psyches, waiting for somebody or some event to spark those latent tastes into action. They are not color-blind. They are aware that interesting Black women are out there, but a lifetime of circumstances and a lack of opportunities have conspired to make them think that the Black women out there do not concern them personally. It's just a habit that developed through a combination of inertia and circumstances. They wouldn't think about dating interracially unless someone else makes the first move and sparks them into action. They won't see Black women as being relevant to their lives until someone at work, a laundromat or in their neighborhood goes out of her way to be friendly. They might become interested if someone just like should flash a little smile on the street one fine day. You can never tell who might be interested. The key point is that, with most such latently receptive White males, the Black woman must make the first move, because their inertia makes it unlikely that they will make the first move. If you're interested in someone, sometimes you are the one that needs to make the first move or your big opportunity will slip by.

White Male Visual Perceptions Of Black Women

"All good looks are a snare."
Oscar Wilde
The Importance of Being Earnest

Women's bodies attract male attention. What you may not know, however, is just why certain appearance factors, and not others, catch men's eyes. The reason is that men are born with a genetically-determined, instinctual capacity for interest and arousal that can be triggered by seeing specific visual cues. Those cues women exhibit are nothing more or less than visual evidence of the likelihood of female fertility. Given that a large proportion of the female body is primarily or secondarily reproductive in nature (such as the ovaries, breasts and womb), it makes evolutionary sense that human males would develop a knack for spotting certain things about women that would increase the chances of perpetuating the species. This instinctual male capacity is a legacy of our hunter-gatherer past, hundreds of thousands of years ago. Hunter-gatherer men were aroused by women showing signs of fertility, and that state of arousal increased the likelihood that men would bond and mate with women likely to be fertile. Women who show visual signs of fertility are more likely, on average, to have the capacity to reproduce than women not showing such signs, and they pass along both the male and female traits in question to their descendants. Over the course of many millions of years, these traits became widespread in the human species. Those lacking such traits were less likely to reproduce, and thus have few, if any, modern-day descendants who also lack their traits. Several aspects of our social mating dances also serve crucial biological functions.

53

The visual cues to which men pay attention provide evidence of both fertility as well as the overall good health that also favors fertility. A good example is a female waist thirty percent smaller than the hips. A woman's curves depend on body fat, and body fat is a crucial element in our reproduction. A woman must have a minimum of eighty thousand calories of body fat in order to become pregnant, or else her body's automatic shutoff mechanisms will prevent her from becoming pregnant, or carrying a pregnancy to term, due to her lack of sufficient calories to support both the pregnancy and her other bodily needs.

Evolution has equipped men of every race and country to spot body fat in terms of visually evident female curvature. Apart from reproduction, another biological purpose of human body fat is to store energy from food for the lean times when our hunter-gatherer ancestors found little or no food, similar to a camel hump's storage of water for crossing desert areas. People accumulated body fat when food was easy to come by, and burned it off in going hungry during lean hunting-gathering seasons. When times were good, hunter-gatherer women accumulated enough body fat to have a biological survival margin that allowed for pregnancy. Thus, body fat storage served the dual purposes of enhancing the chances of both personal survival as well as the perpetuation of the human species.

The other side of the coin is what happens when this physical trait is lacking. Anorexic women usually inspire little male arousal because subconscious male instinctual mechanisms classify anorexic women as unlikely to be fertile, and therefore men are often little aroused in seeing such women. Their instincts make it less likely. Keep in mind that these are subconscious instincts, and are susceptible, within broad limits, to some degree of cultural modification. Thus, cultural conditioning, or developing particular personal preferences, operates to make some men prefer very thin women. It is usually the case, however, that biological programming will override cultural conditioning as regards sexual attraction.

Skin provides evidence of female fertility. Smooth, silky skin is direct evidence of the presence of the female hormones that act to smoothen the skin, providing indirect visual evidence of fertility. Unblemished skin is also evidence of the good health generally associated with fertility, in the sense of lacking blemishes and other skin imperfections which provide visually evident symptoms of fertility-reducing diseases. Good health was important in hunter-gatherer societies by virtue of allowing you to keep up with the rest of the tribe in searching for food. The unhealthy had less chance of being able to find food, which in turn would enable them to make to the point of reproduction.

Black skin has certain advantages over White skin in attracting the interest of certain types of White males. White skin, or any white object, is seen as white because white reflects more light of different wavelengths than other colors. As more light reflects outwards, your eyes receive more photons, which carry detailed visual information about the reflecting object to the brain. White skin contrasts more against many types of blemishes than does dark skin, similar to the contrast you would find with spots of paint against a white canvas versus a darker canvas.

Conversely, dark skin reflects less light, and consequently blemishes and other skin problems are less clearly visible to observers. Unblemished skin, or skin having the appearance of being unblemished, is a visual cue associated with female fertility. Black skin partially masks some types of blemishes, freckles, close-to-the-surface blood vessels, wrinkles and other skin imperfections simply by virtue of being darker than White skin, thereby absorbing rather than reflecting many photons, giving the impression of a smoother and more even skin than the skin of a similarly healthy White woman. Many White women unconsciously recognize this, and get tans to look "sexy," their term for masking visual evidence of skin imperfections that give the appearance of reduced fertility, while risking skin damage from ultraviolet radiation in the process of acquiring such tans.

Black skin withstands aging better than White skin by virtue of having more melanin than White skin, making it more resistant to sunburn damage and the premature aging of the skin caused by overexposure to the various forms of ultraviolet radiation present in sunlight. White and Black women of the same age and in the same state of health will show differing cumulative reactions to sun exposure as the years progress. Sometimes you will hear a White man comment to the effect that Black women do not show their ages as much as White women. Men like smooth skin, or skin that at least appears smooth, and dark skin helps provide that esthetically desirable state of appearance. On top of that, some White men have esthetic tastes that run to women with melanin to spare.

"We women.....love with our ears, just as you men love with your eyes."
Oscar Wilde
The Picture Of Dorian Gray

All of this talk about visual cues for fertility might give you the impression that men don't go for women past the age of childbearing. That is incorrect. Men do go for women of various ages who exhibit visual indicators of fertility, regardless of whether or not she is actually capable of child-bearing. The reason is that the instinctual male sexual drive is aroused by the appearance, and not necessarily the reality, of female fertility. Appearance counts, but only in initial attraction. Just because he finds you sexually appealing doesn't mean he likes you as a person. Sex appeal is only the first step. Personality is a very close second. Men do not choose to spend a lot of time with unpleasant women, regardless of how sexy they are. You need to appeal to a man's sexual instincts, his cultural conditioning and his individual tastes and personality if you want to have the sort of long-term appeal that can lead to a long-term relationship. Sexy is nice, but nice is even sexier over the long run.

Do White Men Only Go For Light-Skinned Black Women?

"I will swear beauty herself is black,
and all they foul that thy complexion lack."
William Shakespeare
Sonnet CXXXII

No. Some White men go for dark women, some go for light women and many go for almost any shade of melanin darker than their own skin tone. Skin tone is most often only one of several physical attributes White men look for in a Black woman, and the sum total of physical attributes sought are in turn just one of several factors a particular White man might value. One man might focus first on intelligence and education, second on personality, third on figure, with skin tone being the fourth factor of interest on his list. Again, they are not looking at you solely in terms of skin color. There's a variety of physical, emotional, intellectual and sociological factors interacting in a given White man's head.

"Love looks not with the eyes, but with the mind."
William Shakespeare
A Midsummer Night's Dream

White men are generally not as color-conscious as Black men and women, because color is not a central factor in their daily lives. The complex, color-related, social-caste gradations that some Blacks like to dwell on mean little or nothing to most White males. This means that a particular White man will home in on a Black woman he finds attractive in terms of his own particular tastes regardless of how the informal Black social caste system slots her. White male tastes vary all over the map.

Some White men find extremely dark women quite attractive, for example. Other White men might go for full lips. Such White men will not ask, or even think of asking, other Blacks for an opinion about her, and probably couldn't care less about their opinions. Even should a White male hear other Blacks' opinions about a particular Black woman, he has no reason to esteem their opinions above his own tastes in women.

White men don't ask other men for advice or suggestions from other men, Black or White, on such matters, particularly in touchy personal situations such as interracial dating. It is more likely that a comet will strike the Earth than it is that a White male interested in a Black woman will ask Black men or women for opinions regarding a Black woman in whom he has an interest.

After dating several White men, you will find that most see skin color differently than most Blacks. It's simply an esthetic characteristic of interest for them. For many White men, just your being Black makes you interesting. As long as a woman is in an esthetically novel, "different" category, meaning darker than he is, the exact shade of black or brown is most often secondary or irrelevant. Black women operate the same way. While some interracially-minded Black women might settle only for men with blue eyes and a certain shade of blonde hair, most Black women are not like that, and are open to a broad range of physical characteristics such as physique, hair, skin and eyes. White men are the same. Their tastes in Black women vary all over the map.

"Here black, there brown, here tawny, and there white; Thou flatterer which compli'st with every sight!"
"Beauty"
Abraham Cowley

White Men Do Not Read Fashion Magazines

Few men, White or Black, read women's fashion magazines, and most have little interest in fashion. Most women learn sooner or later that men have far less interest in clothing and fashion than women, and are sometimes surprised that many men couldn't care less about how they dress. To some degree, this male lack of interest in their own clothing extends to what women wear. To be blunt, men are more interested in what's under the clothing than the clothing itself. If you're relaxed about yourself, you need not worry about your clothing as long as it's clean, not threadbare and looks less than a decade old. Mainstream middle-class attire is often your best bet.

You want White men to focus on you, not your clothing. Dressing up really fancy might even get some men suspicious about you. They might think that you are incredibly narcissistic and spend all of your time looking in the mirror and trying on new clothing. Men are quite aware that women, for reasons quite incomprehensible to men, are often much more interested in clothing than men, but become justifiably suspicious about someone who lives and breathes nothing but fashion, just as you should be justifiably suspicious about a man who lives and breathes nothing but football. Dress to meet middle-class White guys, not to garner applause from catering to the expectations of fashion-minded unattached women.

"Dress yourself fine, where others are fine; and plain where others are plain; but take care always that your clothes are well made, and fit you, for otherwise they will give you an awkward air."
Philip Stanhope, Earl of Chesterfield
Letters To His Son

A corollary of the axiom that White men do not read fashion magazines is that, since they do not read the magazines, they do not know what physically "perfect" women should look like, "perfect" meaning what fashion magazine editors define as perfect, and thus have never warmed up to the idea that women should have anorexic physiques, bones bleaching in the sun. Any woman who thinks that normal men go for skin-and-bones women is way off on a tangent from reality, period. What men consider attractive in a woman differs radically from what women consider attractive in a woman. Expectations that women be ultra-thin originate with other women, not men.

If you want to know what men really fantasize about, look at what most men spend a portion their hard-earned cash on at some point in their lives. These are euphemistically known as "men's magazines." If you've never had the opportunity to peruse such men's magazines, suffice it to say that there is not an anorexic in sight in such periodicals, and there is also little overlap between those models found in men's magazines and the models found in women's fashion magazines.

Men like things about women that are sometimes quite different than what women think they ought to like. Men don't spend their money on fashion magazines featuring pictures of anorexic models because they don't like the way anorexic women look, period, no matter what you and your girlfriends think ought to be the case. An attractive, proportional figure is attainable by nearly all women who exercise and eat right. Eating right does not mean eating almost nothing.

"Preserving the health by too strict a regimen is a wearisome malady."
La Rochefoucauld
Maxims

Thick Figures

White men are attracted to Black women for reasons that include physical attraction. Some White men find thick figures attractive, and will go out of their way to find that particular physical type of Black woman. After being around White women who often exhibit more weight anxiety than Black women, such White men are looking for something different, both in terms of figure and, to a lesser extent, attitude about body weight. If those Black women are otherwise compatible, the men are likely to stick around for the long haul, since they find few real-life women who can match up with the image in their heads. While both Black and White women have thick figures, thick figures are more common among Black women. These

White men are often attracted only to Black women with thick figures, not to Black women in general. White male fetishes for thick figures come in several flavors. Some home in on big busts. Others go for muscular, Amazon types. Still others go for hourglass-figure, proportionately padded Black women, filled out evenly all over.

Yet another type goes for sizable Black BBWs (Big Beautiful Women). While not all White males go for Black women with thick figures, many do go for Black women with various types of thick figures. This fixation may seem a bit superficial, but it is really no different than a Black woman with a fetish for men over six feet tall. To each their own.

"Ah, make the most of what we may yet spend
Before we too into the dust descend"
Edward Fitzgerald
The Rubaiyat of Omar Khayyam

Chapter Five
Ground Rules For Potential Compatibility

"Ultimately the bond of all companionship, whether in marriage or in friendship, is conversation, and conversation must have a common basis, and between two people of widely different cultures the only common basis possible is the lowest level."
Oscar Wilde
De Profundis

Social Class And Interracial Attraction

"Class-loyalty was undoubtedly an ideal with many."
William James
Talk To Teachers on Psychology

One factor that impeded the development of White male/Black female relationships before the last few decades was the social class gap. Blacks usually had fewer good opportunities for education and employment than Whites. However intelligent, attractive and personable a Black woman might have been, should she have lacked a middle-class background and education, many middle-class White men would have thought twice about getting into a serious relationship with her, just as a Black woman today would think twice about getting involved with a White man worlds apart from her in education and income. What would two people from different worlds have in common? Similarities lead to an interest in becoming more closely involved, and the absence of such similarities most often lead in the opposite direction.

When two people from disparate backgrounds do become involved in long-term relationships, their reasons for becoming involved usually involve extensive personality meshing that outweighs outwardly visible social class differences, as in the cases of two people who live and breathe tennis or share a common religious outlook on life. Such people are the exceptions. Statistically speaking, people from similar backgrounds usually turn out to be the ones with the best odds for a good match. Now and then, however, you do hear stories about statistical refugees that stick to your mind due to their uncommon nature. Should two people have nothing more in common besides time on their hands and an itch to get involved, the odds of a long-term relationship developing are not auspicious.

You can avoid a host of potential heartaches by focusing your efforts to become involved with White men on White men of social classes a notch or two or three just above or below you. Social class means a combination of education, intelligence, income level, occupation, lifestyle interests, activities and opinions. The closer your and his social classes, the more the two you are likely to have in common. The greater the social class differences between you and him, the less the two of you have in common in terms of shared background, activities, interests and opinions. Long-term relationships require that two people have some enduring characteristics in common, though the particular characteristics of interest vary all over the map for different people.

By contrast, short-term relationships require nothing in common beyond the desire of two people to spend time together. For some people, education and common intellectual leisure time pursuits are the decisive factors. For others, shared leisure time sports interests are the key. Still others might consider having a white-collar occupation the key factor. Regardless of the specific things you value, there must be some important areas of overlap between you and him or things will not progress very far. Common interests and background are just the starting gate for interaction, not the finish line. Similar backgrounds bring you together, but what you do after you make contact is a completely different ballgame.

Having things in common also provides some personal protection. Certain types of Black and White men have little empathy for women more than one or two steps down the social ladder from themselves. The greater the social class distance, the more such men feel free to lie, play games and use women. While sticking with men similar to you is no guarantee in and of itself that a White man will not con you, you will have some measure of protection in being able to recognize certain common con games that men of your own class use on women. This is regrettable, but a fact of life you have to live with.

The less two people have in common, the more likely it is that the man will see the woman in question as a lesser being than himself, assuming she is the one trying to date a few steps up the social class ladder. Men do not have a monopoly on this.

Similar things happen when White-collar women date blue-collar men. When topics that are central to a white-collar Black woman's life, such as college and office politics, come up in conversations, draw blank looks from a blue-collar man, the woman may become inclined to see him as a sociological specimen rather than a real person. This sort of thing can be overcome if two people have open minds and hearts, but the odds are incalculable. Initial attraction almost always fades when two people have nothing to talk about or do together.

"An illiterate man's my aversion: I wonder at the impudence of any illiterate man to offer to make love."
William Congreve
The Way Of the World

Maturity And Interracial Relationships

White males who get into interracial relationships tend to be more psychologically mature than average. What does mature mean in the context of interracial relationships? Should he have gone out with Black women before, he knows what sort of day-by-day social pressures are involved, and while the pressures may faze him a bit, the pluses far outweigh the minuses for him. Being stared at, pointed at or whispered about doesn't slow him down much. Mature men are less susceptible to social pressures than average. They don't let the potential for social problems overwhelm, paralyze or impede them from getting on with their personal lives.

Should they not have dated Black women before, but be looking to do so, you can be sure they have done some thinking on the subject. True, some younger White males just jump into it without knowing what to expect, but the same can be said about some younger Black women. Maturity means taking on different roles for different social audiences, which includes the ability to tune out irrelevant audiences when preoccupied with the inner audience of one's own preferences. Feeling the need to comply with the social pressures exerted against interracial relationships indicates immaturity in the sense of the inability to tune out external audiences one plays for in taking on a particular role and failing to tune into one's internal, private audience of one's personal interests, tastes and preferences.

Black women and White men too immature to handle an interracial relationship either mature in short order or bail out. Not everybody can manage being in an interracial relationship. Chronological age is not a reliable indicator of personal maturity. Some people can handle interracial dating with no sweat at eighteen, others can't even begin to get a handle on it at thirty.

People also change with time. Someone who can't handle an interracial relationship this year might straighten his head out and be a completely different person next year. No particular blame should be attached to not being able to handle the pressures of an interracial relationship. You just have to be a particular kind of person to do certain things, like mountain-climbing, and some people have just not been pushed enough, either by circumstances or desire, to change as fast as they should. While people can change and grow over time as they learn more, some never learn and never change.

Don't become standby equipment while someone else agonizes about whether or not to mature. You are never under any obligation to commit to someone who has yet to get his act together, or who might never get his act together. You have a life of your own to get on with, and should not put it on hold to wait for someone who might, or might not, eventually mature into someone with whom you can have positive experiences. Should you be the one who needs to mature, the same applies to the man. No one should ever put their life on hold in a world full of fish of both sexes waiting to be hooked. One-sided commitments are about as meaningful as one person standing at the altar.

"No profit grows where there is no pleasure ta'en"
William Shakespeare
The Taming Of The Shrew

Your Type, Or Types

"It is more easy to become acquainted with men in general, than with any man in particular."
La Rochefoucauld
Maxims

What kind of White guy are you looking for? Unless you already socialize with White guys at school, work or in the neighborhood, you most likely won't know what you are looking for until after you get it. You'll probably have to meet a number of guys to get a better handle on your type, or types. The more different types of White guys with whom you have casual interaction, the better able you'll be to develop a feel for such types as might be your types.

There are many different types of White males. The differences can be physical, intellectual, educational, emotional, sociological, or any combination you can imagine. Old and young, short and tall, rich and poor, fat and thin, white-collar and blue-collar, nice and mean, smart and stupid, open and reserved. Should you have lived in an integrated neighborhood, or work in an integrated workplace, this is not news to you, but middle-class Blacks and Whites often live in different neighborhoods, which means they live in different social universes. This keeps them from seeing each other in everyday situations. By default, movies, television news, soap operas, newspapers and even romance novels have rushed in to fill the informational vacuum with a variety of misleading images and stereotypes, positive and negative. Blacks and Whites have numerous media-derived misconceptions about each other, and in many instances, bad news is the media's idea of noteworthy news.

In other cases, fantasy images have rushed in to fill the vacuum. Should the only things you know about interracial dating and White men derive from seeing celebrity couples on television, you are on the wrong track. Most White males are regular guys, and are not rich, movie-star handsome or White Knights in shining armor. They wake up every morning, go to work, pay their bills and scratch around to meet someone just like you. While many details of their daily existence differ from those of Black men, the basics are often pretty much the same. It will take time and effort for anyone to find someone compatible. There's no quick fix.

Some White men will sweep you off your feet at first sight. Most will not. There may be somebody at work, school, the neighborhood, the local tennis court, or just somebody you cross paths with now and then who grows on you slowly, as you are exposed to him bit by bit. This makes sense. You can't really tell what a White male is like just by looking at him, beyond your first glance telling you that you like his face and body. After hearing someone talk a bit, watching him go about some of his everyday activities, and so on, something will click in your head. Or, maybe something about you will click in his head, should he have his eye on you while looking ever-so-casual. Repeated instances of casual contact have a cumulative impact that cuts both ways. Make yourself known and give mutual attraction a chance to sprout. If you get to know a number of Whites men well, something might pop up when you least expect it. Indulging Yourself

"Be as attentive to your pleasures as to your studies."
Philip Stanhope, Earl of Chesterfield
Letters To His Son

Why play it safe and dull, and probably do so unhappily, when you can seek out and indulge yourself in whatever type of man excites you? Should you have a long-repressed fantasy to get involved with a particular type of White male, such as a Scandinavian blonde, an intellectual or an older man, indulge yourself and see where it leads, regardless of what your mother, aunt, girlfriends, neighbors and strangers tell you about what is "right" and "proper" for you. Their gods are not your gods. Only you know what is right for you, and only you can live your life in the manner that suits your needs and desires.

Don't trim down your interests and desires to suit other people's tastes and expectations. Indulge your secret fantasy when a suitable opportunity presents itself. Don't look back and say "I wish I had gotten involved with that guy." If not now, when will you start to come out of your shell? Should it not work out, at least you gave it a try, doing something that might lead to better things, rather than doing nothing, a guaranteed route to nowhere.

"T'is better to have loved and lost, than never to have loved at all."
Alfred Lord Tennyson
"In Memoriam, A.H.H."

Settle the issue of what you like through personal experience rather than by listening to others' opinions. Their opinions can be automatically discounted because those expressing such opinions about you do not have your depth and breadth of knowledge about the things that make you the person you are. The kind of White male you are looking for, even if you are not really sure just yet what type that is, is a preference developed and synthesized in the back of your mind over the course of many years out of the cumulative distilled experience of thousands of little events, decisions and inborn inclinations. You may not even be consciously aware of the exact nature of many of your own preferences early in the game, or even realize that some preferences exist within you until after you meet a White male embodying such traits as you prefer. For example, you might not realize you like artistic personalities until after you meet a real-life artist. Your tastes can also change as you change over the course of time, meet new types of men and have different types of enjoyable experiences. You may find a good match immediately, without repeated random sampling, but you will most likely find yourself enjoying the companionship charms of several less-than-perfect matches while continuing your search. Follow your nose.

"There are many truths of which the full meaning can not be realized until personal experience has brought it home."
John Stuart Mill
On Liberty

He Likes Black Women, But You're Not His Type

You might meet a White guy who seems perfect. But, for some reason, he honestly doesn't think you're his type. This happens. No matter what you think, no matter what your friends think, no matter what anybody else thinks, if for some unfathomable reason (unfathomable to you, not to him) you think he ought to like you, but doesn't, forget it. The most common reason is his idiosyncratic tastes in women. Just because you like him, does not mean his tastes in women automatically complement your tastes

67

in men. There is no accounting for a man's tastes, or, for that matter, your tastes, so don't waste time trying. He may simply have a fixation or fetish for a specific physical or psychological type. Maybe you're short and he has a thing for Amazon types. Maybe you're an engineer and he goes for dreamy, poetic types. There is most likely some little thing about the way you look, talk, act, think or whatever, that turns on a big red "Stop" sign in his mind. You can't peek inside his head to see what's going on there, and he definitely does not want to explain why he doesn't like you. When a man does not like a particular woman, he avoids her or drops her out of her life.

He might like you fifty percent on a scale of a hundred -but he may need to like ninety percent of everything about you to really want to get involved. It's all or nothing for him - if he doesn't like you a lot, he thinks it's best to not like you at all. No matter what the reason is, it makes sense to him, and that's what counts, at least with him. Women do the same thing when they "just have a feeling" about someone, but are slow on the uptake to understand that men do the same thing. This is unfortunate, but a fact of life. Nobody clicks with everybody else, or even with a lot of other people. Just cut your losses and move on.

Older White Men

"Every man over forty is a scoundrel."
George Bernard Shaw
Man And Superman

Older White men, here taken to mean either those over forty or more than ten years above your own age, offer an assortment of pluses and minuses. You might think that older White men offer more in terms of financial security, sexual experience, maturity, personality development and knowing how to treat a Black woman. Some do, some don't. Even older White men can be financially insecure, sexually inept, immature, have underdeveloped personalities and not know how to treat a Black woman. Evaluate older White men on a case-by-case basis.

Older White men are generally less susceptible to the social pressures associated with interracial dating. The older a man gets, the more likely he is to have taken on the multiple roles and responsibilities consistent with

68

adulthood, and to be able tune out external audiences irrelevant to the needs of his inner audience. The opinions of others, including relatives, carry less and less weight with them as the years go on, meaning opinions that obstruct them from potentially positive experiences and relationships. In many cases, they know from sad experience that catering to others' opinions and expectations has gotten them nowhere and produced nothing. If they like you, they will get involved with you. The way they calmly ignore other people's opinions and stares may seem a bit unearthly to some younger women, but it is really just a byproduct of their cumulative life experiences and having seen it all before. You might even learn some new tricks yourself from some older dogs.

A White male divorced from a White woman is less likely to have the fixation that White women are the only way to go. Should he have married young, dating Black women may not have been an option when he was young, and maturity is likely to have washed away the mental roadblocks that impeded interracial dating when he was last unattached. He'll be more likely to check out somebody different who offers the prospect of compatibility, given that he knows all too well just how hard it is to find a really compatible woman. Should he take a liking to you, you can be sure that he has thought about interracial dating and the social pressures involved, even if he never brings up the subject. The reason he doesn't bring up such matters is that he doesn't think that such things are worth dwelling on. Real adults know that being adult requires turning your back on others' expectations to pursue your private interests.

While divorce is common enough among White men, should something about him feel wrong, you might want to look up the divorce court papers to see just why he got divorced. Should he have a long history of physical or verbal abuse, forget him and keep looking. Abusing others as a way of life is a long-term embedded personality trait common among men with mental problems and feelings of inferiority. An abuser at age twenty-five will probably still be an abuser at age fifty. Conversely, someone who is a nice guy at age twenty-five is likely to be a nice guy at age fifty. Past behavior is the best predictor of future behavior. Don't take unnecessary chances. Older White men are off-the-shelf products, and what you see is exactly what you will get. Good and bad habits alike are pretty much set in concrete due to the decades of practice men get in maintaining such habits the time they reach middle age, and nothing you can do will change him in the slightest, though you can annoy him by trying.

Older White men will be picky about who they decide to take a liking to and less likely to settle down in the short run, even should they never have been married. Such men have had a long time to crystallize their tastes and preferences. An older White male might not have dated interracially before getting involved with you, in which case you are a new type for him. While he may have no qualms about becoming involved with you, it may take him a while to assimilate and understand the cultural and psychological differences between you and such White women as he has been acquainted with over the decades.

Even after he understands you, it will take longer to elicit commitment from many older men, some of whom have decades of experience in eluding marriage-minded women. Older men are in no hurry to commit or marry, and a state of hurriedness on your part does not constitute an emergency on his part. He will not commit to you simply because you want commitment. A man will commit when he knows you inside-out and likes most of what he knows about you. It takes a good deal of time to get to that point. There's no fast track to commitment, and women who want instant commitment are on the wrong track. Life is in the details, and older White men want to examine your details in excruciating detail before committing to commingling the details of their life with yours.

Older White men tend to be established in their careers. The careers of some may have peaked, and they may be both interested in, and able to, spend more time on, their personal lives. Should they already have raised children, they will be unlikely to have qualms about biracial children. That assumes, of course, that they want children in the first place. Some, having already raised children, may not want to block out another twenty years of their lives for child raising, and might want a wife or girlfriend all to themselves all of the time. Others might be ready, able and willing to start a new family at age fifty. You can't generalize. There are different types of older White males, just as there are different types of younger Black men, and it takes time to get a feel for what any given individual might want out of life. In many cases, they will not have any really rigid expectations, but will have boundaries you have to learn about and live within. Should both of you have single parent lifestyles, that is one starting point for potential compatibility, given that both of you can appreciate and empathize with the other's problems and scheduling, but you still have to have something more in common beyond both having kids. Try to find some sort of common ground for compatibility beyond both of you being unattached and with kids: sports, church, intellectual interests, the arts, and the like are possibilities for mutual leisure time interests.

It's okay to date an older man if you want a daddy or father figure, particularly if you grew up without a father around. If you're an adult and you want to give it a try, there is no reason to let other people's opinions about a May-December match block you from having a chance at happiness. Your taste in men's ages is no different than race in the sense of concerning nobody but the two consenting adults involved. Wanting a father figure may just be a transitional phase, or may turn out to be what's best for you in the long run. You are the sole judge of what suits you, and the only way to find out what suits you is through experience. The worst thing you can do in life is wither away on the vine due to allowing beckoning opportunities pass you by because you feel the need to cater to "what people think."

What About Black Women Who Look Below Average?

"I have a left shoulder blade that is a miracle of loveliness. People come miles to see it. My right elbow has a fascination that few can resist."
William Schwenck Gilbert
The Mikado

People usually gravitate towards members of the opposite sex who are pretty close to their own general level of attractiveness. If your looks are at the thirtieth percentile, go for the men at your percentile. Everybody needs companionship, and there are plenty of men, White and Black, at your particular percentile. You meet them in the same places as you meet anyone else. Everyone needs to go to work, buy food, go to church, do the laundry, and engage in other activities related to personal upkeep and maintenance. You will just have to work a little harder at meeting men like this, and be prepared to deal with inept social behavior.

Laundromats, food stores, personal ads, computer stores, workplaces, and the like, are some of the places you can meet guys like this. A blue-collar guy might spend a lot of time either fishing or working at home on his car or with power tools, so you meet such men at fishing lakes, racing events and hardware stores, where men usually outnumber women. An intellectual might devote his off-work hours to a hobby or avocation such as computers or books. Find out what guys involved with a certain occupation or hobby do, and that tells you where to meet them. You can meet the technical nerd types on the Internet and at computer industry conventions, where women are still rarities. You meet men who like to read at bookstores and libraries. If you are religious, meet like-minded men at churches. Persevere.

What If Dating White Doesn't Work Out?

"We outgrow love like other things
And put it in the drawer"
Emily Dickinson
"We Outgrow Love Like Other Things"

Why would Black women back off from interracial dating? Some decide that the social pressures involved are just not for them. You alone are the best judge of such things. Maybe you found that White guys are okay, but your curiosity about racial differences has been satiated, and you feel better with Black men. Maybe the novelty and stimulation value of physical differences between the races decreased over time and you just got bored. It was okay, but you decided you like it better back in more familiar social territory. Maybe you find it easier to talk with Black men than with White men. You may have become involved with White players just as bad as Black players, and see no point in taking on the added hassles of interracial dating without compensating gains. Interracial dating is not for everyone, and it can turn out to be less than right for some people. It's a purely individual decision.

Should dating White not work out, you can always go back to dating Black men, or waiting for them to call you. After all, Black men come home from dating and marrying White women. You can go home again, but the lay of the land will look different after you've checked out greener pastures for a spell. Should you have been treated right elsewhere, you have no incentive to ever settle for less again. Should you no longer care for the way Black players treat you, you don't need to play with them any more. Players will sense something different about you. The attitude you radiate will steer game-players around you, with only normal Black men homing in on you.

You Can't Go Home Again
title of book by Thomas Wolfe

Date Whites Exclusively?

You might find you prefer to date White men exclusively. That's okay. You are free to associate or not associate with men of any color as often or as seldom as you wish. Select, don't settle. Dating Whites exclusively doesn't mean giving up your family and friends. Real friends, for that matter, won't come down on you for dating whoever you like. It just means that you date who you want. People who don't like the idea that your life is yours to live as you wish are the ones with problems.

Some Black women who date around might choose to date both Black and White men. Some might try dating White men and, for whatever reason, decide to go back to dating Black men. Others take the opposite tack, and decide to date only Whites. Any approach is okay as long as you are the one making the decisions about which way is the right way to go. It's okay to make mistakes as long as they are your mistakes. Even making a mistake can meet your needs, in the sense that you learn something from your experiences.

Should you have had mainly negative experiences with Black men, and start to have primarily positive, or at least okay, experiences with White men, your actions and attitudes will transform. You will find that as you become more interested in White males, you progressively tune out Black men. Even when one acts friendly, it will take a while for the message to get through to you. Way down the line, you might even get to the point where Black men occupy the mental position formerly occupied by White men: you don't really notice them anymore. This will be reflected in your posture, the way your eyes do -and don't -follow certain kinds of men around, the expression on your face, the tone of your voice when conversing, and so on. You're free to tune out broadcasts sent out by any group of men, and tune in stations more to your taste as you wish.

73

"At times, the whole world seems to be in conspiracy to importune you with emphatic trifles." Ralph Waldo Emerson
Self-Reliance

Chapter Six
Making Yourself More Approachable, Part I

"We have an innate propensity to get ourselves noticed, and noticed favorably."
William James
The Principles Of Psychology

Do White Men Consider You Approachable?

"Everyone affects a particular look and exterior, in order to appear what [she] wishes to be thought, so that it may be said the world is made up of appearances."
La Rochefoucauld
Maxims

Were you to spot the tip of an iceberg off in the distance while at sea, you would assume that the visible part of the iceberg is representative of the ninety percent of the iceberg hidden beneath the surface of the water. Having such information, you would proceed to steer your ship clear of the danger zone where you might hit the submerged part of the iceberg. Conversely, were you to find an invitation note in a bottle drifting out from a tropical island, you would often be justified in assuming that you could dock your ship and receive a warm welcome from hospitable local residents.

Perceptions limit our options for action. White men often perceive Black women as unapproachably cool icebergs best steered around. The unseen psychological parts of such female icebergs are assumed to correspond to their visibly chilly exteriors. If it looks like an iceberg, it is an iceberg, and consequently does not merit further investigation until such time as information is presented that it is not an iceberg. White men are not in the business of warming up icebergs, and are not obligated to investigate further should their initial impression be mistaken. Should an iceberg consider herself approachable, despite the appearances she projects to the contrary, White men still have no visible inducement, reason or incentive to investigate. What they see is what they think they will get, and they are not in the market for towing icebergs home. White male sailors steer their ships of self clear of social icebergs, preferring to steer towards more approachable tropical island paradises which send out notes of invitation.

"The Isle is full of noises, Sounds, and sweet airs that give delight and hurt not."
William Shakespeare
The Tempest

Many White male sailors who find an invitational note in a bottle that exudes the scent of an inviting perfume will go out of their way to steer their ships of self towards an inviting tropical island where an approachable-looking local woman who sent out the note in the bottle can be found waving from the beach, holding a welcome wreath to enchant him away from his passing ship. Such an island paradise offers many more inducements for men to approach than does an iceberg. Should a Black woman appear friendly, inviting, and compatible, White men open to interracial relationships will tune into the subconscious notes in bottles sent out by her appearance which lead men to assume her to be friendly and inviting until such time as they receive word to the contrary. Doing what you can to appear approachable makes things go easier for both the approacher and the approachee.

Beauty and approachability exist solely in the mind's eye of the beholder. It comes down to how men perceive women, not how women think they ought to be perceived, or how they think men ought to try to see through a chilling facade. Appearances are reality from the point of view of the man on the street. It simply is not possible for the man on the street to obtain information beyond the limited visual and auditory information women choose to present to them. Men have nothing to go on beyond appearances before making an approach. Thus, appearing approachable operates to send out visual and auditory notes in bottles to passing sailors to get you past what is often the hardest part of an interracial relationship: making initial contact with an interested White male. While social pressures can cause problems later on, they are more predictable, however unpleasant, than the vagaries of trying to meet someone in the first place. Remember, a note in a bottle has two purposes, and only two purposes: to attract attention to the message inside and to invite a response.

Adults Take On Multiple Roles

"[She] has as many different social selves as there are distinct groups of persons about whose opinions [she] cares. [She] generally shows a different side of [herself] to each of these different groups."
William James
The Principles Of Psychology

While you might not think of your activities in terms of taking on roles, you nevertheless do play different roles for different audiences with different expectations. Typical roles include being an employee, daughter, student, big sister, girlfriend and so on. One keystone of being an adult is taking on, and acting out, multiple roles for different audiences in different parts of your life. Each role you play is an expression of one of the many submerged parts of your total self. These separate audiences usually do not see you perform other roles for other audiences and know you only by the role you play for them. For example, your boyfriend usually does not see the role you play role with your mother, the role you play at the office with your supervisor or the role you play with your girlfriends.

There is nothing wrong or dishonest about playing different roles, any more than there is something immoral about an actress who plays different roles in various movies for different directors with different expectations. You simply cannot always act the same way with different audiences, for the same reason that an actress cannot always play only one role or character, regardless of what the scripts, audiences and director require of her. You must act differently with different people in different situations, because you have no choice but to act out different roles to get through different situations in life, and to acquire the rewards that come from playing different roles, such as a paycheck for playing the on-the-job role your employer expects of you. Acting out scripted roles can make it easier to get through situations where you have no choice about spending time with difficult people, such as dealing with belligerent customers at a customer service desk. You fall back on playing a scripted role and do not take it personally. The social and economic necessities of life require you to play different roles on a daily basis.

You tailor your different roles for your different audiences. In many cases, the different audiences for which you perform will require you to act in particular, specified ways, and only in those specified ways, when they are your primary audience. Acting out roles more appropriate for other social stages and audiences can cause undesirable social friction. For example, your audience at your job would be quite displeased were you to act with them in a manner more suitable for a boyfriend audience. Thus, it should come as no surprise that getting a White male audience to think of you as approachable involves leaving at home certain aspects of the role you play in attracting Black men, as well as a certain amount of rewriting your script to include certain new role characteristics specifically tailored to make you more readily comprehensible to a culturally dissimilar White audience. Should you not want to take on certain role characteristics, don't plan to proceed very far along the interracial dating road. When in Rome, perform as the Romans perform.

Your Personal Billboard

"Bewitched by the charm of looks"
William Shakespeare
Romeo And Juliet

The visible tip of your personal iceberg advertises what men expect to find beneath your psychological surface, be it hot, cold or indifferent. Roadside billboard advertising is a useful analogy for thinking about what sort of iceberg tip you present to your public audience. In driving by a roadside billboard, you have only a few seconds to glance at the billboard, take in the ad, mentally process the information it presents, and think about whether or not it speaks directly to your personal interests before deciding whether or it merits action on your part. When a billboard says that a restaurant with a certain type of cuisine is just down the road, should you have a preexisting taste for their cuisine, you can start steering yourself in their direction after glancing at the billboard.

Drivers get only one chance to see a billboard as they zoom by, so they must take in the advertiser's message in the space of just a second or two. Should the message be hard to decipher or written in a foreign language, potential prospects most often skip over it and drive by, blissfully unaware of what they'll be missing out on. They are not obligated to stop the car, get out and puzzle over what an poorly-put-together, incomprehensible billboard might be trying to say. Nobody owes a poor attempt at communications a second chance, any more than you owe an incomprehensible television advertisement a second chance to confuse you. You just click away on the remote control to look for something easier to take in.

A billboard can't possibly tell you everything you need to know about what it advertises. It settles for making a brief, well-organized, internally-consistent statement that invites selected types of likely prospects to investigate further. Good advertising presents a single theme or message to a well-defined and carefully-analyzed target market without clutter, confusion or extraneous elements. Every part of the advertisement should contribute to reinforcing a single theme or message about the product, eliminating elements of clutter and distraction in so doing. In the context of interracial dating, clutter means subtle cues that attract and interest Black men rather than White men. Such clutter serves only to ward off potentially interested White males, producing no benefits for you in the process.

Presenting your personal billboard to your public audience is just the start. Good advertising involves measuring the response to the advertisement. In the case of toothpaste, advertisers measure response using the numbers sales clerks ring up at checkout counters every day. In the case of a Black woman seeking to meet White men, the standard of measurement for response to your personal billboard is the number of compatible White men who approach you. Approaching you means they try to get a dialogue going as a response to your presentation of self to them. Incidentally, all you really need is one good response to your notes in a bottle from one compatible White male, not an avalanche of prospects. One good one is all it takes.

Dialogue marketing attempts to get a two-way informational exchange going between the prospect and the advertiser about what the prospects are like, what they are looking for, what the advertiser offers, and so on, all of which hopefully leads to insights useful to for both parties. You want to get a dialogue going, some sort of conversational exchange that can lead to things beyond introductory niceties. A dialogue, of course, allows for an ongoing exchange of information between two prospects, a two-way exchange of notes in bottles, allowing both parties to check out each other for possible complementarity.

In walking past men as you go down the street, you have a window of opportunity a few seconds in length to generate initial impressions that the right sort of White males will tune into for more detailed information instead of switching to another some other woman's channel. It is worth a bit of time and trouble to think over what sort of note in a bottle you want to cobble together about yourself to present in walking down the street. Your message has two parts: what you say about yourself as well as what you don't say about yourself. Being approachable means both highlighting certain positive, truthful things about yourself, as well as eliminating certain types of negative elements from your presentation of self. Negative means negative in the context of a given audience, not in some absolute sense of the word. The White male audience requires a different selection of, and emphasis on, elements for presentation of self than does a Black male audience, just as a French audience expects different points of emphasis, style and language of an actress than would a Italian audience. More specifically, certain roles and personal styles that are both common and acceptable with audiences of Black males either fall flat with, or generate negative impressions among, White male audiences.

Should White males not approach you, that reflects only on your advertising, not the product being advertised. The history of advertising, by the way, is filled with examples of excellent products that sank without a trace due to mismanaged advertising. The advertising was mismanaged in the sense of making misguided appeals to misunderstood audiences that wound up not understanding how the products could have fit into their lives. Keep in mind that, whether the subject of a billboard advertisement is yourself or toothpaste, the only thing the prospect knows about the product is what you choose to present, not all the millions of out-of-sight, behind-the-stage details. It's easy to get bogged down dwelling on such details, and think the whole world knows about them as soon as they look at you, something which is definitely not the case.

Should you make a mistake, the good news is that you need not withdraw yourself from the interracial singles marketplace should there be no response to your initial attempts at impression management, unlike a supermarket product that tries to fly, falls, and never gets a second chance. You cross paths with new White male prospects every day, none of whom know what you were projecting about yourself yesterday. There's plenty more where they came from, and somebody for everybody in the singles marketplace. Find your niche and narrowcast, not broadcast, your availability and interest to men in your particular market niche. You can't be all things to all people, so don't waste your time and effort trying. Sometimes the only thing a good product needs to get it moving off the shelf is slightly different packaging tailored to the needs of a particular market, rather than what the manufacturer mistakenly defines as the market's needs.

"We live amid surfaces, and the true art of life is to skate well on them."
Ralph Waldo Emerson
"Experience"

Men respond, or fail to respond, to the role you appear to be taking on. They can not respond to, react to, or even recognize, the real you, which is hidden from the view of casual observers in any event. So, don't take their reactions, or lack of reactions, personally. Men respond to your role-playing efforts, not the real you, just as the audience at a movie responds to the role the actress plays, not the actress herself. This means you need to get a handle on managing the nuances of your impressions, which in turn requires understanding the nature of your White male audience and the tried-and-true roles known to get positive reactions from them. What you are advertising is your availability to play the role of significant other in an interracial relationship.

Should an interracially-minded White male see a Black woman who gives the impression of meeting his definition of approachability and compatibility, he is likely to approach such a Black woman. Appearances are reality in the minds of men, because nothing contradicts such appearances as you choose to put on. The impression you make is the result of your ability to spell out, by means of carefully-crafted visual, verbal and nonverbal impression management, your ostensible prospects for interracial compatibility and approachability. Advertising your availability to play an interracial dating role is done only for the purpose of making initial contact, after which point you drop that particular role and take on a less-structured role for the purposes of getting better acquainted. Focusing your efforts into the right psychological channels can save you time and wasted effort, to say nothing of upgrading the types of men you are likely to meet.

81

Different Advertising For Different Markets

"You are not for all markets."
William Shakespeare
As You Like It

The more elements of familiarity the advertisement includes, the faster the audience slides past the old-hat elements of the sales message to home in on the sales pitch about how the product being advertised meets their needs. They already know what old-hat elements say, so they mentally skim over them. A context of elements of familiarity helps tune the audience into the sales message, because familiar elements are less likely to divert their attention to critical examination of the message. Familiarity operates to put prospects into a relaxed state of mind and become more receptive to sales messages. Conversely, the more irrelevant elements the advertisement includes, such as pictures of Whites in an ad targeting Blacks, the more psychological information processing is required to plow through such extraneous elements in getting to the core message, and the more mental roadblocks get set up. The more irrelevant static mixed in with the message, the harder it is to hear the signal. Should there be numerous mental roadblocks, prospects simply ignore the message, classifying it as not on their wavelength and therefore unworthy of their time. Should your personal billboard become fuzzed up with a collage of extraneous elements, many White male prospects will skip over it as impossible to interpret, and your ad will fail to influence their behavior. They simply walk past you without their interest perking up. When in Rome, advertise yourself as the Romans do.

"An impression which simply flows into [his] eyes or ears, and in no way modifies his active life, is an impression gone to waste."
William James
Talk To Teachers On Psychology

Zoom in on the idea of yourself as a walking billboard that White males drive past on the street and in shopping malls. Should the purpose of your billboard advertising be to induce certain men to take action, in the sense of stopping what they are doing and check you out, then what visual, verbal and nonverbal information would you choose to present to catch the attention of potentially compatible White males? Regardless of what particular type of Black woman you are, or what particular type of White male you are looking for, presenting a consistent personal "front," a sort of psychological package made up of the visual and audible elements of your externally visible self, makes you easy to evaluate. By consciously selecting what you present about yourself to men in public, you can radiate a single, clear-cut advertising theme about what kind of Black woman you are and better attract particular types of potentially compatible White males. Presenting an inconsistent personal front that appeals in part to both White and Black male audiences only confuses your White audience and increases their hesitation. An inconsistent personal front makes about as much sense as making a French movie with Italian subtitles and showing it in Spain. It tries to say something to several audiences but winds up saying nothing comprehensible to anybody.

Meeting White men requires using different impression management tactics than with Black men. The degree to which your message is correctly tailored to the preexisting White male mentality determines in part your success in attracting them. Impression management content that works with a Black men makes different impressions on White men. The psychological, cultural and social differences between White and Black men necessitate different approaches to impression management. In other words, inducing White men to check you out requires knowing something about their hot buttons and cold buttons. For example, presenting yourself as a cool Black woman is acceptable with certain types of Black male audiences, but not with White audiences. Whites react very differently than Blacks when you take on a cool role.

Good advertising tries to fit into the preexisting mental framework of the audience, meaning what is already in their heads. You can not educate somebody on the spot from scratch about what a totally new and different type of person you are in the space of the few seconds he gets to look at your personal billboard. Men understand new things best when such things are phrased in terms of an old and familiar concept-system. You attract the right kind of attention when your message can be readily understood using the terminology of a familiar, existing category. In your case, this means using impression management to state that you have a number of social and psychological characteristics in common with Whites, differing primarily along the esthetically desirable dimension of racial characteristics.

The Basics Of Impression Management

The sum total of personal information you make available to those you pass by on the street, or with whom you engage in initial conversations, is your personal front. The elements of your personal front should ideally add up to a consistently positive impression or theme. You can also think of your personal front as your visual, verbal and nonverbal packaging. Packages present messages. Packages are stylized representations of carefully-selected characteristics of the products within the packages. Packages give you a lot of product information at a glance, including the product name, function, the color scheme of the package design, and so on. The package tells the prospect what the manufacturer wants the prospect to know first about the product. Although you may not have thought of it before in such terms, product packaging is also a form of advertising, in the sense of presenting a miniature billboard with a short sales pitch to prospective buyers. Remember, the purpose of a billboard, or any other form of advertising, is to move the product off the shelf, and out of standby equipment status.

The package is not the product, however, and there is a lot more to you than your personal front. The problem is that anything other than your personal front is hidden from view, so by default your personal front represents what you are to the rest of the world. Men's minds automatically classify what they see and hear, and they go on to make inferences about a woman based on such information about her personal front as she happens to present in public. Information does not mean things like statistical reports and analyses, but rather visually-presented qualitative information such as the color and make of a woman's clothing, her hair style, her posture, as well as certain types of auditory and nonverbal information such as her vocabulary, her tone of voice, her accent, her smile and so on, such information as a man might see and overhear when a woman speaks with a sales clerk. While this information is qualitative, it is nevertheless rich in the sort of information men use to make decisions about potential compatibility. They makes inferences about your personality based on your personal front and take action, or not take action, based on those inferences. Some might decide to applaud your impression management performance by making an approach to join you off-stage where the two of you take on different roles for a redefined interpersonal situation. Impression management is a two-way street, and you likewise react to the impressions men generate.

Your personal front is the small slice of your total self you choose to present in visual, verbal and nonverbal form to single White males in public. Many elements of your personal front can be changed on short notice, such as your clothing and facial expressions. Other parts, such as your speech patterns, can be changed only over an extended period of time. Your personal front determines in large part who will be attracted to you. It tells them what kind of woman you are, which in turn largely determines what kind of men might be interested in you. If you dress and talk as if you live on Fifth Avenue, men from Fifth Avenue are most likely to home in on you. If you dress and talk as if you live in a trailer park, men from trailer parks are most likely to home in on you. If you look depressed, depressed men will sense a kindred soul in you. We all seek out, and home in on, people like ourselves. Personal fronts are our initial means of attempting to influence our social situation by interactively screening certain types people into, or out of, our social circles.

It makes no difference whether the front you present comes about by design or by default. Should you put on old clothes because you are in a rush, people will inevitably make automatic assumptions about you based on how you present yourself. No one cares whether or not you had the time to express carefully-crafted thoughts through your appearance. All that matters is what is presented, not how it happened to get to the point of being presented. You may think that is somehow unfair, that the way that life ought to be is that others should be able to look into your head and see what you are really like, and not judge you by the clothing you happen to throw together when you are in a hurry, or by your posture and expression when you are tired. Yes, life should be set up differently, but unfortunately life is not actually like that right here and right now, and is not likely to be like that in your lifetime. Wishing that life was easier will not make it one bit easier. You have to play the hand that life deals you, and knowing the rules of the impression management game is one way you can make it more likely to go your way. Understanding that people make inferences about you based on what they see and hear about you is the basis for managing the impressions you create. Consciously choosing the information you present about yourself when making impressions allows you to manage the favorable impression you want to make in your audience of single White males to some degree. Presenting yourself as interracially receptive cuts through layers of White male caution and makes you more approachable.

"Life isn't fair."
attributed to John F. Kennedy

The extent to which a woman is unconsciously and automatically slotted into a favorable category is the extent to which she matches up with a particular White male's preexisting mental slotting system. Different types of men have different preferences. One style does not fit all types of men, so there is no sense in even trying to appeal to everybody. Thus, the impression your style of dress, hair and the like makes in the minds of White males should take priority over your personal opinions about making an individualistic fashion statement. Do what it takes to meet men. After you get something going, show your wilder side. If you want to be considered for a particular role, dress the part, and let your hair down after you get accepted to fill the part of significant other. An actress expresses her individual idiosyncrasies at times other than when she is auditioning for a particularly important part.

Why White Men Do Not Approach Black Women More Often

Most White men see approaching Black women as a social situation filled with unknowns. The potential for embarrassment and rejection is believed to be high. For a variety of reasons, they see the potential for a social payoff as low. While a small number of adult White males have enough nerve to just leap into the unknown, most prefer to look before they leap. Looking at unfriendly women, or women perceived to be unfriendly, creates stress and makes them unlikely to leap.

White men unconsciously classify women by the extent to which they exhibit elements of familiarity in their choices of garments, carriage, expression and other elements of their personal front. They want to be reassured and enticed onwards, not shocked or left befuddled. Familiarity reassures, unfamiliarity engenders caution. This is analogous to the considerations that pass through their heads in making other types of major investment. Let's say an adventurous White male looking for a car happens to be receptive to foreign cars. Keep in mind that just by virtue of being open to foreign cars, he is sticking his neck out to some degree. While he is willing to take certain types of calculated risks, he still prefers to be reassured that there is really not much of a risk at all, and that the time, money and emotional investment made are all well spent. Taking a risk needs to justified in terms of some sort of compensating payoff or benefit. Taking risks equals stress, and stress is to be avoided wherever possible.

Taking a perceived risk on one front, that of being in the foreign car category in the first place, is compensated for by reducing perceived risks on other fronts. He automatically screens out cars with steering wheels on the right side instead of the left side. Such cars are just as good as cars with steering wheels on the left side, but he sees no advantage in sticking his neck out in that additional dimension of risk on top of already sticking his neck out by virtue of being in foreign car territory in the first place. The lack of familiar guideposts also makes him seek out familiar brand names. What does he wind up with? A foreign car manufactured abroad by a foreign division of a domestic automobile company embodying symbols of reassurance, such as a familiar trademark, all in one package. He takes a limited risk along one dimension, while taking almost no risk at all along other dimensions. White men see financial and emotional investments in much the same way. If they are going to stick their necks out, they minimize overall risk and accompanying stress. They stick their necks out only for what looks like a pretty sure thing, something they have some realistic basis for thinking of as being okay.

Chapter Seven
Making Yourself More Approachable, Part II

"Our hearts should well agree with our external parts."
William Shakespeare
The Taming Of The Shrew

Black Women Are Unknown Quantities To Most White Men

Black women are foreign psychological territory for most White men. White men who have not dated Black women beforehand have little real information to work with, and back into classifying Black women as high-risk/low-probability-of-success prospects for companionship. Few have friends who have gone out with Black women. When their subconscious tries to put together a composite mental picture of Black women involved with White men, most White men draw a complete blank, except for a few mass media depictions of interracial celebrity couples.

While any unknown woman represents a package of numerous unknowns to any man considering approaching her, a Black woman presents more unknowns to the minds of White males than would a similarly unknown White woman. The more unknown and unpredictable elements presented in any social equation, the less likely are White males to try to understand the unknowns and solve the equation. They do know one thing for certain about Black women, however: a large percentage of Black women they see on the street, the subway, in fast food restaurants and the like show little or no reaction to the White men they pass by. By contrast, the majority of White women they pass by typically exhibit at least some minimal level of nonverbal reaction to White men they pass by on the street, if only to take a fast glance. Black women typically exhibit few of the reactions that White men recognize as indicating an interest in being approached.

"Your face.....is as a book where men may read strange matters."
William Shakespeare
Macbeth

Black women act cool as a result of social conditioning within the Black community against Black women showing any interest in White men. White men thus perceive Black women in general as evidencing little interest in White men. They think Black women would not welcome their attentions, and thus don't bother trying. They reach this conclusion by generalizing from what they know about White women to include Black women, concluding that lack of reaction translates into lack of interest. Lack of reaction means the lack of eye contact, lack of smiles, lack of turning the head or body in the direction of White men, and so on. Regardless of what goes on in the heads of Black women, White men have only what they see of the personal fronts of Black women to go on. Just as Black women do not understand that White males' basic framework for understanding Black women is usually derived from past dealings with White women, White men do not understand that Black women's framework for reacting to White men have been primarily shaped by their dealings with Black men, as well as being spiced with various cultural differences. These perceived differences are compounded by seeing many Black women in different styles of dress than White women, which seemingly provides visual confirmation of their prior perception of social differences.

A White male considering approaching a White female has some idea about whether or not she is on his general social level by looking at her manner of dress, posture and other visual elements of her personal front. Her facial expression, degree of eye contact and expression of smiles round out his impression of her emotional availability and consequent approachability. He uses that information to decide whether or not she is worth the emotional expenditure of sticking his neck out to make an approach. Men do not like being rejected, and weigh their probability of success before making an approach. The more elements of familiarity and reassurance a Black woman projects, the more likely a White male is to evaluate the Black woman in a positive light. Unfamiliarity breeds disinterest.

Another consideration is also at play in their minds. White men believe that Black men are generally more aggressive than White men. They suspect that, were a White man to approach a Black woman, or date Black women, some nearby Black men might react negatively. White men think that Black men as a group are possessive about Black women in general, and frown on White men moving in on the Black male's exclusive social "territory." They may have seen Black men who usually maintain cool exteriors become quite worked up on seeing Black women with White men. Men are prone to assume the worst about other men as a matter of course, and the negative impression White men get of Black men from the mass media accentuates this. While violence is quite uncommon in real-life interracial dating situations, White men subconsciously assume it to be a real, if slight, possibility. That perception keeps some from approaching Black women. The on-the-edge-of-anger way that certain types of Black men stare at Black female/White male couples reinforces this belief. As a result, few White men will approach Black women when Black men are in the vicinity. Don't hang around anywhere near Black men if you want White men to approach you.

The White Male Definition Of Approachable Black Women

"You ought not to aim at changing the tone of company, but to conform to it."
Philip Stanhope, Earl of Chesterfield
Letters To His Son

Being interracially approachable comes down to whatever White men think makes you approachable. Not fitting their definition of approachable means they will not approach you, period. As a general rule, the perception of social and psychological Conversely, the lack of familiar social and psychological elements discourages White men from making overtures. Racial differences are an esthetically desirable dimension of differences welcomed if the other dimensions of the woman's personal front confirm the existence of substantial social and psychological similarities. This means similarities that fit into their preexisting ideas about women. While this may seem obvious, many Black women assume that White men are no different than Black men except for skin color, and thus act the same around White men as with Black men. This is completely wrong. Black women need to take on somewhat different roles for White male audiences than for Black male audiences. Should the White male fail to see any of the elements of approachability usually exhibited by White women of his acquaintance, he is unlikely to approach the Black woman. Thus, unless the Black woman exudes the impression that the White male is welcome to join her, it will probably not occur to him that he is welcome at all. It takes two to tango, and it has to be clear to both parties that both want to tango. Do things to make him feel welcome.

The more elements of reassuring social familiarity Black women exhibit, the more likely White males are to approach them. Having social and psychological characteristics in common with White women makes them feel more at ease about approaching you by virtue of reducing the number of unknowns about you. Thus, if you are looking to attract a middle-class White male, the more closely the central tendency of your dress, speech, posture, facial expressions, body language and visible emotions resemble that of a White woman of his social class, the more elements of familiarity you seem to offer and the better your chances of being approached. Conversely, the more elements of unfamiliarity you radiate, the less your chances of striking a responsive chord and of being approached. All of this is for the purposes of making initial contact only. Yes, you and he do have differences, but it is best to play them down in the short run, because the two of you will have plenty of time to discuss them over the long run. Sort out the details later.

All of us are most comfortable with people who think and act a lot like us. Our coping energy for dealing with wholly different types of people is limited. People like us are less likely to turn out to be full of unpleasant surprises. Men like to feel that they have something in common with women they are considering approaching, if only to have a few hooks on which to hang the initial conversation. After all, what would you talk about with someone you know absolutely nothing about? Using impression management techniques deliberately gives them clues about what you are like, no different than sending out a note in a bottle from your island of self. Given that a Black woman on whom they might have their eyes is a total stranger, all they have to go on is her personal front, meaning her mode of dress, posture, expression, and other easy-to-observe characteristics. They will inevitably make automatic, endless inferences about you based on your personal front.

White men have some idea about how to deal with White women within a given radius of social class around their own social class. They automatically assume that what applies to White women more or less applies to Black women as well. They have nothing else to go on, so, by default, that so that is all they have to use. Thus, White men seeking Black

91

women for long-term relationships are initially likely to home on Black women they perceive as being something like themselves. White men seeking short-term relationships with Black women have little concern about long-term compatibility and are thus less discerning about the details of your personal front.

Upper-class White men will home in on upper-class and middle-class Black women. Middle-class White men will home in on middle-class Black women. Working-class White men will home in on working-class Black women. It is easier to get inside the head of someone who is like you in some readily-observable manner than to try to understand the mindset of someone who gives the impression of being from a completely different background. When men see you exhibiting certain characteristics and recognizable symbols of their own lifestyles, they fill in the blanks to form a consistent mental picture of you using what they do know about women they think are like you. If you manage the impression you give them, the assumptions they make will operate in your favor. If you look like you could be one of their neighbors, they tend to be more relaxed about approaching you.

Casting Yourself In A Role

"In the joy of the actors lies the sense of any action."
Robert Louis Stevenson
"The Lantern-Bearers"

Think of yourself as an actress playing the role of a Black woman receptive to White male attentions. While this may not be the way you think of yourself round the clock, given that you have other roles to play at other times, keep in mind that this is a role you can take on for the limited purpose of meeting White males. It requires dressing and acting the part. The job of an actress is to play the role she has selected for herself, not think it is the job of the audience to understand her despite her failure to really develop the elements of her personal front to flesh out the details of the role so that the audience can better understand it. This is no different than the structured role you take on for the limited purpose of a job interview. You dress and act the part for the limited purpose of getting the job. Once you get the job, you can relax and let down your hair with co-workers who also once acted much the same way for the limited purpose of getting the job, and dropped that particular role once they had the job offer in hand and the new everyday demands of the job required them to take on other roles.

Were you the casting director for a movie or television show and auditioning actresses for a part, you would immediately screen out any would-be actress who had not bothered to at least flip through the script and get a feel for the emotions it called for her to express, as well as those who similarly failed to make some effort to dress for the part. You would tune out those perceived to be incompatible for the role and just keep looking for a better match. White men do the same. They want Black women who seem to fit the role of being interested in, and available for, interracial dating. If you don't look like you fit the role they have in mind, you will not get much further along in the process. They want some readily visible evidence that you might be interested.

White men automatically fill in the blanks about women in predictable ways with odds and ends from their private mental storehouses of information about women. The sum total of admittedly superficial information you project in making impressions gets added up with what's in their heads to form an instantaneously-generated, composite mental picture of you. Since you can safely assume that most White men you pass by on the street have not dated Black women before, it means that they are comparing you primarily along certain limited, specific dimensions to White women of their own social class whom they have dated or otherwise been acquainted with. After all, that is where they have gotten most of their information about women, so what else would you expect them to use? Men compare their impressions of you with their composite information about various other women they have known and decide whether or not to approach you based on their level of comfort, familiarity and perceived compatibility. If you embody symbols of reassurance, such as familiar styles of dress, patterns of speech, facial expressions and the like, you are halfway there already. When little information about a new category is available, what little information is available, or seems to fits, expands to fill the informational vacuum and cultural differences.

"In admitting a new body of experience, we instinctively seek to disturb as little as possible our pre-existing stock of ideas. We always try to name a new experience in some way which will assimilate it to what we already

93

know. We hate anything absolutely new, anything without any name, and for which a new name must be forged."
William James
Talk To Teachers On Psychology

White men do make use of a secondary source of comparative information in evaluating you besides comparing you to White women. This source of information is Black female celebrities who date, or marry, interracially. They get this information from the mass media. Black female celebrities who date interracially are typically entertainers of one sort or another, and their White male companions are similarly not representative of the population of White men as a whole. Men generally do not follow the activities of such celebrities as avidly as do women, but nevertheless do retain certain general impressions about Black women in such interracial celebrity pairings. The Black women in such celebrity couples appear to be emotionally expressive in such news coverage as the mass media give them, in the sense of looking happy when with their White male companions. They don't act cool or disinterested. Have you ever seen such a Black female celebrity look unhappy when with her White male companion? Actresses, rock stars, models and the like are all superb at managing their personal fronts, of course. The nature of their work as public performers operates to screen in Black women good at such things, and thus their well-managed impressions stick out in the minds of men. You can learn a few things by observing the personal fronts of such accomplished performers.

Don't Typecast Yourself As Cool

"I have hid my feelings, fearing they should do me wrong."
Alfred Lord Tennyson
"Locksley Hall"

Black men take on certain roles to influence their Black and White audiences at work, play and in public. Some Black men take on the role of being cool in part as a reaction to their perception of ill-treatment by White society. Being cool is a coping strategy designed to bolster Black male confidence and pride, and is a psychological defense mechanism that involves taking on the role of an unflappable, tough, aloof, emotionless performer on public stages, and often on private stages as well. Being cool is a role with several components, such as developing individualized styles of dress, but the primary psychological component of interest here is that of wearing an emotionless mask.

Being cool is the psychological equivalent of being a character actor, actors who consistently play only one role, such as cowhand or bad guy, and thus never become the star of any production, because they can only play one role. If you can play only one role, that limits your options both in acting and in real life. Being a one-note character actor is not an adult role in real life. Cool people typecast themselves, work at fitting that typecast role, and must live with the consequences.

The cool front is an act, a pose, a mask that covers an underlying rage and sense of insecurity. While being cool starts out as an act to impress adolescent, street-corner peers, the mask often becomes permanently embedded in the core personalities of many Black males, and becomes progressively harder to drop in front of any audience, White or Black, male or female.

After a decade or two of being cool, cool men find themselves preempted from playing other roles because being cool turns off audiences who themselves take on roles other than cool every day. Being cool is most pervasive in the lower socio-economic classes, but middle-class Black men often take on some aspects of being cool in the sense of not wanting to reveal their feelings, and seeing interpersonal relationships as a chessboard game, and not as something involving real people with real feelings. Blacks do not have a monopoly on being cool, and certain types of White males also develop analogous White styles of cool in reaction to similar types of environments and treatment.

Being cool is a coping mechanism developed by adolescents involving maintaining the monochromatic personal front of being cool. Being cool is a full-time role that precludes taking on non-cool roles. Taking on roles other than cool is not cool. Since becoming an adult requires taking on multiple roles and responsibilities, the extent to which an adult Black male insists on being cool as the primary, or sole, style of personal front in his repertoire is the degree to which he falls short of being an adult.

The inability to present personal fronts other than cool is a social handicap except with other cool individuals. Being cool is a self-imposed handicap that prevents one from even learning how to take on other roles. Being cool offers few rewards outside the society of street-corner peers, and excludes one from large parts of the non-cool, adult world. Being cool is a big negative in the job market, which looks for employees who can play other roles besides being cool. Being cool excludes cool individuals from getting into real relationships with real adults. Real adults sense immediately that those preoccupied with being cool are non-adults and avoid them in favor of those perceived to be more emotionally available. Cool precludes becoming emotionally available.

"Do not kill the spirit of love with a perpetual dulness."
William Shakespeare
Sonnet LVI

Being cool is a Black male psychological blizzard that freezes parts of the Black social environment into an ice-cold adolescent emotional mold. The aftereffects of Black men being cool ripple through audiences as well as performers long after the performances are over. While the primary audience for cool performances is other Black males, a very close secondary audience is the audience of Black women. Black women who socialize primarily with cool Black men take on some aspects of being cool themselves in response to its pervasiveness in certain segments of the Black social environment. Association breeds imitation. Even a Black woman who grows up in a middle-class neighborhood where cool is minimal, might have a father who tilts her development by acting cool, or might see cool being depicted as acceptable behavior on music videos.

While not all Black women act cool, some degree of being cool is nevertheless all too common. It takes on two forms. First are those Black women who actually are cool, female analogs of cool Black men. After years of associating with cool Black men, a Black woman's personality warps in reaction to the cool Black men with whom she socializes. Her personality becomes fine-tuned to the Black male social environment making her as ill-adapted to other social environments as a fish out of water. Since being an adult involves taking on multiple roles and responsibilities, the degree to which a Black woman takes on a cool role as her primary role in life is also the degree to which she is less of a multidimensional adult capable of, and open to, playing multiple roles. Being cool blocks off the psychological oxygen necessary to breathe life into the adult habit of taking on multiple roles by virtue of freezing one into the cool adolescent social role. Cool is a role that prevents one from learning, or taking on, other roles.

The second type of cool Black woman, while not quite cool, nevertheless has a certain type of callused reaction-to-cool personality that discourages intimacy, and develops in psychological reaction to contacts with cool Black men. Should you have few opportunities to deal with men who themselves take on multidimensional adult roles, you get little practice in taking on multidimensional social roles yourself. If you deal only with men who are emotional adolescents, it's hard to develop the social skills you would have developed from dealing with adult men on a regular basis. The primary characteristic of interest is the taking on of one role in most social situations, though the particular role taken on is not in and of itself a cool role.

Black women often react to cool performances by donning blizzard-proof personal fronts that ward off the worst effects of dancing with emotionally cool Black male polar bears, but which do not allow room for future adaptation to non-arctic social environments. Blizzard-proof emotional clothing is not much fun to try to move around in on a daily basis, and only those wearing similar garments will try to dance with Black women so clad. This is also not the way you would expect a woman who has had positive relationships with men to behave. Exposure to one adolescent coping style generates a different sort of incompletely adult coping style in those with whom they have contact.

Immunization Against The Cool Virus

"False face must hide what the false heart doth know."
William Shakespeare
Macbeth

You become immunized against a virus by being inoculated with a less virulent killed version of the virus. A killed virus protects you from the live version of the virus by tricking your immune system into developing antibodies. The process of developing an immunity against it thus involves

97

taking some measure of the disease into your system to prevent even more widespread damage. Cool is an adolescent personality virus against which you can vaccinate yourself to prevent complete emotional destruction. But using the vaccine creates side effects. Reaction-to-cool is a psychological defense system that involves some measure of taking on, and reinforcing, aspects of the cool virus to develop psychological antibodies. Black women inoculated with a killed version of the cool virus acquire some measure of protection against it. But vaccination blocks off some measure of the capacity for taking on other adult roles. Certain parts of the personality become frozen into an adolescent mold as part of the psychological defense process developed in reaction to continued exposure to cool men, like a childhood smallpox vaccination leaving scar tissue that remains visible in adulthood. While vaccinations can help, the best way to treat a disease that offers no benefits is to leave the quarantined area for more hospitable, uninfected areas and let the virus slowly work its way out of your system.

"There is something terribly morbid in the modern sympathy with pain. One should sympathize with the color, the beauty, the joy of life. The less said about life's sores the better."
Oscar Wilde
The Picture of Dorian Gray

Such Black women might not seem cool, but that is just a part of the reaction-to-cool facade. A single role developed in reaction to cool defines their lives, and any single role that blocks one from taking on other roles is part of an adolescent personality structure. One common form of this reaction-to-cool personality is the "strong, independent" Black woman who says she doesn't really need men in her life, and is too busy playing the single role of being strong and independent to waste time with them anyway, is an example of such a Black woman. Her life revolves around playing a strong and independent role that is trotted out on all occasions for all types of audiences. The degree to which a Black woman fails to take on multiple roles is the degree to which she is an incomplete adult, regardless of how well she fills her one-note role of choice. While it is not really her fault, given that she has no choice about being exposed to immature, non-committal cool men on whom she can not depend for anything, it nevertheless remains a coping style for incompletely adult women. Being self-supporting, and nothing else, is not a well-rounded adult life.

Being cool creates endless barriers that impede the development of interracial relationships with no compensating gains. Being cool reduces your chances of meeting adult White or Black males capable of taking on multiple roles, because such men usually see little of interest in cool women. White men have better things to do than attempt approaching a cool Black female iceberg. Being cool means you are not emotionally available, and thus offer no prospect of long-term compatibility. Cool is a limitation, not a plus. Interracial relationships require wearing many more social hats than being cool allows, and being cool makes interracial relationships less likely to develop in the first place, because one of the cornerstones of cool is that it is developed in reaction against the values of White society and Whites in general.

"Too much sadness hath congeal'd your blood"
William Shakespeare
The Taming Of The Shrew

The first step in becoming interracially approachable is to stop playing the role of a cool Black woman. Being cool offers nothing of interest to middle-class White males. Thinking of the world as something other than a vale of tears peopled with emotionless hulks walking around is the first step towards developing an outlook on life that makes being cool unnecessary. Being cool automatically and inevitably means only cool, non-adult males will approach you, the one thing you do not want. White men do not enjoy trying to chisel their way through cool masks, and are unlikely to even try approaching a Black woman who looks cool. Once you start taking on other roles, opportunities that have always been present, if unnoticed, start presenting themselves. While shedding cool characteristics will not in and of itself get you into an interracial relationship, it does nevertheless remove the biggest of all obstructions from your path. You open yourself up to a broad spectrum of emotional possibilities and emotionally available men when you stop being cool and become a more complete adult.

"There is a local propriety to be observed in all companies; and that what is extremely proper in one company, may be, and often is, highly improper in another."
Philip Stanhope, Earl of Chesterfield
Letters To His Son

Chapter Eight
Making Yourself More Approachable, Part III

"We shall be the more marketable."
William Shakespeare
As You Like It

Positioning Yourself In The Minds Of White Men

"Any object.....may become interesting through becoming associated with an object in which an interest already exists."
William James
Talk To Teachers On Psychology

Our minds come with inborn capacities for sorting out the deluge of information that comes into their heads every day. We must winnow through the people, things and events to which we are exposed every day. Positioning means that, for whatever category you can think of, adults have little mental ladders in their minds for evaluating people and products. These cognitive structures tend to be arranged in terms of some sort of real or perceived level of quality. For example, the leading brand of cola would be at the top of your mental ladder for soft drinks, the second leading brand would be a close second, and generic brands would be at the bottom of your mental ladder for soft drinks. The higher on the mental ladder something in a given category is, the more preferred it becomes in most situations, so you pick the number one brand over the number two brand most of the time.

As men accumulate information about any sort of category, they start sorting things out. For example, we might classify auto mechanics and doctors of our acquaintance as "really good" (top of the ladder) or "okay" (somewhat lower on the ladder). It is helpful for everybody, including you, to be able to sort things out and classify them on the basis of partial information. So, if you see a new brand of car from an established auto manufacturer, you usually assume it is okay until you hear otherwise. The reason is that the manufacturer's name is associated with certain positive qualities. When their name is put on a new product, you usually make a lot of positive assumptions about the new product due to the mental associations carried over from the other products with that name on it. Advertisers go to enormous lengths to try to insert their particular products into the preferred slot at the top of customers' mental ladders by showing off their products in ways designed to get people to think it is top-of-the-line.

Assume you work at the Melanin Beverages Company and are trying to market a regional blackberry cola that has done well in the southern territory, into the northern territory, where that particular product is relatively unknown. That company also makes a vanilla soda that has been around the northern territory market for a long time. The way to introduce the blackberry product into the northern territory is to create a package for the blackberry cola that suggests that it is similar to, or related to, the package for the same company's vanilla soda, differing only in the color of the packaging, or personal front. The blackberry cola is considered to partake of the associated qualities of the vanilla product. Why? The more familiar elements the blackberry product package contains, such as a similar company name, package shape and design, trademark, and so on, the more likely people are to simply classify it as a slightly modified version of the regular product they drink all of the time. Prospects will mentally slot the new product at the top of their new mental ladder for the blackberry cola category, parallel in rank to the vanilla soda.

The new product is assumed to partake of all of the positive qualities of the more familiar product by association, because we fill in the blanks with preexisting information that seems to fit until we see a reason to do otherwise. The blackberry product is perceived to differ from the vanilla product only along the esthetically desirable dimension of taste, and in the personal front packaging that advertises that esthetic characteristic. Adventurous male prospects with a taste for blackberry colas are likely to automatically turn to the product packaged in this manner because everything about it says it is the same as the more familiar vanilla product with which they have years of experience, while having the added virtue of being novel, and therefore of interest to that part of the market looking for something new. Perceived similarities thus create mental associations between the old and the new. The singles marketplace is no different than the soft drink marketplace. From the point of view of the prospect, you partake of the qualities of self of the others in singles marketplace by presenting personal front qualities that link or associate you with those positive characteristics of others. It comes down to taking whatever male prospects already have in their heads as a given, and linking or associating yourself with it. Similarities focus their attention, differences lose their attention.

"Take the tone of the company you are in."
Philip Stanhope, Earl of Chesterfield
Letters To His Son

Most White men do not have mental ladders for Black women because they generally know little about Black women, and thus have no information to work with. White men do, however, have mental ladders they use to slot White women with whom they come into contact. The greater the degree of similarity an unfamiliar White woman has with such positive categories as are already in his head, meaning his mental ladders for slotting and arranging women, the more readily the man can evaluate that new woman. Positioning slots an unfamiliar woman into a particular rank on the mental ladder within that category. The basis for slotting her is the extent to which she exhibits key personal front characteristics that others on that mental ladder have usually been observed to have. This applies to Black women as well as White women.

Take On Roles Consistent With Your Social Reality

"We should gain more by letting ourselves be seen such as we are than by attempting to appear what we are not."
La Rochefoucauld
Maxims

All of us are members of one social class or another, and this is usually determined by some combination of education, occupation, income and lifestyle. We are good at sensing whether or not someone is on our general level or not based on their personal front, meaning external characteristics of their social class. People tend to get along best with others just above, just below or at about the same level within their own social class. We are all aware of this in a general way, which is why we are surprised when a millionaire marries a waitress, or when a millionairess marries a construction worker, and why we are not surprised when they break up a few years later. They have nothing in common.

Each social class has its own ladder, and the social ladders for different classes run parallel to each other, but do not bump into each other very much. You have to work at bumping into someone from a different social ladder, because they tend to live in different neighborhoods, have different types of jobs, different lifestyles and just not bump into each other very often. Men classify women as being either on their own particular ladder, and therefore relevant to their lives, or as not being on their ladder, and therefore not of real long-term interest.

A Black woman should project a consistent personal front image skewed towards the top of the social ladder she lives on in a manner consistent with her social class. The more consistently the elements of the Black woman's personal front add up to a top-of-the-line image for women among her social set, the more positively White male in that social set will regard her. Thus, a working-class Black woman might shop for clothing at major retailers, but avoid both discount stores and preppy attire shops, both of which are inconsistent with the other parts of her personal front, such as her accent and education, to say nothing of possibly scaring off potentially compatible working-class White males by inducing them to see her as too rich for their blood. It's a mistake to try to position yourself at the top of your ladder by trying to look like you are from a more affluent ladder than is actually the case. You won't be able to carry it off for very long before others sense that the truth about you is something different than what your personal front projects.

"Nothing so much prevents our being natural as the desire of appearing so."
La Rochefoucauld
Maxims

Avoid giving the appearance of being something you are not. As soon as you open your mouth, people will sense whether or not you really are what you make yourself out to be. The other details of your personal front will confirm their suspicions one way or the other. Deceptions usually can not be carried on for any length of time because few people have the depth of knowledge of what they pretend to be to carry it off for an extended period of time. It is okay to take on personal front characteristics of people a notch or two above you. Women do this all the time when they use

104

prestige speech patterns to avoid being classified as lower on the scale than their actual social class. But, when you try to take on the personal characteristics of people from another social class ladder altogether, you are being deceptive because you are not authorized to play such roles by virtue of your background.

"This above all: to thine own self be true."
William Shakespeare
Hamlet

Take On Only Those Roles You Are Authorized to Play

The role you decide to take on determines the details of the personal front that go with that role. Your details need to be consistent. Inconsistencies between details tells others that you are some sort of a phony, because the pieces of your personal front are as mismatched as pieces from two different jigsaw puzzles. There is a difference between taking on an authorized role versus an unauthorized role. An authorized role is one you can play by virtue of it being an actual part of your life. If you work as an accountant, it is okay to talk shop with other accountants, since being an accountant is a role you are authorized to play by virtue of your education, employment and life experiences. If you are not authorized to play the role of accountant, you are free to try to pretend you are one, and others are free to inflict a variety of negative social consequences on you when they find out that you are acting without authorization. Pretending to be what you are not is bad business. Don't pretend to have a job, an income level, education or lifestyle that you do not have in reality. If you tell people you go yachting all of the time, you'd better have the depth of experience necessary to pull it off around people who really do go yachting all of the time.

"Thou hast the power and own'st the grace to look through and behind this mask of me."
Elizabeth Barrett Browning
Sonnets From The Portugese

Playing a role means you have the depth of experience necessary to fill out the role, in the sense of someone who has lived the part and has a wealth of depth of experience to draw on. Playing a role is a two-way street.

105

Whenever you play a role, audiences analyze and react to your role-playing. They will not accept it, lock, stock and barrel on your say-so. They will feel free to interact with you to test their assumptions. If you can show that you really do live up to all of the expectations of your role, at that point both you and your male audience can drop most of your role-playing and relax. Being truthful makes it easy to be consistent, because you have an endless number of real-life experiences to draw on to fill out the details of your role. Do not pretend to be what you are not, because you do not have the depth of experience to bluff your way through a role you are not authorized to take on.

"We are never so ridiculous from the qualities we have, as from those we affect to have."
La Rochefoucauld
Maxims

Whatever role you take on, audience members in the know about what that role involves will feel free to pass judgment on you and about their judgment with others. There are a thousand little verbal and nonverbal clues that will tip them off to whether or not you are an impostor. You may have heard of one particular type of impostor yourself. Suburban White males sometimes pretend to be cool White males. Cool Black males can spot such frauds at a glance. If you're still in the process of discovering yourself, be what you know you are already, not what others expect you to be. If you are in some sort of dead-end job or life situation, don't be ashamed to tell others. Just state it in a matter-of-fact way and move on with the conversation. Lies are much harder to live with than just getting it out and moving on.

Attracting Interracial Lightning

Bolts of lightning find lightning rods particularly approachable because the metallic composition and physical arrangement of the lightning rods are specifically designed to attract, and conduct, electrical discharges from surrounding environments crackling with electrical potential. Interracial lightning is about as far from cool as you can get, and requires playing by the rules of psychological electricity, not the rules of cool. If you want to attract interracial lightning, become an interracial lightning rod. Getting White men to approach you requires managing the impression that you are

106

both interracially approachable and have the potential to conduct interpersonal emotional electricity. Catching interracial lightning in a bottle requires attracting it using impression management to position yourself atop White male mental ladders, where interracial lightning is most likely to strike. Playing for the Black male audience drains your potential for conducting interracial electricity.

Tune Out Irrelevant Audiences

"A preoccupied attention is the only answer to the importunate frivolity of other people; an attention, and to an aim which makes their aims frivolous."
Ralph Waldo Emerson
"Experience"

Don't act embarrassed about being interracially interested and available. This might take the form of hesitancy or a sheepish sort of attitude about the whole thing. You must tune out Black audiences to reach your White male audience. You have an unlimited right to pick the audience you want to play for, and complete autonomy in your choice of role. Don't cater to a Black audience if you prefer to spend your time taking on a different role for a White audience. Different roles have to be fine-tuned to the needs of different audiences, and playing for one necessarily excludes playing for another at the same time.

It doesn't matter what others think unless you see a need to pay attention to them. Others are important only if you let them become important by dwelling on them. Those who seek to prevent you from taking on your role of choice are really trying to prevent you from being an autonomous adult by virtue of getting you to take on their expectations as your own and thus freeze you in the role that they choose for you, rather than the one you choose for yourself.

You may feel somewhat embarrassed in going against the grain of years of experience at living up to others' social expectations at home, in school and on the job. Living up to other's expectations is simply one of many habits you have unconsciously taken on over the years, and one over which you have an unlimited freedom of choice about compliance. Interracial relationships do mean going against the grain of the past, and that is the right way to go. Human beings come with an instinct to want to be in harmony with their social reference group, but the net effect of living up to the expectations of group instincts is to level you down to the group's lowest common denominator of behavior that does not make others jealous or envious, providing no compensating benefits to you in the process. It is simply a childish form of conformity. Limiting yourself only to those personal choices that do not make others jealous or envious is no way to go through life. Aim up the scale of individual preferences, not down the scale of contorting yourself to avoid provoking others' jealousies and envy.

Being an adult necessarily requires taking on multiple roles, and anything that prevents you from taking on one or more desired adult roles is just another counterproductive obstacle to maturity. Becoming an adult means moving beyond adolescent conformity to consciously analyze and plan what is best for you, not what others think is best for you or expect of you. No one knows what is best for you better than you. Get enough practice tuning out group opinions and doing what you know is best for you and you will find you don't miss catering to others' opinions one bit. That means being unembarrassed about making your availability known and unembarrassed about responding the right sort of advances from the right sort of White males.

Embarrassment just means that you still have some residual inhibitions remaining from years of unwarranted sensitivity to the attitudes and expectations of those around you. Do your own thinking and develop your own dating preferences. There's nothing to be embarrassed about unless you have the conformist attitude that others' opinions take precedence over your own. After acting as if there is nothing wrong with being interracially receptive for a while, such behavior becomes automatic behavior. A lot of other things about your personal front will fall into place automatically once this becomes ingrained behavior. You are not doing anything wrong, so there's nothing to be embarrassed about.

"What I must do is all that concerns me, not what the people think."
Ralph Waldo Emerson
"Self-Reliance"

Your Dress, Hair And Accessories

"The apparel oft proclaims the [woman]."
William Shakespeare
Hamlet

Your personal front should differ from those of White women only along approved dimensions, and your mode of dress is the easiest thing to adjust should you want to encourage White men to approach you. White men are more likely to take notice of you when you dress in a manner similar to White women at, or near, the top of the social class ladder the two of you have in common. Dress is just the start. They notice other things about you besides how you dress. Should the other pieces of your personal front be inconsistent with your mode of dress, or show you to be an unpleasant person, you are wasting your time. They will sense from a distance that something is not quite compatible about you as regards themselves. They will not explain this to you, they will just avoid you.

For the limited purpose of expediting initial meetings with White males, avoid red-black-green Afrocentric attire or accessories. Your mode of dress is a symbol of what you are and the sort of associations you want to come to mind when they first see you. To White men, multiple elements of Afrocentricity portray you as desiring to exclude yourself from interracial socializing. Afrocentric personal fronts advertise that you focus on Black culture, which to them means that Whites need not apply. Since they don't have a lot to go on, they use what little you choose to present to them to evaluate you. Again, all of this is for the purpose of a getting a first meeting going only. You can take on a more relaxed role after the two of you become acquainted, but in order to get to that point you have to play by certain rules.

Avoid positioning yourself sexually. This means not wearing short skirts or low-cut blouses, which men see as a way of saying that you are being blatantly sexual because you are not looking for a long-term relationship. Remember, what counts is how the men think of you, not how you think they ought to be thinking about you. Wear middle-of-the road, possibly understated, clothing. Don't wear a lot of jewelry.

What if you have no idea at all about how to dress for some reason? Your fallback position should be to dress as if you were a nice, middle-class Black woman going to a suburban church. If you belong to a church where the women dress like something time-warped out of the past, update your wardrobe. While dressing like a church girl might not be quite appropriate for all occasions, this is something that your typical White male can recognize and tune into, and shows that you are at least from the same planet as he is, even if you are not necessarily from the same neighborhood. You can fine-tune your wardrobe later on.

Be Sure to Smile

"One who smiles so has no need to speak To lead your thoughts along"
Elizabeth Barrett Browning
"Two Sketches"

Regardless of social class, White men prefer to approach emotionally-available Black women who exude the appearance of being approachable. When visiting unknown territory, they show a marked preference for places that hang out welcome signs. Smiling is a greeting signal that advertises your receptiveness to advances and emotional availability, and this part of your personal front is no exception to the rule that you attract what you advertise for. Be aware however, that you should not flash the sort of face-splitting smile that lets him inspect your wisdom teeth. Show your front teeth, but avoid the extremes of showing all or nothing.

Good feelings are contagious to some extent, since we are all imitative and suggestible to some degree. For that matter, being smiled at actually releases certain hormones that trigger off instinctual affective social responses within the mind and body of the recipient of the smile. We are programmed by our biology to be social creatures, and we react to others within our social sphere. Thus, the overall attitude reflected in your smile is a form of invitation to certain types of men to enter your personal space and soak up more of the personal atmosphere you exude. If you have trouble smiling, just practice. Sooner or later, your thoughts will follow in the trail of your actions, filling in your mental blank spots in a consistent manner after you fill in the first blank with something positive.

The lines of your face should go up, not down, positive expressions reflecting a positive state of mind. You should look like a smile goes naturally with the rest of your face, and you should definitely smile when you see somebody interesting looking at you. How else would he know that you would welcome an advance from him?

Fine-Tuning Your Personal Front

Your posture, facial expression, tone of voice and degree of eye contact reinforce the other parts of your personal front, and your personal front should be organized around expressing social class similarities and emotional availability. Express your emotional availability. Don't act cool. Cool is a personal front that advertises you as being unavailable to take on adult roles with non-cool companions, and means you are unavailable to play the adult role of interracial dater, which necessarily involves having the psychological and emotional flexibility to open up to the new emotional experiences that go with new roles.

Adult White and Black men value indicators of emotional availability, and your facial expressions are a primary indicator of this characteristic. An unhappy expression will screen out unpleasantly large numbers of interesting men who don't want to be around a woman with a sourpuss expression. Expressing oneself in an open manner is not a White or Black thing, but an emotionally adult thing. Facial expressions express your personality and show what kind of person you are. The best dress in the world will not hook in any men should your facial expression make you look like a tough nut to crack.

The greater your range of facial expressions, the better you can communicate a wide variety of emotions, and that capability will operate to attract men who share your ability to have and express various emotions. Should you think this is an exaggeration, consider the opposite situation. A cool woman who expresses no emotion will find only cool men gravitating towards her, sensing a kindred cool soul in her.

Eyes are the windows of the soul and your emotional availability. Eye contact tells White males that you are curious about them, and possibly open to being approached. Let your glance linger, and sometimes a man might approach you without a word ever being spoken. Such is the power

111

of eye contact. Incidentally, don't wear sunglasses. They obscure your eyes, and the expressive muscles around your eyes, from being observed by potentially curious men, as well as advertising that you are not open to eye contact, along with everything else that goes with not being open to eye contact.

Body language, posture and gestures vary all over the map, both between and within cultures. Nevertheless, there are some basic principles applicable to interracial dating. You should use your body language, posture and gestures to show that you are interested and available. Turning your head and body when you see a really interesting man is one example. Waving to a total stranger is another example. Both let the men know that you are interested and probably are secure enough in yourself to openly and directly express your interest in man, about as far from cool as you can get.

"You'll catch more flies with a drop of honey than a barrel of vinegar."
attributed to Abraham Lincoln

What If You Have Nothing To Be Happy About?

"I show more mirth than I am mistress of."
William Shakespeare
As You Like It

Don't be stern faced. Avoid hangdog, sad-beagle expressions and attitudes. But what do you do if you don't feel very happy? Method acting techniques emphasize drawing upon past experiences and previous role-playing experiences to add depth of expression to the role you are playing at present. Recapturing a positive feeling you had in the past will add luster to your expression in the present moment. If you can't think of anything that has made you happy lately, maybe think of a Christmas present you got as a little girl or how you felt on a summer vacation at the beach a few years ago. Reliving the experience in your mind will replay on your face some of the feelings that you had at the time. Of course, after you have a few positive contemporary experiences, you probably won't need to reach too far back into the past to find something to lift your spirits.

112

"Assume a virtue, if you have it not."
William Shakespeare
Hamlet

Two Examples

Assume you have twin sisters who grew up together and went their separate ways after high school. The first Black woman has medium-length straightened hair, wears a Beethoven sweatshirt and a plaid wool skirt, has a pleasant, calmly direct (not cool) expression, and wears no jewelry except small gold earrings, a class ring and a wristwatch. She looks at White males in walking through a shopping center, making some degree of momentary eye contact, flashing little smiles at some and turning her head to look at a few particularly interesting White males. She might even wave to one. Her personal front appeals to White men. She is a hundred times more likely to be approached by White men than her twin sister who acts cool, wears loads of jewelry, has an Afrocentric hair style and wears Afrocentric black, green and red clothing.

Her sister has a personal front suitable for certain types of Black male audiences, but unsuitable for facilitating initial meetings with most types of White male audiences. She has an Afro hair style, wears red-black-green Afrocentric clothing under a black leather jacket, Afrocentric jewelry and looks cool. She does not smile, and the lines of her face go down. She wears dark glasses that hide her expression. When she talks to a sales clerk, her voice is deep and unemotional. Her posture is slumped over, as if a bit depressed. She talks in a deep monotone. She does not look men in the eye, does not return their eye contact, never smiles in public and does not turn her head or body should she see somebody interesting. She is at the low end of the approachability spectrum as regards White males. Although she has probably not given it much conscious thought, most of the elements of her personal front add up to the general impression that she tunes out White males and is neither friendly nor approachable.

Having a personal front with one or two Afrocentric elements is okay. Some Black women just look better in Afro hair styles than with straightened hair, for example. But a personal front with multiple Afrocentric elements results in the perception of unreceptiveness among

113

men of other ethnic groups. The more closely you seem tied to an Afrocentric self-definition or role, the less interracially approachable your personal front makes you appear to potentially interested White males. Any sort of self-determined ethnic focus automatically seems exclusionary, because the more tightly you identify with your race, the more tightly that bond with members of your race seems to exclude outsiders. This situation might be easier to understand if you look at White males from the same perspective. If you saw a White male dressed in traditional Italian, Polish or Greek garb in an ethnic neighborhood or at an ethnic street festival, you would probably think of him as a low-probability prospect for an interracial relationship, because the more closely he identifies with his particular ethnic group, the more exclusionary his personal front appears to those who are not members of that ethnic group. Such a White male might actually be open to an interracial relationship, but there is nothing in his personal front to make you think of him that way. Rightly or wrongly, his personal front advertises that he is locked into a culturally and racially exclusionary role where outsiders are not likely to be welcome because they lack the social bond he shares with the other members of his social reference group.

"All the world's a stage, And all the men and women merely players."
William Shakespeare
As You Like It

Chapter Nine
Where And How To Meet White Men, Part I

"Where The Boys Are"
movie title song by Neil Sedaka and Howard Greenfield

The Easiest Way To Meet White Men

"There is an incessant influx of novelty into the world, and yet we tolerate incredible dulness."
Henry David Thoreau
Walden

Men most often become involved with women who live in either their neighborhood or immediate vicinity. The further apart they live, the less their odds of meeting in the first place. As your distance from a man increases, your chances of meeting him drops like a rock. If you never meet him, you'll never go out with him, period. The rule of thumb is that, should a woman live more than twelve blocks away from a given man, odds are they are unlikely to cross paths in the course of their neighborhood business and become involved.

The opposite is also true: the closer you live to large concentrations of men, the better your chances of making initial contact with one or more of them. People who live geographically close to each other, meaning within walking distance, have numerous opportunities to cross paths with each other in the neighborhood, make initial contact and try to get a relationship going. The implication is that the best way to encounter large numbers of potentially compatible single White males is to go to where they already live. Men spend a large proportion of their time close to home when not at their places of work, and you have numerous opportunities to meet them near their homes.

The easiest way to meet White men is thus to live in a neighborhood full of them. This puts you into everyday contact with single White males walking by on the street, waiting for the bus, buying food in the supermarket, eating in the restaurants, doing laundry in the laundromat, worshipping at church, browsing books in the bookstore, relaxing in the park and various other places in the neighborhood where they go about their everyday activities. Even if you are not particularly outgoing, if you pass by a large number of men in the neighborhood in the course of your daily business, a few will take notice of you unless you give the appearance of being energetically unfriendly.

In addition, since neighborhoods tend to be socially homogenous, meaning they attract people of similar educational and income levels, some basic social screening has already been done for you. This means that, while you are not guaranteed meeting the perfectly compatible man of your dreams just by virtue of living in a particular neighborhood, your odds of meeting someone on your own general level, or someone with whom you will have some things in common, increase dramatically simply because you have opportunities for exposure to large concentrations of socially similar White males in integrated or primarily-White areas. If living in an area with a large proportion of Whites males is not an option, visit such areas on weekends to go shopping, browse in the bookstores, and lounge about afterwards in a local coffeeshop. Should you meet a White guy while so disposed, and he asks why you do your shopping so far from home, tell him it seems like a place where you might want to live someday, and the friendliness of at least one of your prospective neighbors is a definite source of encouragement. Who knows, your crystal ball might just turn out to be on target.

Some words of caution are in order. Not all White neighborhoods welcome Blacks. As a general rule, as you go up the education and income scale, you will find far less overt or covert racism, and increasingly more potentially compatible prospects. The other side of the coin is that as you go down the education and income scale, the opposite happens. This does not mean that all of the people in a given neighborhood don't want Blacks around. It does mean that you should closely scrutinize certain types of blue-collar neighborhoods before signing a lease and save yourself from embroilment in a host of avoidable problems. Take a walk around on a busy Saturday and see what sort of notice you attract from the locals, as well as whether or not you see any other Blacks around. If all you get is hostile stares, it's best to look elsewhere. Not too many prospective compatibles in places like that anyhow.

A different sort of problem is presented by places where you might be comfortable, but where nearly every man you might meet is already married. As a general rule, the more private homes you see, the more likely it is to be a bedroom suburb full of married couples with children. Single White men tend to live in rented apartments in cities and suburbs until they get married, in part because they know that nearby apartments, bars and laundromats are filled with single women looking for single men. Meeting single people of both sexes is a lot easier in urban and suburban neighborhoods full of apartment houses filled with single people than in a sprawling bedroom suburb with one-twentieth the singles population density of a big city neighborhood. Remember, the key demographic characteristic you are looking for is the presence of large numbers of single White males, not the number of dress shops or the landscape architecture in the local parks. You can move to farther reaches of suburbia after you get involved with someone.

Should you choose to live in a primarily-White neighborhood, make your preferences known to the locals. Mention it to people who work at the local coffeehouses. Mention it in conversations with people in your building and the neighborhood. Mention it at the post office when you buy stamps. You might become known as "that Black girl who's looking for a White guy." Should it lead to you meeting someone interesting, what do you care what some people think or whisper? While there are no guarantees, publicizing your preferences might eventually find their way to receptive ears you might want to nibble on.

Your primary singles marketplace is the city you reside in, and big cities usually have more women than men. Although the imbalance between the numbers of men and women might seem a bit intimidating, keep in mind that there are several times more White men interested in Black women than there are Black women available for interracial dating. Your match is out there, but it's up to you find a way to run into him, or make yourself available in a manner that he is likely to run into you. Almost any activity besides staying home with your girlfriends will give you some sort of opportunity to meet men. If you are thinking of living in particular neighborhood, walk around during the weekend or a weekday evening. Should you see no coffeeshops, bookstores, laundromats or other such places where single women can bump into new acquaintances, it may not be the place for you, regardless of how good a deal you get on the rent.

117

Small- and medium-sized cities with less than two hundred thousand people, and rural areas out in the sticks, tend to have more men than women. If you don't seem to run into too many single men in the big city you reside in, you might try overnight visits to smaller cities a hundred miles or more away during the weekends. You might even subscribe to a small-city newspaper to get listings of events such as county fairs, street festivals, fund raisers, church events and the like. Remember, all you need is one guy, not a boatload of them. You might even arrange to get a weekend temporary job at certain events as a ticket-taker or hostess to facilitate initial contact.

The Second Easiest Way To Meet White Men

"We ought not so much to apply ourselves to create opportunities, as to make use of those which present themselves."
La Rochefoucauld
Maxims

Lots of women have met compatible dates and mates at work. You could lose your job tomorrow, but a really good relationship that develops out of initial contact made on the job might last forever. Should you be like most women, you are probably interested in gainfully employed single men, and you are guaranteed to find many such men at their places of work.

Huge numbers of Black and White women meet men at work. The reason is obvious. Most people work at least eight hours a day, half or more of their waking hours. Not very surprisingly, a lot of people use their workplaces as informal social centers, if only because they spend so much time there in addition to there being so many people around them. In any large group of people, there will probably be a few individuals with whom you have something in common. The bigger the company you work in, the better your chances.

There are two obvious problems with this rosy scenario. First, even if you pretty much keep to yourself, you probably don't want the office gossips whispering about you, especially if what they are whispering is completely inaccurate and might find its way to your supervisor. Some people can find this a bit unnerving, especially in small companies where everybody sticks their noses in everybody else's business. Second, you can be absolutely sure that an interracial romance will attract ten times more attention than a same-race office romance. Third, if the relationship does not work out, you and he have to look at each other for a long time to come. You are the only one who can weigh to pros and cons of your particular situation and decide which way to go.

One way out of the problem with dating men from work is through temporary jobs. If you know in advance that you will only be at a particular place of work for a week, a month or whatever, the details of a long-term office relationship are obviously a secondary consideration. And, should the pickings in one place be somewhat slimmer than thin, you can always move on to other places of work for other temporary assignments. While you can meet eligible White men in almost any kind of setting, it's probably better to get placed in a large company than a small company, if only because the large company's cafeteria has more single men sitting around the company cafeteria during their lunch hour than dozens of small companies put together. Load the dice in your favor.

Your workplace situation also gives you indirect opportunities to meet White men, should you not find anyone worthwhile at work. Working with other people plugs you into a social network of sorts. There are probably a few people with whom you might get together after work for a drink. If a group goes out for a drink, go with them a few times and see what sort of crowd gathers around them. Some of them might have interesting friends from elsewhere drop by.

The White women with whom you work should not see you as competition, because White men who go for Black women have probably either tuned White women out completely or are in the process of doing so. Someone who is on the same wavelength as you might even offer to introduce you to some men they think are your type, probably in the context of some sort of low-key party or other event. Recently-married White women are so ecstatic about having gotten married that they often want to help everybody they know attain the same state of marital bliss, so be receptive should such a woman offer assistance or suggestions.

119

The Third Easiest Way To Meet White Men

"Opportunities make us known to others."
La Rochefoucauld
Maxims

Should you work in the downtown of a big city or a major suburb, your lunch hour is a great opportunity to get out of the office and check out the millions of single White males walking around during lunch time. You might even spot a few White guys dating Black women. If you're actively looking, the worst thing you can do during lunch is stay at the office, eat at your desk and talk with other single Black and White women doing the same thing as you. Unless you work in some large company with huge numbers of single male employees piling into the company cafeteria at lunch time, get out of your office for lunch. The second worst thing you can do is go to a fancy restaurant with lots of girlfriends and sit in a quiet corner of the restaurant where White guys can neither see you nor run through your private blockade of girlfriends. Leave your girlfriends at the office. You are looking for a boyfriend, and "three's a crowd" from the perspective of unattached White men, who rarely approach women when they bring an army of girlfriends with them.

There are a number ways to meet White guys during your lunch hour. One way is to go to a fast food restaurant and try to get a conversation going with someone on line. Comment on the length of the line or ask if he knows whether a certain menu delicacy is any good. If he pays no attention to you, you will never see him again, so who cares? Another approach is to sit down next to a White male who is not sitting with anyone else. Ask him if the food tastes okay, compare it to what you get at another restaurant, and so on. If he's interested, anything will suffice to get the conversation going. If not, just check out the other guys walking by. If someone on line talks with you and you think it might lead somewhere, anything you choose to say can suffice to get the conversation going. After you get your food, walk over to where he's sitting and ask if this is a good place to sit down. After all, you've already been sort-of introduced.

Yet another approach is to just sit down by yourself with a few empty tables near you and see if anyone interesting notices you. If so, flash him a little smile and make some cyc contact. Whatever you do, don't sit near a group of chatterbox women. For that matter, avoid restaurants that seem to be filled mainly with groups of women. Men hate having to deal with groups of women in making initial contact, and will often walk away without trying to cut through the blockade. Some White guys will actually sit down with you if you look friendly, make eye contact and sort of invite them to take a fancy to you. The first thing you should say is hello, I don't believe I know your name. After that, ask what he does or where he works. The conversation may or may not lead to the two of you exchanging telephone numbers but sometimes just talking with someone who's interested in you to some degree can lift your spirits if you've had a long dry spell.

If the local parks are safe, sit on a park bench to eat your lunch and check out the White guys passing by. Who knows, one or two might be thinking about you the same way you're thinking about him and ask a question about your lunch, or even whether there's room for two on the bench.

The Fourth Easiest Way To Meet White Men

Coffeehouses and laundromats are good places to meet White guys, and seem to be designed to facilitate initial social interactions. Though seemingly dissimilar, both laundromats and coffeehouses have certain underlying similarities. Both seem to be popular wherever there are lots of single people living nearby, and both have clienteles that typically stick around for an hour or less per visit. You find them almost everywhere these days, from downtown to city neighborhoods to the suburbs to college towns to shopping malls. Except for a few budding intellectuals, you can be sure that a good proportion of the guys who go to coffeehouses and laundromats are on the prowl, maybe for someone just like you. Some insightful laundromat owners have recognized the mating dance function served by laundromats and have set up bars and pubs directly adjacent to laundromats, so that pickups and picker-uppers can have a drink with each other in the bar next door while their clothing spins away.

By the way, you need not limit yourself to visiting the local laundromat once a week. You'll find a lot of men tend to do their laundry on Fridays, Saturdays and Sundays, especially if they're not involved with a female-type person who keeps their weekend schedules filled. Should you accidentally happen to get several pieces of laundry dirty every day that the laundromats coincidentally happen to be filled with men, nobody in the laundromat will ever know that you were in there the day before.

But exactly how do you go about meeting someone in a laundromat or coffeehouse? You need to get a conversation going somehow or other, or you are wasting your time. Now and then a guy will make a move on you before you realize it, but don't count on being hit by a bolt from the blue. If you want to conduct interpersonal electricity, make yourself into a lightning rod. Dress either preppy or middle class. Don't wear a lot of jewelry. Don't wear much of anything that is Afrocentric, since that might be perceived as your way of saying that you tune into Blacks more readily than you tune into Whites. This is visual reassurance that you are "safe" to approach, meaning you do not look like a militant who will lecture him on race relations instead of investigating the prospects for an interpersonal relationship. Bring one or two newspapers with you for casual browsing while you simultaneously check out every White male that comes in the door. Sit in a place where you can see men coming in, as well as where there are some empty seats around you. Don't sit near other women under any circumstances, or allow them to sit near you, because men will see you as unapproachable by virtue of assuming that you and whatever women they see you talking with are inseparable friends and that it is thus a lost cause to even try to intrude on your private conversation. Like it or not, most men consider groups or women to be unapproachable. Men hate trying to get what they hope will be a productive private conversation going while unwelcome third parties stand by listening, gaping and slowly growing envious that nobody wants to talk with them.

Should someone suitable catch your eye as he comes in the door, make eye contact with him and flash a little smile. If he makes eye contact back at you, smile a bit more and maybe wave casually, as if he were someone you know. If he's interested, he'll make an effort to sit near you. Ask him if he'd like the sports section of the newspaper you are reading. Sports sections are a good bet for many males. Tell him that you don't read the sports section and you're wondering why men like it so much, one good conversation opener. If he's interested in you, he'll be glad to explain it to you at length. Should you come into the coffeehouse and see someone you like already there, try to sit right next to his table and use the routine with the newspaper. Do more or less the same thing in a laundromat. Sit in the part of the laundromat where you have a few empty seats around you, and don't sit near other women if you want men to come near you. One sure-fire way to attract interracially-minded White males in a coffeehouse or laundromat is to be seen holding up and reading a book or magazine with a cover that depicts Black women involved with White men or whose title involves interracial relationships. Something like that advertises what's on your mind.

One big mistake women, especially students, make is to bring big, clunky, dull-looking books on philosophy or some other esoteric topic with them cover up the coffeehouse tabletop and hunching over the table. This advertises that you are so caught up in the world of the mind that you can't be bothered with the social world around you. First of all, you can't share a book the way you share a newspaper. It's a bit difficult to slice a book up into sections. Second, a specialized book on philosophy or the like tunes out non-philosophers, who tend to have difficulty getting a conversation going on topics they know next to nothing about. The more obscure the topic, the less secure a male feels in commenting on it because he is unlikely to know anything about the topic. By contrast, the front-page news and sports sections, as well as any section of the newspaper other than the fashion section, is likely to interest many men and offer some prospect of common ground for discussion.

The male counterparts of such women who bring philosophy books to laundromats and coffeehouses are the computer geeks who bring small computers to work on while sipping coffee. They are obviously unclear on the concept that a coffeehouse is about trying to pick up someone, not to exhibit their award-winning electronic gadgets collection. Taking on the role of nerdy computer user necessarily excludes other people from involvement in such inward-directed performances.

Computers are not a conversation-opener, and few people of either sex outside Silicon Valley will try to start up a conversation about electronic equipment. Another mistake to avoid is wearing a radio or cassette player with headphones. Covering your ears with headphones makes you look unreceptive to being approached, because headphones are perceived as your way of tuning out the people around you. Dark glasses cover the eyes, hide your expression and make you look both unapproachable and emotionally unavailable.

123

The Hardest Way to Meet White Men

Stay home with your girlfriends to talk about the low quality of men and you are guaranteed to meet zero White men while so engaged.

Men Who Share Your Values And Lifestyle Interests

"Intimate society between people radically dissimilar to one another is an idle dream. Unlikeness may attract, but it is likeness which retains; and in proportion to the likeness is the suitability of the individuals to give each other a happy life."
John Stuart Mill
The Subjection Of Women

While it's nice to think about finding men whose personalities are compatible with your own, the basic problem with that notion is that you can not tell what a guy's personality is like from looking at him as he walks down the street. Get around this by becoming involved in activities that suit your values and lifestyle. Such activities attract men with whom you have things in common because their lifestyle interests derive from underlying similarities of personality and outlook on life. Since there's a lot more White men than Black men out there, if you look in the right places, you will probably find a few men who share your interests, outlook and lifestyle.

If you are a religious Black woman, you probably go to church at least once a week. You might also go to prayer meetings, retreats and similar activities of a religious nature that derive from your underlying religious orientation to life. That underlying religious orientation to life also determines other things about you. You probably do not wear revealing clothing in public. You probably do not drink much and do not smoke at all. You probably believe that there are ground rules for behavior for life and sexual conduct to which both you and a compatible male should both subscribe. You probably would not find too many compatible men at boxing matches, bars or heavy metal concerts.

To meet religious White men, go to a church of your denomination in an integrated or White neighborhood, preferably in a neighborhood with plenty of singles living in apartments. You might want to volunteer to work at some of the functions and events sponsored by churches. The sort of White males who attend, or volunteer, at such functions are likely to share many of your views and your overall outlook on life. If you enjoy religious activities outside church, men who share your enjoyment can probably also be found at such events. You might find suitable men at Christian singles events, Christian concerts, statewide religious conferences, Saturday night prayer meetings and related activities of interest to those with a strong religious orientation towards life. You might want to investigate volunteering to work at such events. Christian bookstores also attract preselected types of Christian males likely to share a particular outlook on life. Visit Christian bookstores and maybe even get a job in one.

If you have humanitarian or social-action interests, volunteer to work at a social services agency as a volunteer caregiver, get involved in a blood drive or work at the local animal shelter. Such activities bring you into contact with similarly-involved men whose outlook on life drives them to volunteer for such activities in the first place. Environmental groups and other types of social-action groups likewise tend to bring the like-minded together.

The problem with intellectuals is that they stay home to read and watch public television, worthwhile activities that somehow fail to bring them into contact with very many other people. Again, the key is to get out of your apartment and take it from there. If you're an intellectual, you are most likely to find people like yourself in bookstores, libraries, public radio and public television fundraisers, poetry readings, art film theaters, museums, symphonies, art exhibits, academic conferences, lectures, evening classes at colleges and similar sorts of mind-expanding activities. Whatever the particular flavor of your intellectual interests, there are sure to be other people like you out there somewhere, and such activities bring intellectual singles together.

If you're into science fiction, go to science fiction fan conventions or big-city bookstores that specialize in science fiction, fantasy and horror. If you like technology, you can meet men who like the same sort of thing at computer stores and computer industry conferences and logged in for conversations on the Internet.

125

Be aware, however, that people take on certain type of unconventional roles when logged on, roles often quite different than their everyday reality. Should you meet such a person in real life, don't be surprised if they are not ten feet tall and have social maladjustment problems that induce them to spend much of their lives online. Use your head in dealing with people you cannot see or hear, and go really slow on giving out your phone number and other personal information. That goes double for meeting someone from online in real life. Do it in public and have someone stand guard on the sidelines. Never give your real name, address or phone number out to somebody from online until after you get to know them really, really well. Play it safe, not fast.

Social and recreational activities of any specialized type attract a pre-selected audience of potentially compatible men who share those interests. Be aware, however, that certain types of events, such as football games, attract such broad cross-section of the male population that it is impossible to generalize about what kind of men attend such events. Football games attract everybody from college professors to illiterates. The only thing you can do in such cases is play it by ear.

At concerts, sports events and parades, you can usually tell at a glance whether or not they have wives or girlfriends by seeing who sits next to them, whether they wear wedding rings or have women on their arms. If you want to try to get a conversation going, all you have to do is get close to them and ask a question about the ongoing event, maybe letting your gaze linger a bit longer than usual while so doing. If he tries to get a conversation going, he's interested in you. If he doesn't try to get a conversation going, move on. Be aware that most men go to games to watch the game, and expressing an interest might catch them off-guard.

Beware of professional sports fans. Enthusiasm is okay, but the sort of guys who fill their lives to the brim with sports memorabilia and knick-knacks are probably not for you. Men who make a career of being professional spectators are somewhat hollow at the center. There's something wrong with someone who can't find anything else in life more interesting than rowdy enthusiasm for a team engaged in physical exertions. Such an obsession is an indicator that he is immature, in the sense of being so focused on external things that he has not really developed much of an internal mental life. Their identification with a team seems to preclude identification and development of their own interests and identities.

Such men are just little boys in grown men's bodies. You need psychological maturity and a sense of individuality to make it in interracial dating, and men who focus on enthusiastic, adolescent-style behavior rarely have what it takes to cut it outside the stadium. Overwhelming enthusiasm for group activities is usually a sign of having neglected to develop the individual capacities and judgment interracial dating requires. Such men often have little else in their life from which to derive satisfaction and status beyond identification with "their" team.

Certain lifestyle and leisure interests attract few men. Women are often interested in things that are incomprehensibly foreign to men. The fact that you are interested in certain types of activities does not require men to show up for something in which they have no interest. Adult education is one good example. Ballet classes are a one-way ticket to meeting other women, not men. Knitting classes are more of the same. Now and then, however, a man might show up for a cooking course.

Woodworking and machine shop courses are much better bets. If you like to go shopping on weekends, the only men you will meet in the women's clothing departments are the sales clerks and married men buying gifts for their wives. Hardware and sporting goods sections attract men who might be receptive to a woman seeking advice on what to buy for a specific problem at home. Incidentally, men only go shopping when they have something specific in mind, not for the fun of it. Shopping is not a preferred leisure time activity for most men. Whatever the activity, if most participants are women, you won't meet too many men there.

Offer Or Ask For Assistance

Help!
title of Beatles movie directed by Richard Lester

Should you see a White guy struggling with bags of groceries, a couple of packages from the post office or trying to get a cart of whatever up the stairs in your building, ask him if he needs any help. Don't do this near hotels filled with out-of-towners passing through town. Some men don't want to be helped by anybody for any reason, but most will at least thank you for asking and some will take you up on your offer. The period of time in which you assist him will give you a few minutes, and maybe a lot longer, to ask him what's in the bags or boxes the two of you are bringing along, where he's going and so on. It's a two-way process, by the way. If he's interested, he'll look for ways to prolong the conversation, which might include stopping off at a local coffeeshop to recharge your neural batteries. Don't let yourself be induced into going into his apartment an hour after you meet him, because while most White men are not mental cases, any one particular guy could turn out to be a refugee from the law of averages.

You can also be the one who asks for assistance. Asking for the time is bit tacky, but can be an okay lead-in to a conversation. When you ask for the time, most men think all you want is the time. You must follow it up with something specific, such as asking if he has the time to sit down for coffee with you. If you don't spell it out, most men will not make the connection. Spelling it out means following it up with a question or a suggestion, such as asking whether he has time to drop into a coffeeshop with you, after first detecting some glimmer of interest in his eye.

Asking for directions is an even better tactic, even if you know perfectly well where to find for which you are asking for directions to actually is. This is a sort of conversation, and men will tune into your wavelength a lot faster than when you ask for the time. If you can carry off asking for directions in a sufficiently enticing tone of voice, some guys will walk you to your destination themselves, which gives you an opportunity to get something going. You can use these tactics almost anywhere in public without feeling guilty about being too forward.

If you have a long-term problem, sometimes you can meet White guys as a byproduct of seeking to solve that problem. For example, if you are a recovering alcoholic, joining a support group such as the local chapter of Alcoholics Anonymous, can plug you into a social network of people with the same problem. Parents without Partners is another example of how having a mutual problem can lead to initial contacts with similar men.

What If A White Guy Makes A Move On You?

"What passion hangs these weights upon my tongue?"
William Shakespeare
As You Like It

Should a White guy who is neither visibly psychotic nor otherwise undesirable make a move on you, go out of your way to look as friendly as possible. "Friendly" does not mean freezing up and looking the other way or at the ground. It means forcing yourself to show him some sort of a smile, looking him in the eye, and saying something, meaning anything that shows that you are interested. Should a White guy say something to you, be sure to give him some sort of response immediately, regardless of the tumult going on in your head. Should you say nothing, or give the appearance of playing hard to get, he'll most likely just forget it and move on. Remember, a White male who approaches a Black woman is going out on a limb, and your failure to give him a reason to continue the conversation will induce him to just walk away. Should there be something wrong with him, you can always dump him later on, but your number one priority is to get some sort of back-and-forth conversation going so that you have an opportunity to evaluate him further. It's also important to not talk in monosyllables, as women often criticize men for doing.

"In action, everything continually depends upon deciding promptly."
John Stuart Mill
The Subjection Of Women

Any normal White guy who approaches you is going against the tide of social convention in making an approach on you. Most White males are likely to see Black women as being, at best, of neutral friendliness, and possibly as "high-risk" in terms of approachability. Risk is defined as the possibility that you will just walk by and ignore them, as they have seen Black women do to Black men from time to time. A guy on the edge of moving in on you might give up a nanosecond before doing so because you look unfriendly, unresponsive or too tough to chew on. If you are with your girlfriends, start putting some distance between you and them - he does not want an audience listening in should he try to pick you up. This

129

will give you a few moments to mentally change gears and try to come up with a few things to talk about.

Your first priority is always to get a private conversational exchange going. A very close second is exchanging personal contact information that will allow the two of you to maintain contact. This could be your office telephone number, e-mail address or whatever. Once the two of you start talking, the routine is the same as when you make the first move.

Making An Approach

It's okay to try to pick up a White guy. If he likes you, anything will suffice to get the conversation going. If he doesn't like you, nothing you can say will change that, and you will never see him again, so who cares. Sometimes you have to be the one who makes the approach, or a perfectly good catch who might never have known that you existed will slip through your net. Should you decide to approach a White male, don't sneak up on him from behind to ask or say something.

Men like to see who's talking with them. In addition, coming on to him from the front allows him to check out your face, figure, and the like, and maybe allows him a chance to start formulating something to say to you, very possibly before you even have a chance to open your mouth. Men are like that. Men can sense if you are about to come on to them, even if you work at hiding it from them. They can see your intentions on your face, eyes, expression and body language. Sneaking up from behind is also a way of saying to them that you are not confident about yourself for some reason, and this just gets their minds rolling in the wrong direction. Women don't like wishy-washy men, but have a blind spot for the same fault in themselves.

It's best to approach head-on, face to face. If that is too much for you to handle, the second-best approach is from the side, which remains a definite improvement over slinking in on him from the rear. Let's say that you see someone walking down the street you decide you want to make a move on. Follow him along to the point to where he is waiting for a light, looking in a store window or looking at a newspaper machine. Anything that slows him down is a good thing, in that it gets his mind off walking. When he slows or comes to a stop, more of his attention is available by virtue of not being focused on walking and avoiding obstacles encountered while walking. Men tend to be a bit slower to change their mental gears than women. Ask him for directions or if he knows the way to a certain place. Time permitting, he might even take you there himself. Should he go out of his way to bring up various conversational topics of any nature whatsoever, that means he is definitely interested in you, so be sure to give him some sort of contact information, such as a phone number or e-mail address to allow him to contact you later on.

Should you see someone checking you out from top to bottom, without being totally consumed with nothing more than lust, smile, walk up to him (you can be pretty sure that he will not turn you down) and suggest that the two of you sit down for a caffeine injection in a local java emporium. Who knows, maybe he was thinking about the very same thing when you beat him to the punch.

"There are lots of good fish in the sea."
The Mikado
William Schwenck Gilbert

Chapter Ten
Where And How To Meet White Men, Part II

"The eyes are the windows of the soul."
Author Unknown

Making Eye Contact

"Her eye discourses; I will answer it."
William Shakespeare
Romeo And Juliet

You need to learn to make eye contact with men who happen to be strangers or near-strangers, or else they will most likely remain strangers forever. Men in general are very visually oriented, and White men are no exception. Eye contact advertises your approachability and emotional availability. White men are turned off to some degree by Black and White women alike who won't look them in the eye. Adult White men often say that they have a bad feeling about a woman who will not look them in the eye. Younger Black women might have trouble looking men in general in the eye. Blue or green eyes can add an unsettling measure of unfamiliarity into the eye contact equation and might take some getting used to. While this problem with making eye contact is common enough, from the male viewpoint it remains a barrier to communication. Should your stomach develop butterflies when making eye contact, an old interviewing trick might help. Looking at the bridge of the nose comes off as almost the same as eye contact. It allows you to make initial contact and gives you opportunities for extended contact and to work your way up the scale to more complete forms of eye contact.

Over the long run, however, you need to systematically desensitize yourself against reacting to eye contact with queasiness. Systematic desensitization means that whatever gives you butterflies in your stomach is the thing to which you deliberately, but gradually, expose yourself in slowly increasing dosages over time until you lose your original queasiness. You become less sensitive to what bothers you because being exposed to it in small doses makes you gradually realize that there is nothing to be afraid of. As you get more practice responding in the new manner, that new, non-queasy response slowly but surely becomes your automatic response. Over the course of time, your old queasiness response gradually vanishes, or becomes extinguished, and a new type of response takes its place.

Maybe you have a secret fascination with blue eyes, but looking directly at a man with blue eyes makes you freeze up, or worse. Start off small. Try looking at pictures of a movie star or rock star with blue eyes. Then start taking fast looks at men with blue eyes passing by on the street. A week or two later, try flashing a smile at someone with blue eyes walking by on the street. Further down the road, try to get a conversation going with a guy with blue eyes you see on the bus every day or on line at the fast food restaurant where you eat lunch. Moving up the scale of increasing eye contact exposure in little increments makes your original reaction fade over time as you build confidence in making eye contact.

Don't Be Overtly Sexual At First

"I am not a slut."
William Shakespeare
As You Like It

Don't try to hook a White male by being overtly sexual when you first meet. For that matter, don't make any verbal references to anything of a sexual nature. It smacks of two things you definitely do not want to exude in making a first impression: desperation or (even worse) the appearance of being "easy." The verbal and nonverbal information about yourself that you provide will both shape his initial perceptions of you will as well as his overall perception of the kind of person you are. Initially, you are a blank slate to him. When you first meet, he has very limited and partial information about you. Fill in some of the non-sexual blanks in his mind first. Don't bring hormones into the picture unless all you're looking for is sex. Should the two of you get along, you'll have plenty of opportunities to fill in the sexual blanks later on.

Your typical White guy has not had an overwhelming amount of experience dealing with blatant or overt sexual suggestions from White women. The sorts of White women with whom he generally associates typically have a more subdued style of coming on to men than do Blacks,

133

even when they're rarin' to go. What sort of behavior should you avoid? Don't engage in any sort of physical contact beyond shaking hands when the two of you part (after exchanging phone numbers, of course). Beware of White men who seem a little too eager to make physical contact. They are probably looking for only one thing. Don't make the opposite kind of mistake by swinging to the other end of the spectrum, acting arctic when you feel tropical. That gives him nothing to be interested in, and he will go away assuming you don't like him. Be happy, pleasant, energetic, feminine, open to possibilities, but not overtly sexual. Why would you want the first thing he knows about you to be something sexual?

"The Moving Finger writes; and having writ, Moves on: nor all your Piety nor Wit Shall lure it back to cancel half a line, Nor all your tears wash out a word of it."
Edward Fitzgerald
The Rubaiyat of Omar Khayyam

Most Whites Will Avoid Racial Issues

Race and color are usually not hot-button issues for middle-class Whites. Blacks must often think about some aspect of being Black every day, while circumstances rarely force Whites to think about being White. Thus, since racial issues rarely have rarely had any personal impact on them, even well-informed, well-intentioned liberal White men tend to be a bit slow on the uptake understanding what it means to be Black on an everyday basis. The Black experience is something they have read about or heard about from others, but not something they have experienced themselves. For example, when you talk with a White about slavery, the general connotation for them is something they read about in high-school history, not something that actually happened to their great-great-grandparents, the memory of which has been passed along within the family by oral tradition.

This has implications for interracial dating. Whites generally prefer to avoid talking about racial issues with Blacks, at least in the early stages of a relationship. If you don't bring up racial issues, he probably won't either. If you're tired of constantly talking and thinking about race, many White guys will oblige you, glad to avoid the issue for the time being. Whites are generally reluctant to bring up racial issues with Blacks because, somewhere along the line, they were probably on the receiving end of a high-temperature conversation with a squeaky wheel, and went away with the impression that some Blacks get steamed up fast about racial issues, so they don't bring up racial issues with Blacks unless they like to elicit verbal pyrotechnics. Whites who have had limited social contacts with Blacks will generalize from single events of this nature, just as some Blacks who have had a few unpleasant run-ins with certain types of Whites will be wary afterwards.

Even White men who have dated Black women usually avoid discussions of racial issues early in the game after learning from experience that it has the potential to raise the room temperature. Go easy on social issues at first, particularly so if you have a personal stake in them. Most White men are looking for women who can bring positive feelings and experiences their way, and will act reasonably if you explain your viewpoint in a calm and factual manner as the relationship progresses. Being angry about how Whites in general have treated Blacks in general will not get him interested in you. A drop of interpersonal honey will catch more flies than a barrel of social-issues vinegar.

Some younger White men from sheltered backgrounds go to the extreme of not even acknowledging that you are Black, despite the reality in front of them. These men are a particular type of color-blind liberal, in the sense of believing that race should be a completely neutral factor in their interest in women. Most were probably taught in school something along the lines of they should not consider race or skin color in their evaluations of others as people. Since they think race is always supposed to be a neutral factor in social relations, they have no experience in getting a handle on talking and thinking about racial issues.

Somewhere in the back of their minds is also the unacknowledged desire to sidestep what they dimly perceive as a hot-button issue. These men prefer to circle around the edges of unknown territory for a spell before entering the door. They can't just jump into thinking and talking about racial issues all at once, though they have no problem socializing with Blacks from similar social backgrounds as long as racial topics do not come up. Some sheltered Black women hold analogous viewpoints, and are similarly uncomfortable discussing racial topics with a White person early in a relationship. These individuals gradually learn to have honest discussions of racial issues as time progresses and they become more comfortable with discussions of racial topics.

Beware Of White Men Who Bring Up Racial Issues

"My mind is no more shocked at seeing a man a rogue, unjust, or selfish, than at seeing vultures eager for prey."
Moliere
The Misanthrope

Beware of White males who bring up racial issues within a few minutes of meeting you. They will overstate their interest in you, or Black women as a group, for the purposes of hustling you into bed as fast as possible. If that is all you are looking for, you won't have to look very far. But most Black women are not of that persuasion.

White men who do this have predictable topics of discussion. The most common is strangely-phrased interest in Black women. Younger men will say something like "I find Black women attractive" (why doesn't he say it's you that he finds attractive?) The younger men give the impression of being repressed nerds living in some sort of sexual fantasy land where Black women are their ideals of forbidden-fruit sexuality. The less contact they've had with real-life Black women the more likely they are to have such ideas.

Older men might say something like "I've got a lot of respect for Black women" as a prelude to a sexual advance. Of course, some Black women with a history of limited social and sexual contacts with White males might see White men in much the same nerdish manner. Another common type of phony will start mentioning his support for affirmative action, civil rights, and so on. Even avid supporters of such policies will not bring such topics into a purely social conversation unless they are trying to hustle you. In general, White guys who stick to nonracial issues early in the conversation game are better bets for real relationships.

"Real friendship is a slow grower."
Philip Stanhope, Earl of Chesterfield
Letters To His Son

136

Meeting White Guys In College

"All went there because their friends went there."
Henry Adams
The Education Of Henry Adams

You will probably never have an opportunity to meet as many single White males in your own age range, all with free time on their hands, as you will have in college. Even should you be in a historically-Black college where women outnumber men several to one, you can still meet White men by hanging around the libraries at nearby integrated colleges. There are several ways to take advantage of the large number of unattached White males running around colleges waiting for someone like you to scoop them up.

One of the easiest ways to meet White guys is through a part-time job on campus. Avoid jobs that isolate you in a backroom. Work at the book checkout desk in the library. Work at the information desk in the student union, a good way to meet new guys on campus the first few weeks of school. Work in the student bookstore. Such jobs give you an opportunity for casual contact with hundreds of people on a daily basis, and some of them might have their eye on you. These jobs give you an opportunity to initiate casual banter that can lead to extended conversations and arrangements for further contact off the job.

For example, should you work in the library or the bookstore, ask him about courses and professors in the field for which he's buying textbooks or checking out library books. If he's interested, and is convinced that you're really being friendly with him beyond what clerks usually do, he'll find an excuse to hang around and prolong the conversation. You must act a shade more friendly than the other clerks or he simply will not get it that you are available and interested. Suggest that the two of you talk after you finish work either in person, over the phone or via e-mail regarding you taking courses in the same department. This will keep the conversation going until the point where you tell him how boring your weekends have been to date and you'd really like to find someone to go out to the movies with on weekends. Be low-key, but stay pleasantly direct. If you're too subtle, most will have no idea you're really interested. If he turns you down, there's plenty more where he came from. You might even drop by his dormitory room on talk on some bogus pretext.

Become his friend, but don't become a female study buddy, one of those sexually-neutral girls, quite common in schools of engineering, who spend a lot of time working with boys on group research projects and homework assignments, but who never seem to get beyond superficialities with those guys. Study buddies don't date their personal study buddies, it's almost like incest. However, being a study buddy does give you access to his friends and various types of male buddies who drop by for parties and to shoot the bull. Work on the friends, but not the guys you actually study with.

When you get into a one-on-one conversation with a guy, drop a few low-key but direct hints that you're looking to someone to go out with. Do not do this if anybody is eavesdropping. Men hate audiences. If necessary, spell it out in a friendly sort of way for him. If you feel really daring, catch him when you know that he doesn't have any exams or other minor crises coming up and suggest that the two of you go to a movie together, each of you paying your own way. That takes some of the pressure off him, since not paying for you means he can still continue to check you out without making a commitment.

Some guys might want to go out with you as part of a group to relieve some of the perceived pressure of solo date with someone new. That's okay the first time out, but sooner or later you have to get into some sort of one-on-one date, or get relegated to a variation of study buddy status, meaning girls who date in large groups but who never get into one-on-one relationships. Remember, most college-age White males are not used to Black females expressing any interest in social contact with White males outside the classroom. Most think that "Blacks tend to stick with other Blacks," so they see no reason to pursue the matter unless and until they see evidence to the contrary. What little they do knows fills up all the room in their minds regarding the interracial dating issue. Disabuse him of that exclusionary notion by making your interest in him known. Don't focus all of your hopes on any one guy until after the two of you are actually going out on a regular basis. Remember, most guys are also quite aware that there are plenty of female fish in the local sea, and feel free to shop around.

Consider working in the dormitory cafeteria. Most of your student co-workers will be White. While many Black students refuse to work at cafeteria jobs that involve cleaning, serving and mopping, it's "just a job" for White students. This type of work allows you to meet both a number of White male co-workers as well as the numerous dorm residents for whom the cafeteria workers prepare food. Student cafeteria workers tend to eat their meals together either before the cafeteria opens or after it closes, giving you a chance to become better acquainted with your co-workers. Should your work involve serving food or checking off meal cards at the cafeteria entrance, you will have daily opportunities to meet large numbers of people on a regular basis. Try to avoid out-of-sight jobs like cooking food in the kitchen and working in the dishroom.

When in public contact situations, try to look cheerful and maybe become known for a sense of humor or cute little remarks. Direct carefully-tailored remarks and hints at boys of interest. Since you will probably be working in the same place every day, a White guy who wants to make a move on you will have ample opportunity to check you out, test the waters in successive increments and see how you react to him over the course of time. Be sure to encourage him and drop some hints. Be aware that White boys do not like to have anyone listening in when they try to invite you out, especially if they are not really sure as yet whether your apparent friendliness goes beyond the superficial.

Should you have a White girl as a roommate, try to be friendly with her (assuming it is possible for the two of you to get along with in the first place). Mention that you like White guys and are looking for one. She will probably see you as "safe," meaning she will not think of you as "competition" for the types that go for her. Women often socialize with physically dissimilar females who attract men with different physical preferences in women, because women compete with other women for men. You might get to meet some guys from her classes or her sorority functions who drop by her room or while the two of you eat in the cafeteria.

White fraternity boys are often a little too much into living up to group behavior expectations to conform to do something as radical as date interracially, but now and then you might come across an exception who thinks for himself. The other side of the coin is that you might get a

139

roomie that wants you to help her meet Black guys! Roommates with nasty dispositions can scare boys away. If things don't work out with any one roommate for some reason or other, find a pretext to make a fresh start with a new roommate in a new room in a new hall.

In classrooms and lecture halls, sit down next to, or at least near, a guy you're interested in. Ask him a question about the homework, when the next report is due, etc. Try to get a real conversational exchange going, not just questions with yes and no answers. As open-ended questions, such as how did he find time to do all the homework and go to the movies on weekends. Don't maintain suspicious hackles up. Ask for his e-mail address so that you can ask him a few questions about the homework assignments when you run up against a brick wall.

This will enable the two of you to get better acquainted, and maybe give you an opportunity to drop a few hints via e-mail, a low-pressure medium of communication, that you'd like to become a bit better acquainted. Mention that you have more time than you wanted to work on the homework last weekend because you have nothing else to do lately. Ask him about a book that you know he doesn't bring to class, and ask if you could drop by his room later in the afternoon to take a look at it.

Should he give you anything beyond short, simple answers, or proactively ask you questions on his own, keep it up, you may have a live one. Should you see an unattached White male keep looking at you without saying anything or making a move, he may be a live, however subdued, prospect. He may be interested but not sure whether he needs to say or do something different in making a move on a Black girl as compared to a White girl. Sit near him in class and ask a few classwork-related questions in relaxed, business-like manner. Keep it low-key so you don't scare him off. If he warms up, keep it up. Should he seem to avoid sitting near you or coming near you, it's probably a lost cause. Be sure to say hello to boys from your classes outside of class, even if you don't know their names. They may recognize you and that might suffice to get an initial conversation going about classwork or homework or coming exams. If he likes you to start with, any pretext is okay for getting a conversation started. If he doesn't like you to start with, nothing will work.

140

Try sitting in the student union cafeteria where the off-campus students eat lunch. Bring a newspaper with you. Sit down near where you see an interesting unattached guy sitting or where you know guys will drift by to sit down later. Offer one a copy of the sports section, especially if you see him looking at you with a gleam of interest in his eye.

Most college libraries have lounges where you can get drinks and munchies. These are often well-known local pick-up spots. Ask boys in the vending-machine area if they need change for the vending machines. If a guy sticks around, ask him what sort of paper or exam he's working on in the library. Should you recognize him from a class, ask him how the homework assignment or term paper is coming along. Any pretext of any kind is okay to get a conversation going. If one guy doesn't work out, there's always plenty more where he came from thirty seconds later.

Join a student club with a large membership related to your interests. Examples might include a political group during the campaign season, a blood drive, or working as a student government election monitor, all of which serve to bring you into contact with large numbers of single White males. It's okay to join the Black student groups as well, but you won't find too many White males involved in those activities. Whatever you do, don't ignore Whites when with Blacks, no matter what the local group consensus is on such behavior. Whites can sense the chill a mile away and will definitely remember you as someone who tunes out Whites when Blacks are around. Conversely, steer clear of White males who ignore you when they are with other Whites.

White guys in college are generally not used to women coming on really strong to them. Talk directly, but don't get brassy, laugh like a foghorn or show one of those smiles that make it look like your face is going to crack apart. Be low-key. Go easy on the perfume. Yes, he can tell you're a female of the species without it. White boys usually do not like girls who wear a lot of jewelry. Stick with small earrings, a watch, maybe a small necklace. Dress preppy or suburban middle-class. No really short skirts. Stick to clear or subdued nail polish. If you are not sure how to dress, observe how the White girls at your school dress, and go for the middle of the road as regards fashion.

There's a lot of peer pressure in college from other Blacks to limit your social contacts to other Blacks. This often means rooming with other Blacks and eating only with them in the dining hall. There are many subtle social pressures to get you to do what other Blacks expect of you. If you don't, they'll punish and stigmatize you by spreading the word to give you the cold shoulder and the silent treatment. Oddly enough, this sort of treatment is rarely extended to Black men with several White girlfriends, only to unattached Black women who are supposed to go through college and ignore the thousands of unattached White males who surround them in college while college Black men fail to invite them out. If the Black men can get away with a double standard, they will do so. People who perpetrate such social pressures are not your friends, and you don't owe them anything if they imply, or state overtly, that they will pull this on you if you don't conform.

The cold shoulder treatment is very rarely applied by Whites to White males who date Black women, although a quite a few Whites will stare at such boys. A few of his friends may ask some questions for a spell, but that's about it. Keep in mind that for most college-age Whites, seeing someone dating a Black woman is a social novelty. Except for a few cracker-barrel schools in the deep South, social ostracism for interracial dating is rare among White males, though you will find that some college fraternities go out of their way to discourage interracial dating. Men pretty much do not question other males' choices of girlfriends, seeing it as a private matter that White men do not discuss with other men. In addition, any college-age White male that gets involved with Black women is both likely to be more mature than average, and those with whom he socializes are likely to be of a similar cast of mind.

Why Would a Nice Black Girl Like You Place A Personal Ad?

Personal ads are a supplemental, low-risk way to attempt making initial contact with interested parties. They are not for everyone, and come with an assortment of pluses and minuses. It can help you get a feel for how White males respond to you. You can also get a feel for what sorts of White guys are looking for Black women. See it as a learning experience, not a make-or-break situation. You'll be okay if you don't expect too much from it.

142

Should your self-confidence be generally devastated, an ad is one small way to try to rebuild. Black women who are hesitant, cautious or have mixed feelings about interracial dating can use personal ads as a low-risk way to dip their little toes into what may look like a big White pool of pretty cold water. You can talk about what you're like, what you're looking for and see what comes in, and nobody will ever know your name unless you choose to tell them. Most personal ad services in newspapers and on the Internet provide for various forms of anonymous response mail boxes or masking your real name and e-mail address. For some women, getting any sort of responses from White men, even if not quite what they are looking for, makes them feel better about interracial dating and gives them the added confidence to move beyond personal ads, possibly without ever having any real-life contact with respondents to their ad.

Some Black women prefer to browse ads placed by others instead of placing one of their own. Unfortunately, some Black women become intimidated by what they see and sink further into isolation. If they fail to see any ads placed by Black women, they think something must be wrong here and don't place one of their own. Should they not see ads by White males specifically seeking Black women they think nobody's looking for Black women and become more depressed. The problem is that when everybody waits for somebody else to make the first move, everybody loses out.

Black women who see nothing wrong with going after what they want on the job do a complete about-face when it comes to their social lives. At some point, somebody has to make a move, so it might as well be you. Just by virtue of being a Black woman who places a personal ad, you create the possibility of changing your situation. Doing nothing, or being afraid to do anything, becomes a self-reinforcing vicious cycle, increasing your inhibitions. The problems remain unsolved until definite action is taken to correct the situation. No amount of thinking it over will ever lead to a solution unless and until it includes definite action. Let's face it, if you're afraid to read or place an anonymous personal ad, you really have problems. You have to start somewhere, and writing an ad can be your training wheels.

The Basics Of Writing An Interracial Personal Ad

Advertisements For Myself
title of book by Norman Mailer

The basics of writing the text of a personal ad are pretty much the same regardless of whether it's being placed in a local newspaper, a national magazine or on the Internet. The most basic principle is to provide factual information about yourself that will alert and tune in potentially compatible prospects. You can include other types of information beyond the factual, but factual information tends to work best.

First, include your age, height, weight or weight range, hair color and length, eye color and related information. Keep in mind that men are visually-oriented creatures and that a particular feature can be a turn-on for some White men, or a turnoff for others. Don't waste your time and theirs if they have a set-in-concrete fetish for height or some other feature. No matter what you say or think, you're not going to change their minds. Just state the facts. Including your skin tone is optional (light/medium/dark). You might also include your body type: slender, medium/average, thick or BBW (Big Beautiful Woman). Include your marital status: single/divorced/widowed. If you have any sort of distinguishing physical characteristic or handicap, mention it and save yourself time further down the road. Men have a variety of fetishes for certain physical characteristics, and these fetishes tend to become carved in stone by a certain age. Should your most noticeable physical characteristic be your bust, you might add the word "buxom" to your list of physical characteristics.

Second, say a few words about what you do for a living. Don't call yourself a "professional." Just state what you do for a living - teacher, programmer, secretary, nurse, student or whatever. You might also mention how far you went in school - "college graduate", "master's degree." Many White men have a decided preference for women with educational backgrounds similar to their own.

Third, include a dozen or so words about your leisure time interests, such as (but not limited to): movies (which kind? action, musicals, science-fiction, romance, etc.), exercises (aerobic dancing, skating, jogging, etc.)

reading (specify what you prefer: classics, mysteries, science fiction), television (what kind of shows?) restaurants (what kind of cuisine are you partial to?) Remember, long-term relationships require some common interests.

Fourth, be sure to include your geographical location. This is particularly important on the Internet, which has millions of users worldwide. You don't want any penpals in Australia, do you? Even within the confines of a major city such as Chicago, which has dozens of far-flung suburbs, location can be important to a young guy without a car who lives fifty miles away.

Fifth, say a few specific, truthful words about your personality as other people have told you they see it. This is crucial. Saying that you are "pleasant, feminine, giggly and intellectual" will bring in very different types of responses than saying that you are "strong, independent and assertive". Keep in mind that you should talk about personality characteristics that would be of interest to a romantic companion, not a prospective employer. Most men like women with a sense of humor as well.

Sixth, state what you look for in a White male as far as race, age, religion, occupational group ("white collar" is okay), leisure time interests, location/acceptable distance from you, personality characteristics, and the like. Keep in mind that the pickier you sound ("must be over six feet tall and have blue eyes") the fewer responses you will get. You have to decide where compatibility leaves off and being picky begins.

Last, but not least, is the headline for your ad. The purpose of a headline is to provide a capsule form of some crucial piece of information about yourself. Saying something like "I love cats" is not likely to bring in too many responses, though it might be included in the text of the ad as secondary personal information. The most common meaningful headline for an interracial personal ad is some variation on "SBF ISO SWM," the abbreviated way of saying Single Black Female In Search Of Single White Male. You can also write the headline as on "SBF seeks SWM."

Why provide so much information? The more factual information you provide about yourself, the better your chances of catching the eye of someone to whom those characteristics are important. If you don't say it, they don't know about it, and won't respond to the ad, and response is the name of the game. While providing a lot of information will screen out many unsuitable men, it also operates to screen in more of those few with whom you are likely to be compatible. Remember, you only need one good one, and you don't care about the huge number of incompatibles out there. Quality over quantity. Conversely, avoid putting in cutesy-poo information that really says nothing important.

"Omit needless words."
William Strunk
The Elements Of Style

Below is an example. Your own ad need not be as long as this one, but it does give you an idea of what sort of personal information is important in a personal ad.

SBF, 33, 5'6, 150 pounds, average build, medium brown skin tone, short hair, regular facial features. Have bachelor's degree, work as programmer in North Shore suburbs of Chicago. Casual dresser outside of work. Nonobservant Catholic. Enjoy classic rock, jazz, romantic movies, ice skating, Chinese cuisine, ballet, light jogging. Favorite movie: Casablanca. Favorite rock groups: Rolling Stones, U2. Casual dresser, non-smoker, light drinker, no drugs. Politically liberal/Democrat, giggly, relaxed, intellectual. Seeking: SWM/DWM, age 30-40, 5'7+, average or athletic build, non-smoker, light drinker. No children at home or bisexuals, please. Must have a bachelor's degree. Open on leisure time interests. Need not have dated interracially before. Should be open to possible LTR. Liberal social values, history of positive relationships with women, emotionally open, gentle, humorous. No control junkies.

It takes a while to write an ad like this. Write down as much as you can and sit on it for a few days, look at it again in broad daylight and revise and rewrite it as necessary. You'll be surprised at how what looked like a stroke of genius last night looks like gibberish the next day. Rewriting is always a good idea.

By contrast, look at a really bad personal ad -and why it's bad:

Strong, independent, professional Black woman seeks mature, financially secure, professional or independently wealthy White male. Must be over six feet tall.

What's wrong with this ad? It sounds like she is seeking an acquisition for a portfolio instead of a person. Among the more notable things she left unsaid are: no age, no height, no weight, no location, no occupation, no education, nothing about her personal appearance, nothing about her personality, nothing about her leisure time interests. The only thing you know about her personally is that she has an elevated self-opinion and provides nothing to back it up with. Last, but not least, what she's looking for sounds like a picture of a man lifted directly from the back cover of a gothic romance: tall, mature, lots of money. Note that a man's personality, leisure time interests and history of relationships with women all seem to be irrelevant to her. Take a guess how many years it's been since a woman who placed an ad like that has gone out on a date?

Common abbreviations in personal ads: ISO = In Search Of S = Single D = Divorced WW = Widowed W = White B = Black M = Male F = Female P = Professional LTR = Long Term Relationship N/S = Non-Smoker N/D = Non-Drinker BBW = Big, Beautiful Women C = Christian

Note 1: Never use the word "generous" in your ad or respond to an ad that mentions that word. "Generous" is a common euphemism in ads for the exchange of money for sexual services!

Note 2: The jury is out on whether or not you should specify "no drug users." While you probably don't want to get involved with one, just the fact that you mention that you don't want to meet such men might raise some questions about what kind of people you've associated with in the past such that you feel a need to mention the subject. Why bring it up?

Note 3: Specify what "financially secure" means to you, should you choose to include it as a desired characteristic for a man. Does it mean having a job? Owning a house? Being independently wealthy? Specify what it means to you, or leave it out.

Chapter Eleven
Mistakes To Avoid

"There are follies as catching as contagious disorders."
La Rochefoucauld
Maxims

Exceedingly High Standards

You can set your standards for suitable men as high as the moon. But unless your booster rocket has a million pounds of personal-characteristics thrust, you're more likely to remain sputtering on the launch pad, held earthbound by the gravitational pull of social reality, rather than orbit into a lunar rendezvous with a celestial male body. A deliriously exaggerated self-opinion uncorroborated by similar opinions from single men fuels only ships filled with private fantasies. Should you persist in setting exceedingly elevated standards, you can plan on spending your leisure time with other unattached, high-standards women rather than with real-life men.

Women with high standards forget that high standards are a two-way street. High-status men have high standards of their own, and may not set their standards low enough to include poor, little medium-status you. There is one thing of which you can be sure. Affluent men are quite expert at sniffing out, and avoiding, women on the lookout for men like them for no reason beyond their incomes and assets. Affluent mice can smell hungry cats a mile away. Mr. Rich and Famous White Guy may come your way, but don't plan your life around him sticking with you. Check out the White guys in your own league first.

"Certain men affect us as rich possibilities."
Ralph Waldo Emerson
"The Uses Of Great Men"

The supply of high-status rich men, Black and White, is limited. There is an inverse correlation between supply and demand: the greater the demand, the less supply offered, and most such men do not remain unattached for long, except by choice. Rich men are hard to find, and your chances of getting involved with such men is as statistically meaningless as the average man's chance of hooking up with a centerfold model. If you persist in thinking this will happen, dwell for a spell on what you can offer someone like that, unless you are already on their social level.

One little-discussed inverse correlation is that, the fewer men with whom a Black woman has been involved with in the last few years, the higher she sets her standards. Should she never have been involved with anyone in her life, she claims that only royalty could possibly hope to meet her stratospheric standards. Royalty, of course, couldn't care less about what reclusive workaholic women a mile below them on the social ladder think or expect, and have better things to do with their time anyhow. Such women are evading taking responsibility for their social lives. Their evasions often take the form of working so many hours that no sane male would waste his time trying to fit into her crowded schedule. Men "file and forget" such women. Such female hermits are disengaged bystanders in the singles marketplace. The more elevated their standards, the longer they will remain bystanders. If men do not ask you out on a regular basis, sky-high standards are a one-way ticket to spending your life in a private fantasy world or, at best, with other women. Black women who emerge and descend from their hermit mountain caves will find numerous pickings to be had in the well-populated orchards spread out below their solitary hideaways.

"I lived with visions for my company instead of men"
Elizabeth Barrett Browning
Sonnets From The Portugese

Do You Live In A Fantasy Land?

Your ideal of a compatible White male might be someone over six feet tall, rugged looking, went to an Ivy League college, a professional man or independently wealthy, has loads of leisure time he wants to spend with you, knows how to dress, great dancer, poised, articulate, passionate, romantic, and has hair that is always just right. If this sounds vaguely familiar, it is because your subconscious mind has pieced together this composite picture of a perfect man from bits and pieces of romance novels, soap operas, old time movies, wishful thinking and outright fantasy. When you know little about a subject, what little you do know expands to fill all of the mental space available. Even Miss America would have trouble finding such a guy, and very few of the Black women you see reflected in your bathroom mirror each morning are in any danger of winning that award anytime soon. Were such a guy to exist, you would not be able to get within a hundred feet of him due to the crowds of admirers and groupies swarming about him. He's guaranteed to already have more lady friends of every race than he can handle. You'll be well along in years if you're holding your breath waiting for Mr. Romance Novel Cover Model to waltz into your life and dance the night away with you into your blissful future together. While everyone fantasizes from time to time, fantasies can become a crutch to hobble along on when you should be walking around and seeking real-life men with just as many warts as you.

"Women in solitude, and with troubled hearts, are pestered with unaccountable delusions."
Nathaniel Hawthorne
The Scarlet Letter

Checklists

You'll miss out on a lot of interesting White men if you've spent too many Saturday nights at home with your girlfriends developing detailed checklists of "must-have" characteristics for men with whom you would deign to consider associating: age, height, occupation, income, and other readily measurable characteristics. Sounds a lot like a personnel department requisition form, doesn't it? Outside of the workplace, however, life isn't like that. The singles marketplace does not play by workplace rules. Suitable men can not be ordered up from a catalog, however much that would uncomplicate life for the socially unlettered.

"In the catalogue ye go for men."
William Shakespeare
Macbeth

Homemade wish lists usually say little about the man's personality beyond vague generalities, indicative of the list-writer's general lack of experience with men. When such lists do include details of personality, the descriptions sound as if they've been lifted verbatim from a romance novel. The more detailed the checklist, the more out of touch with reality is the person drawing it up. The less social contact a woman has had with men, the more time she has had to refine such checklists with the aid of other women in similar social situations. Blind women lead other blind women, and probably to a place where single men are nowhere to be found. No amount of drawing up lists, or talking over such lists with your girlfriends will make compatible men materialize. No matter how much you want your wish list to be a magical lamp you can rub to have your wishes granted, that does not happen in the real world. Wishes only come true for those who go out and work at making them come true, not those who stay at home thinking about how nice it would be if wishes did come true.

Would You Rather Dwell On Not Being In A Relationship Or Work At Getting Into One?

"No blessed leisure for love or hope,
But only time for grief."
Thomas Hood
"The Song Of The Shirt"

The longer you are not in a relationship, the more acclimated you get to being in that state and the more your entire lifestyle contorts itself around your not being in a relationship with a male of the species. For example, you might plan on meeting with your girlfriends every Saturday night in one of your living rooms to drink coffee and discuss the low quality of the male population, rather than going out where you have some chance of meeting a guy. Keep doing things like this, and eventually even the thought of looking for a relationship will stop intruding on you. Everything in your life is set up to keep thoughts of men from intruding. The same old stale thoughts continue to circle endlessly in your mind until you put new thoughts in to take their place. Dwelling on not being in a relationship becomes a sickly, space-filler substitute for actually being in one. You develop an overall total lifestyle into which men can not intrude.

"Find expression for a sorrow, and it will become dear to you."
Oscar Wilde
The Critic As Artist

The time you spend living in such an unwholesome lifestyle is better spent looking at, and working at, ways to get into a relationship with a White male. Even if a new relationship does not dramatically spring into being, just the act of moving in that direction will make you feel better and operate to push you into circulation in realms where the possibility of meeting someone exists. As your outlook on life improves, you will appear more desirable. White guys steer clear of women with hangdog attitudes about life, with the possible exception of those who are similarly bogged down. As you start tuning into White men, you will find that some start to tune into you in as well. This will not happen overnight. But you can get the ball rolling in a small way at any time of day or night by starting to think differently.

For example, you might pick up a newspaper and read the personal ads, noticing how many White men are looking for Black women. In any big-city newspaper, you'll probably find more than a few such ads. That starts putting some new information into your mind, and it slowly circulates through your neuronal network. Do something different and see what happens. Maybe go to a church service on a Saturday night in an integrated neighborhood. Go out to a music store and browse the clientele as well as the merchandise. These are small actions in and of themselves, but anybody can start doing them at almost any time. Doing such things gets you into the habit of taking actions that have the potential to increase the number of White males with whom you will come into contact. Work at getting into a relationship instead of staying home thinking about the futility of trying to get into a relationship and finding consolation in your sorrowful state of existence.

"Unmuzzle your wisdom."
William Shakespeare
As You Like It

Playing Hard To Get

Playing hard to get is not likely to get you anywhere worthwhile with most White guys worth being around. Keep in mind that if a White male approaches you, he is sticking his neck out for you. Make him feel comfortable or he will move on. Playing it cool will probably guarantee that he will go away. If he is someone you see in the neighborhood or at work on a regular basis, he will probably avoid you afterwards, because he assumes that you were expressing your true feelings, and so he moved on to find other fish to fry. A bad first impression is hard to erase later on. By the way, this also happens to White women. Normal White men usually avoid women who play hard to get.

Getting into an interracial relationship takes a bit more effort than an same-race relationship, to say nothing of maturity. You can spend quite a while getting to the point where you are all psyched up about getting into an interracial relationship, have figured out where and how to meet White guys, have gotten to the point of talking with a stranger.....and then come to a dead stop just before you get to the finish line, by playing hard to get for some inscrutable reason.

This is a mistake. If the guy is wrong for you or plays head games, just stop communicating with him. If he's right for you or at least okay, why would you want to let him know by your attitude that you're not interested? True, to some extent you are putting yourself on the line because you decided to play hard to get - but since you have a personal value independent of others' perceptions, it will not be the end of your world of it does not work out perfectly. If you're playing the same old sandbox games with new partners, you might as well go back to your old sandbox.

Don't Be A Resume Nerdette

"Nothing but work, work, work."
Henry David Thoreau
Life Without Principle

Are you a resume nerdette? That's the type of Black woman who like to spout off about how she's strong, independent, hard-working, can run her own business, can take care of herself, and so on. The rest of her conversations center on details of what she does at work. Remember that this is a personal conversation, not an office memo or job interview. This kind of talk might make some people see you as a fast-track professional. It does not make you look interesting to White men considering you as a romantic and sexual possibility, with the possible exception of a small minority of hopped-up, fire-breathing White male workaholics who are so

153

similarly caught up with their career plan that nobody takes them seriously for anything other than grinding out the work.

While this personality style can have some effect on Black men who encounter such pretentious Black women all the time, it is a surefire turnoff for most White males, who can get plenty of it from similarly socially inept White women. White men are looking for girlfriends, not briefing sessions.

"Resume talk" makes you look so wrapped up in your work that you sound like you don't have time to relax, or maybe you never really learned to relax with a male of the species. Either way, the impression you make is negative, and nearly every White man you encounter will take you off his list of possibilities. Adults need to take on multiple roles to get through life, and this particular role is incompletely adult in the extreme.

It's okay to talk about your work with someone interested in you after you get to know something about each other. But work shouldn't be the first, last and only thing you talk about. Drop a few not-too-subtle hints about yourself and what sort of things might turn you on. Maybe a romantic old-time movie, maybe some romantic oldies music by a group you like. If he's interested and available, he'll pick up on your hints after a few minutes. Put the shoe on the other foot. How long would you want to hear him talk about his resume and how intelligent, strong and intimidating he is? That doesn't give you much to work with, and you don't give him much to work with when you talk like that.

If your love life is bad or nonexistent, you may be tempted to throw yourself into your work until your job becomes your life. Should your career be all you want out of life, that is the way to go. After a few years, you will be in no danger of getting involved with anybody, Black or White. Men will sense that you don't "waste" time on silly things like relationships and will not even come close. It's up to you to give them something to be interested in.

"It is very vulgar to talk about one's business. Only people like stock brokers do that, and then merely at dinner parties."
Oscar Wilde
The Importance Of Being Earnest

Suspicions

Some Black women are suspicious of any White man who is interested in Black women. Such women think all they're out for is sex. Some are, some are not. Needless to say, such women will probably meet few, if any, normal White men, since such men have more enjoyable things to do with their time than waste time on suspicious women. Black women who bristle with suspicion soon find that the few White men they do meet are exactly what they expect.

The normal ones steer clear of them, because normal men do not enjoy being with suspicious, emotionally unavailable women. If you start out suspicious of White men, you will get what you expect. If you start out expecting something positive, you are more likely to eventually find someone positive than Black women who start out completely negative.

"Our mistrust justifies the deceit of others."
La Rochefoucauld
Maxims

Suspicious Black women get that way because they've let the propaganda espoused by certain types of Black men become lodged their minds without critical filtering. Sometimes, however, suspicions may be justified. If there is a major social class gap between the two people, suspicions are well-founded, since totally different people have little prospect for long-term compatibility. If all he talks about is sex and getting you into a motel room, you have good cause to be suspicious. Make up your mind about such men on a case-by-case basis.

"Extreme distrust is not less harmful than its opposite; the greater part of men are useless to [she] who will not risk being deceived. "
Vauvenargues
Reflections And Maxims

Leave Your Bad Experiences Behind You

Don't Look Back
title of Bob Dylan documentary film directed by D.A. Pennebaker

Many Black women walk around filled with resentments about how men have treated them. Years of mistakes have colored their outlook on men. Being hurt is a bad thing. Should all of your experiences with men have been bad, your first reaction to any man will probably be to react with suspicion, coolness and maybe even hostility. While this may seem valid to you, the end result of such attitudes will be that White men with whom you might have had positive experiences will automatically classify you as "bad news", and look elsewhere for female companionship. Nobody is obligated to become your punching bag, even if you think that life "owes" you after all you've been through. Bad experiences are things to dwell on for a spell and put behind you, and not for wallowing in as a substitute for getting your life going. In addition to scaring off normal men, an unexpected side effect of a bad attitude is that it probably guarantees you meeting more bad-news men. Certain types of men seek out women who wear their bad experiences on their faces. They have a lot of experience with such women, and know which strings to play to get them to sing their tune. Bringing bad experiences with you means you will pick up the worst kind of unwanted baggage in your travels.

"What a great heap of grief lay hid in me."
Elizabeth Barrett Browning
Sonnets From The Portugese

Don't Talk About Other Men

White men see conversations differently than Black women in several respects that may be news to you. Should you mainly converse with other women, you have probably developed little unconscious conversational habits from talking primarily with women that make men want to walk away from you. Both the style and content of certain types of female-on-female conversations can be turn-offs for men. Of particular note is the way you talk with a female audience about men. Transplanting this form of conversation to a conversation with a male is a recipe for a disaster. Talking with a new-found White male acquaintance about men as if you were conversing with one of your girlfriends is a social disaster. The role and conversational style you take on with women is inappropriate for White male audiences. There are certain things you should never talk

156

about, or bring up, when first meeting someone, unless you want to give him an excuse to put one, or both, feet out the door.

Never bring up a past relationship - your ex-fiancée, your ex-husband, ex-boyfriend - with a new male acquaintance. Never. You and your girlfriends probably spend endless hours psychoanalyzing men and past relationships to death, so it is a topic you feel comfortable talking about. This makes White men uncomfortable. Men do not want to hear you talk about other men, period. If you talk about, or even mention, one or more old relationships in the course of first conversation with a new guy, he automatically assumes that you are going out of your way to do so because you have no interest in him. If you think otherwise, that is just too bad for you.

Again, talking about other men, with the possible exceptions of your father and brothers, is a major, and possibly fatal, strike against you. Continuing to mention other men in the course of an initial conversation with someone new probably spells the end of the conversation. Even such have been the case for you, there is no advantage in telling a White male that Black men, or men in general, are bad news. Why bring it up at all? He may think you don't like men in general or that you are trying to prove something to yourself. While women talk like this with other women all the time, telling a White male this sort of stuff makes him assume that seeing and talking with him makes you think of those other unpleasant characters for some reason. The only White men that want to hear such things is the type that plays along with you because he wants to get something out of you by making a show of commiserating with you. Send out bad vibrations and you'll get echoes.

Get Rid Of Your Girlfriends

Leave your girlfriends at home if you want to meet someone. White men generally do not approach groups of unfamiliar women. Women who watch movies where this happens think this happens in real life, but such is rarely the case.

That goes double for women of another race, which adds an additional layer of caution to their minds. Bringing your girlfriends with you everywhere you go is a surefire way to lose out on opportunities to meet men. If he's thinking of approaching you in a bookstore or laundromat, and you've got one or more of your girlfriends chattering away with you, he'll just forget it and move on. Why?

First of all, if he's interested only in you, your girlfriends may become enviously huffy about being ignored. That is a problem from the man's viewpoint. The atmosphere gets strained when your girlfriends catch on that he has eyes only for one member of the group. Because most men do not approach women very often, they do not have a lot of practice at clearing the atmosphere, so they just forget it and don't bother trying. How to deal with people who are talking to you at the same he is trying to break into the conversation is a real problem.

"She can only look with envious eyes on the accepted lovers of others."
Moliere
The Misanthrope

Second, if you tell him in so many words to get lost, he does not want an audience while being rejected (would you want an audience?), all giggling and whispering like teenagers. Being rejected or ignored is quite a common experience for men who try to pick up women, and they don't like the feeling.

Third, since he knows zero about you before approaching you, even should he have gone out with Black women before, the racial difference makes him a little more cautious about who he decides to approach. Bringing along your portable support group of girlfriends makes him classify you as a higher-risk possibility. Men can sense right off the bat if your sagging confidence is dependent on having a group to hold your hand. Interracial dating is no place for people who need minute-by-minute group therapy.

Fourth, women take on a different role when surrounded by other women than when one-on-one with a single male of the species. They act out the role other women expect of them. The role you take on to meet the expectations of other women has little or no appeal for men. Remember, living up to group expectations levels your individuality and expectations for yourself downwards, not upwards. The way you have to behave to get group approval from other women is of no interest whatsoever to men.

When you are with your girlfriends, you are a part of a group, and play a role for that group. It is rarely a completely adult role. Your dealings with men are different, precisely because a one-on-one relationship excludes the group. You don't need your girlfriends' seal of approval to be interested in anybody. If you are with your girlfriends and see someone who you get a certain feeling about, break away from your girlfriends and try to make contact. Sometimes you have to walk away from the crowd or one of life's big opportunities may pass you by that day. If you don't pursue it, you will regret it later. If you are so unsure of yourself that you need your girlfriends' approval to like someone, you definitely need to exercise your backbone muscles and move away from the herd.

White men will make more moves on you if you leave your girlfriends at home. Bringing your girlfriends with you is like advertising that you either don't want White males to come near you or don't have the social skills to deal with them or with men in general. Some things you just have to do all by yourself. Last but not least, have you ever approached one man in a group with a serious proposal to get better acquainted? Think it over.

Don't Let Your Girlfriends Screen Your Boyfriends

"Friendship is constant in all other things Save in the office of and affairs of love."
William Shakespeare
Much Ado About Nothing

Don't bring your White boyfriend over to meet your Black girlfriends early in the relationship. One of your girlfriends might make a play for him. The second reason to not have him over to meet your girlfriends is that he might start thinking that you need social approval from a group of women in order to become involved with him. Men have a hard time understanding why any woman would need approval for a relationship from other women. No matter how you explain it, doing this makes him see you as a wishy-washy type who needs to get permission from the local dating permissions committee to go out with him. Some Black women, especially those who spend an excessive amount of their time at work, really think that it's okay to seek "permission" from a group of girlfriends (none of whom are dating anyone) to put their seal of approval on the

159

relationship. Such behavior is grossly immature and an indication that a woman can not tune out the expectations of her female audience even when with a male audience.

It is okay to bring him to meet one or two of your girlfriends and chat. But group meetings often have a way of turning into grilling sessions, the kind that men can smell a mile away. This reflects poorly on you in two ways. First, he thinks that you're exceedingly immature and unable to come to your own conclusions about him without reassurances from others. Interracial relationships are no place for the immature. Second, he wonder what you and your girlfriends say about when he's not around. Rightly or wrongly, he'll assume absolutely nothing is private as regards you and your girlfriends. If he thinks that you need to get personal decisions ratified by a committee, he'll also think that you tell your best friends the most intimate of private details. Men hate that, and hate talking with your girlfriends with the suspicion lurking in the back of their mind that there isn't anything about him that you don't tell your girlfriends.

By comparison, should he really like you, he will not tell other men much of anything about you except that the two of you are involved and spend a lot of time together. Men are like that. The more they like you, the less they tell other men about you. Men know that other men are morbidly and vicariously curious about the sexual aspects of relationships. That goes double for interracial relationships. Other men never let up on barraging him with sexually-oriented questions, so he will block off all access by never giving other men an opening. Who he dates, and what he does when he is with her, is his business alone. If the two of you are intimately involved, you'll probably meet some of his buddies along the way, but it would never occur to him to solicit their opinions about you, let alone discuss really private matters, unless he is socially warped. Should you have the misfortune to become involved with a White guy who does discuss intimate matters with other men, dump him, because he obviously does not take you seriously, and is more interested in catering to his buddies' expectations than to any of yours.

What If I Don't Know What I'm Looking For?

It's okay to not be sure exactly what you're looking for. Don't become paralyzed with indecision. You probably won't know what you really want until after you get it, and you won't get to that point until you do a lot of bouncing around in the process of getting there. It takes time to piece together through reasoning and experience even a general description of your needs and tastes, and even longer to figure out how to satisfy them.

You will probably first develop an interest in such White guys as you cross paths with by chance. You initially need to acquire information about White men which you can use as a basis for more focused searching. You have to experiment to get the raw data you need to reach some conclusions, and it is unrealistic to expect all such information-gathering experiments to pan out. Don't be a Nervous Nellie, so afraid of making mistakes that you never do anything to start with. You've got to start somewhere, so get on with it and start shopping around.

If you've never gone out with a White guy before, that's okay. Few Black women are born with interracial dating experience already under their belts. Everybody has to get their feet wet for the first time. If you swim like a swan the first time you're thrown in the water, that's okay. If you sink, try again tomorrow. You won't sink from sight forever the first time you take a dunk in the interracial dating pool. If you go out with one guy and it works out, that's great. If it's not a good match, or even a positive experience, you can still pick up a few pointers for future reference. At the very least, you will retain some general impressions about how White guys talk and act in a one-on-one situation. Knowing a few things gives you a basis for moving on to more informed and focused attempts at socializing. You must start your learning curve somewhere, so go ahead and do it. It will not develop of its own accord when you lounge about on your living room couch.

Although many would consider the point debatable, should you have had little, or no, social contact with White men due to having grown up in a single-race neighborhood, it may be a good idea to go out with the first friendly, non-deranged, nonviolent White male who comes your way. First of all, if you know nothing about White men beyond what you see on television, you have to start getting a feel for how they differ from Black men. There are different types of White guys just as there are different types of Black guys. The perfect White guy will not come your way by accident. They can sense immediately if you're not comfortable with them, not used to being around them, don't really trust them or if all they get from you is strange looks whenever they say something to you. The more you socialize and go out with White men, the better that new prospects can sense that you are both approachable and comfortable with them. Your prospects will upgrade as you upgrade yourself in terms of cumulative experience. Since you are unlikely to start off with a really good match, just accept that the first guy or two you meet is not going to be a match made in heaven. Enjoy it for what it's worth, but don't go in expecting the world.

"Something or other is to be got out of everybody."
Philip Stanhope, Earl of Chesterfield
Letters To His Son

Second, having low-magnitude positive experiences, such as going to the movies with a guy who is not really a great match for you, will nevertheless make you feel considerably better than staying home with your girlfriends or being home alone waiting for the ultimate relationship to drop down on you from the sky. You will at least be moving in the right direction. Remember, White guys don't want to stay home either. At the very least, you will develop a few positive associations that will make you feel better about yourself and prepare you to move a step or two up the ladder to ever better relationships. You might even meet a potentially compatible friend or two of his while out on the town with him. You have to start your learning curve somewhere, and you will probably not do so with the man of your dreams. You can always end a relationship if it goes nowhere, but that's hard to do if you're not in one to start with.

"Snatched in haste,
Is laid down at the first ill-sounding note."
Elizabeth Barrett Browning
Sonnets From The Portugese

Don't Become A Demagogue's Spear Carrier On The Slavery Issue

"The present generation of Southerners are not responsible for the past, and they should not be blindly hated or blamed for it."
W.E.B. DuBois
The Souls Of Black Folks

If you keep up with world events, you may have heard about parts of the world where ethnic conflicts regarding issues hundreds, or even thousands, of years old have kept those countries embroiled in tensions or even war. Who benefits from these conflicts? The only identifiable beneficiaries are always the top honchos, who have a vested interest in keeping old hatreds alive as a way of keeping people of their particular ethnic persuasion under their personal control. The bosses always seem to be out of harm's way and sitting in the lap of luxury. All the spear carriers get is death and taxes. Interestingly, you often find a lot of socialization and marriage restrictions imposed on group members from above in these types of local dictatorships. Sound like anyone you know?

What happened to Blacks under slavery is a valid issue for anger - but don't let yourself be contaminated with the unexamined secondhand opinions of others. Get the facts and do your own thinking on the issue. Demagogues have axes of their own to grind on this issue, and are looking for eager volunteer spear carriers to spread the word, and have no qualms about asking you for money. Yes, a lot of really bad things happened to Black women before 1865. The men who did those things are long dead. Their sons are long dead. Their grandsons are long dead. Yes, they were guilty. Unless you believe that their guilt was transmitted genetically to their descendants, it's time to move on. Nobody gets to pick their ancestors. Racism continues to exist today, but is on a gradual if, uneven, decline. Remember, individuals, not groups, are the only parties concerned in interracial relationships, and there are no benefits or pluses from catering to group expectations and opinions. You wouldn't make sweeping generalizations about Blacks as a group, so why do so about Whites? Make up your own mind, but get the facts first. People of any persuasion are a mixed bag. There are racist Whites and racist Blacks in every era. Seek out the good apples, throw back the bad ones, and nibble only on those that suit your personal tastes.

"There's small choice in rotten apples."
William Shakespeare
The Taming Of The Shrew

Chapter Twelve
The Scarlet Letter Of Interracial Dating, Part I

"The man, and still more the woman, who can be accused of either of doing "what nobody does," or of not doing "what everybody does," is the subject of as much depreciatory remark as if he or she had committed some grave moral delinquency."
John Stuart Mill
On Liberty

The Sexual Scarlet Letter

"Our judgments concerning the worth of things, big or little, depend on the feelings the things arouse in us."
William James
Talk To Teachers On Psychology

The Scarlet Letter is a classic novel about a single mother in a town of New England witch hunters. They forced her to wear the symbolic scarlet letter ("A" for Adultery) on her dress for engaging in the impermissible sexual activities by which she became a single mother. Her crime was having had a sexual relationship and a child with a man whose name she chose not to reveal. Her hypocritical lover became so consumed with guilt about his unwillingness to reveal himself as her lover, as well as his unwillingness to be seen with her, that he worried himself into an early grave. Wearing the scarlet letter made neighbors and strangers alike recognize her on sight as a pariah guilty of violating the witch hunters' community norms for sexual behavior. They were so obsessed with the supposed importance of their opinions about her sexual behavior that they wanted everyone who saw her to know their opinions as soon as they saw her, making her into a sort of human- billboard projection of their warped opinions on sexuality.

The world is full of bullies who want you to think that you need to get their permission to do anything of a sexual or personal nature. Witch hunting was simply a superficially plausible pretext of convenience for sexual neurotics to accuse others of a variety of imaginary sexual sins as a means of diverting attention from their personal mental and sexual problems. An obsession with punishing the bedroom behavior of other people is definitely an indication of underlying individual and community insecurity. If the sight of someone who chooses to act differently than others, while not infringing on others' rights, is a cause for outrage, the problem lies in those outraged, not the object of their wrath. If a million people do a stupid thing, it remains a stupid thing. The scarlet letter is thus an externally visible symbol of community pressure for conformity in sexual and social matters that are really private concerns. The pressures for conformity exist solely to assuage the psychological problems of an envious or otherwise disturbed community. Misery loves company and will pressure those not yet miserable to join the envious herd.

Why do people act like this? Why do some people persistently stare at interracial couples? Why do some rare people become physically enraged about total strangers dating interracially? Why does interracial dating elicit such visceral reactions from some people? Most important of all, why do others see interracial dating as a matter that concerns them in the first place? Consenting adults who happen to be of different races are free to get together with anybody they wish. Interracial dating and interracial marriage are well-known as perfectly legal behavior in most civilized countries, yet the visibly shocked, and sometimes irrationally angry, reactions that interracial daters sometimes experience make them feel that some others regard them as guilty of some manner of unspecified crime. Parents of both races, as well as parts of the community at large, engage in various sorts of behavior that let interracial couples know of their disapproval.

You don't have to burrow very far into the caverns of the subconscious to find subterranean psychological parallels between interracial dating and the tale of the scarlet letter. Both wearing the scarlet letter and dating interracially publicly advertise that your choices of social and sexual companions differ from the choices of many people you pass by on the street. They see you as a nonconformist-by-choice. Some stare, and some go beyond staring, in reaction to seeing you because you behave differently than others, and for no other reason. The perception of nonconformity arouses certain peculiar forms of behavior in different types of perceivers.

"Jealousy; it is the green-eyed monster, which doth mock the meat it feeds on."
William Shakespeare
Othello

Neurotics become irrationally disturbed at the sight of others enjoying what they are not, for the same reason that an anorexic becomes irrationally agitated at seeing others eat full meals. The more mentally disturbed the individual, in the sense of secretly thinking of themselves as socially inferior or sexually frustrated, the greater the degree to which interracial dating confronts them with visual reminders of their own sexual shortcomings. They are frustrated because their mental problems have led them to set up their lives so that they cannot enjoy themselves. Interracial relationships force them to think about the novelty and excitement absent from their own lives. The sight of physically different people being together accentuates the monochromatic dissatisfaction of their own lives. Frustrated neurotics whose own sex lives are in shambles hate to see others enjoying themselves. Not having what you have, they'll either try to keep you from having it, or try to manipulate you into feeling bad about enjoying yourself. The sight of tantalizing sweets beyond their reach enrages neurotics. Interracial dating thus engenders visceral, emotional reactions in others because it is linked to frustration of their sex drives. It comes down to envy and jealousy. Wherever you have this, you have irrational behavior along the lines of ranting about the scarlet letter. Envious people will react to you as if you were wearing the scarlet letter of sexual immorality, meaning nothing more than their own thinly-disguised neuroses.

"Envy is more irreconcilable than hatred."
La Rochefoucauld
Maxims

When casual bystanders see interracial daters, they immediately note them to be of physically different races, wonder what brought them together, think about what they see in each other, and so on. The duller their own lives, the more vacant mental space they have for dwelling on such things. Since the majority of the population have not themselves been in interracial relationships, all their minds have to work with is what they already have on hand, meaning rumors about interracial relationships being vaguely illicit hot stuff, their limited personal experiences and idle fantasies. They assume Black female-White male relationships are illicit because they almost never see them. They go on to assume that the reason interracial couples are not seen very often is because they are illegal, prohibited or forbidden in some manner. They fill in the blanks with whatever low-quality mortar their own subconscious minds happen to have floating around at the moment. The lower the quality of the mind, the lower the quality of the mortar used. Low-quality mental mortar puffs up to fill all of the mental space available for its expansion.

The appearance of external physical differences automatically leads some to project the supposition that physical differences brought interracial companions together, and that the excitement of sexual novelty is the main factor in their mutual attraction. The end result is that many casual bystanders fill in all the blanks with the fantasy mortar of steamy, red-hot interracial sex. In their minds, interracial dating automatically equals red-hot interracial sex. Most people who think like this repress expressing these thoughts, but you can tell from the rapidity of their facial reactions that something that relates the sight of interracial daters to sex is what's on their minds. That is why some people seem a bit embarrassed and look away a bit too fast. For such people, seeing others dating interracially is one step away from peeping into their bedroom window.

"When an uninstructed multitude attempts to see with its eyes, it is exceedingly apt to be deceived."
Nathaniel Hawthorne
The Scarlet Letter

While most people just take a fast look at an interracial couple and go back to whatever they were thinking about before, such sexually projective thoughts nevertheless simmer one or two steps below the surface of consciousness. The sight of interracial daters makes people project whatever is in their minds. It shines daylight on whatever witches' brew of emotions lies bubbling beneath the mind's surface. The more psychologically disturbed the individual, the more vehement and angry their reaction. Seeing others dating interracially, meaning others whom they suppose to be on their way to enjoying interracial sex, brings the sexually frustrated to a psychological boil because they themselves are not on their way to any such enjoyable thing. Those who snigger or laugh are

167

really revealing their own attitudes about sex and relationships in general, because they have nothing to draw on beyond what little resides in their minds. Both anger and sniggering are slightly modified forms of expression of envy and jealousy.

Psychological steam pressure builds up within when brought to a boil by the lack of social status or a sense of inferiority. Jealousy can erupt at the sight or sound of any random stimulus that results in forcing disturbed individuals to think about the pleasurable things in life they are not enjoying and probably have no prospect of enjoying. This psychological frustration is part of the reason why some people hate sexually suggestive music and movies and seek to prohibit others from partaking of such entertainment, because such makes them think of things they do not have and therefore want to push out of their minds. The sight of people who have caught interracial lightning in a bottle enrages such losers. These losers are the modern-day descendants of witch hunters, walking cauldrons of sexual and social resentments waiting for opportunistic public targets of convenience to let their persecuting spirit bubble over onto. They don't like anything that even hints of novel relationships or sex because, if they don't have it, they don't want anyone else having it either. Misery loves company.

"Envy is a madness which cannot endure the good of others."
La Rochefoucauld
Maxims

The woman who wore the scarlet letter wanted no part of the sexual misery that was the norm among witch hunters. They nevertheless insisted that she partake of their misery by turning her into someone both shunned by the community and stigmatized on sight as a pariah. In essence, they said that pleasure is bad unless we control it, and punished her for enjoying herself without permission from the envious mob. The witch hunters expressed an extreme form of a two-sided instinct buried deep within us, an instinct that makes us both pressure others to conform as well as modify our own behavior to conform to obtain the approval of others. Human beings are social animals, and being a social animal means associating and communicating with our fellow creatures. Social pressures are a limited form of communication, and stares, shocked facial reactions, looking the other way when someone comes and the like, are all forms of

168

such one-sided communication, the object of which is social control and conformity. The aim of social control is to level us all downwards, not raise us upwards. Wearing the scarlet letter was simply an extreme form of community disapproval of nonconformist sexuality expressed as punishment for past behavior and as a warning for potential future transgressors.

The sexually repressed witch hunters forced a woman who had in engaged in unlicensed sexual activity outside of marriage to wear the scarlet letter as a badge of community dishonor and disapproval. Modern-day interracial daters encounter less intense forms of social disapproval, but simply by virtue of being in a relationship with a physically different person, they wear a different sort of scarlet letter. This scarlet letter exists only in the minds of frustrated, disturbed individuals who believe that being envious gives them the right to try to control the social and sexual relationships of total strangers they happen to see on the street. Interracial dating is normal behavior, and neurotic intolerance is abnormal behavior. The sexual scarlet letter of interracial dating exists only in troubled minds where a mixture of rumors, fantasies and an anger born of neurotic repression puff up like a hot air balloon to fill the mental vacuum available for such neurotic delusions. Both sexual witches and the scarlet letter exist solely in the psychological recesses of those who want to believe in them, and nowhere else.

Why People Stare At Interracial Couples

All the world may love a lover, but interracial lovers seem to be exceptions. You can't escape getting get hit with stares everywhere you go. Sorry. Even people in interracial relationships of their own will automatically take more than a passing glance at other interracial couples. Your eyeballs will swivel, as if possessed of minds of their own, to track interracial couples you see on the street. This is a normal reflex. Our mental radar tends to skip over, or tune out, the familiar and, conversely, sends out screeching alerts when something "different" pops up on our sociological radar screen. Differences make us stand up and take notice. The more physically different two people are, the stronger the alert signal sent out by that radar signal processing center inside your head. If you usually see matching pairs of chocolate or vanilla radar reflections walking in formation down the street, seeing a vanilla reflection paired

169

with a chocolate reflection will give you a jolt. Should you be in an interracial relationship yourself, however, your reaction to interracial couples presumably expresses something other than unadulterated shock. Visual contrasts catch the eye simply by virtue of differing from the threshold of difference we usually encounter. This is the way our brains process the information the eyes send to the brain, and is not susceptible to conscious control. What bystanders do after seeing an interracial couple, however, is another matter altogether. You can expect several predictable types of responses from predictable types of people.

Most onlookers take a fast peek out of curiosity or surprise before snapping back to their business-as-usual mode. Seeing an interracial couple evokes little from them beyond a brief eyeball reflex and maybe some minor swiveling of the head. If the notion of sex crosses their minds when seeing an interracial couple, it fleetingly skims the fringe of consciousness before their internal censors clamp down on it in short order. Sexually normal people have other things to dwell on besides extrapolating about what total strangers who happen to be interracially involved do in bed. They might or might not have an opinion one way or the other concerning the propriety of interracial relationships, but don't see it as an issue that concerns them personally any more than any other slightly-out-of-the-ordinary thing they encounter in their daily routine. Sometimes people with no particular interest keep staring because situational circumstances make it impossible to not do so, as in facing an interracial couple when seated on a subway car or in a restaurant. Black women who think there is something wrong with taking a look at interracial couples should check their own automatic reactions to seeing Black men with White women before casting the first stone.

Different types of bystanders continue staring. Their faces show what's on their minds. There are several different types of bystanders. Some are adolescents in mind, if not in body. First are the young nerds, and some not-so-young nerds. What they see on the street becomes a lightning rod that attracts electrically-charged bolts of sexual imagery from the stormy depths of the subconscious. Neurotic, repressed nerds stare on seeing an interracial couple because the novelty brings adolescent sexual fantasies to the forefront of consciousness, and visions of sexual sugarplums dance in their heads. While sex is a part of any good relationship, nerds see and think only about sex when seeing an interracial couple. Knowing little about relationships due to not having been in any themselves, they don't have anything else to work with.

When inhibited nerds see something not on display every day in their narrow social universe, such as a couple where the partners are decades apart in age, their minds fill in the blanks with red-hot sex. They project their fantasies and preconceptions to fill the many unexplained gaps in their sadly-lacking understanding of relationships, and automatically paint sexual auras around people visibly involved in interracial relationships. Whatever they don't understand immediately, or are afraid to dwell on, the instant, all-purpose answer to what ails their understanding is always red-hot sex. The interracial aspect raises the level of steaminess by adding elements of the unfamiliar, novel and exotic, which are assumed to be unbearably exciting until proven otherwise. The sight of an interracial couple might even keep looping around in their neural circuits for days on end until the sexual electricity generated gradually dissipates. They have yet to reach the stage of personal development, regardless of chronological age, where they can get a handle on what real relationships are, and so interracial relationships are just another offbeat flavor of sexual fantasy come to life right in front of their eyes.

Why do nerds act like this? In the final analysis, interracial dating is a way of advertising both your physical preferences in men as well as your potential sexual preferences. Should people see you with a member of the opposite sex, many will assume that you are likely to wind up in bed with them eventually. Physical differences which are a source of attraction for you are a source of instant fantasies for them. Adolescent sexual thoughts pantingly expand like a hot-air balloon until they lift off the ground to sail through a sky filled with hormonal fantasies. Nerds won't cause any problems unless you are bothered by turning heads and jaws that drop a notch or two. Caucasian nerds will sometimes actually get red in the face just looking at an interracial couple, though public meltdowns are rare.

Sometimes you encounter people so low on the mental scale that they keep staring because they can't believe what they are seeing, like backwoods yokels popping their eyes out on seeing a two-headed dog at a circus. Don't waste time thinking about such people. It is a waste of time even trying to analyze minds at the bottom of the scale of simple-mindedness.

Nerds, however repressed, react to interracial relationships and the prospect of interracial sex in positive terms of a sort, even if those thoughts overload their circuits in the short run. A very different type of bystander doesn't like the idea of interracial relationships one bit. They stare at interracial couples out of anger, envy and jealousy. Storms of evil thoughts brew in their minds. The sight of an interracial couple ignites minds laden with combustible racial and sexual prejudices, triggering off subterranean psychological explosions. You can actually hear some of them muttering under their breath. Most keep their opinions to themselves, though their disapproving looks give you a pretty good idea of what's going on upstairs. You will probably not personally encounter very many people like this, but an encounter might rattle you a bit. You might not understand why the sight of you out on a date has such an effect on them. They probably come from the ranks of the twenty-three percent of Blacks and thirty-nine percent of Whites who oppose interracial marriages. Most are older people, but these attitudes are also found among the young, especially at the bottom of the social scale.

First, such people can dredge up lurid sexual-fantasy projections at the snap of a finger. When they see a Black woman and a White man walk down the street, hand-in-hand, they don't see two casual acquaintances strolling along on their first date. They see two sexually supercharged human containers of bubbling hormones on their way to jumping into bed and engaging in illicit, exotic red-hot interracial sex all night long and maybe even all day long. Sexually adolescent minds see such things in, around and under, every bed. Unlike the nerds, however, they don't like the idea of red-hot sex one bit. Most such people will give you little more than an unpleasant look, though some will mutter under their breath to the effect that they don't like what they see, it's disgusting, it's wrong, it's immoral, what's the world coming to, and so on. Such backward people act like this in part because that's how they are socialized among their like-minded brethren. When among the heathen general public, however, they tend towards restraint, probably due to having learned the hard way that when in Rome they should at least restrain themselves and do as the Romans do. Laughing, whispering, sniggering and pointing are simply different forms of expression of their thinly-disguised envy.

Second, envy and jealousy are major factor in their lives, not minor events. Their sex lives simmer with neurotic frustrations and inhibitions.

172

Interracial couples give the public appearance of enjoying deviating from dating norms, and are thus assumed to similarly enjoy happily deviating from unexciting sexual norms as well. Happy nonconformists really get their danders up, and interracial dating is the most publicly scarlet of scarlet letters they can imagine. Interracial sex is "different" and therefore "excessive" or "too much" to even look at when seen from the point of view of a frustrated adolescent mind in an adult body. They just plain don't like the idea of uncontrolled relationships and sex between consenting adults of different races. They don't enjoy their own lives, and don't want to see anybody else enjoy themselves either.

"People hate those who make them feel their own inferiority."
Philip Stanhope, Earl of Chesterfield
Letters To His Son

The older they get, the more time such neurotic old maids of both sexes have had to dwell on their frustrations and resentments. The only satisfaction they can find is in trying to control or wipe out what makes them burn. Some such people are envious of one member of the interracial couple in the sense of wanting what they see that person enjoying but cannot have for themselves. They can't stand the idea of some one of another race, someone totally physically different than themselves, someone with whom they can not identify in the sense of that other person being a sort of surrogate or psychological extension of themselves, enjoying what they are not. The sight of people enjoying the exotic delights of an interracial relationship accentuates the misery of their own deprivations. If you don't have even plain old everyday ice cream, the sight of someone else enjoying exotic, imported flavors just adds to their outrage. Envy will seek any pretext for expression, and racial differences are a ready pretext for coming down on easy-to-spot targets on the street. They come down on interracial couples because they see them as social pariahs they mistakenly suppose to have little social support for a supposed grossly impermissible level of enjoyment of life.

"The propensity of human nature [is] to tell the very worst of itself, when embodied in the person of another."
Nathaniel Hawthorne
The Scarlet Letter

Third, misery loves company. Dammed-up sexual impulses will explode somewhere, sooner or later, and the trigger is often the sight of non-neurotics enjoying life. Exploding with anger is one way to control, repress, censor or intimidate such people and activities as constitute real-life dramatizations and reminders of their personal deficits, internal conflicts and assorted other problems. The envious and jealous always want to control others' relationships. They become seethingly angry at seeing others merrily get on with their lives without paying any attention to their problems. Whatever ostensible reason they trot out, the real reason for their behavior is that they want to control other people to satisfy their personal demons and neuroses. This is no different than an anorexic who can't stand to see others enjoying food and who thus says that eating food is evil and that she'll stop others for their own good, a psychological transformation of jealousy into the slightly more socially acceptable, but still odious, form of claiming to know what's best for others.

Preventing you from enjoying yourself is their way of controlling you. It means that they, not you, control the pleasure spigot of your life. The more lacking their lives, the more they want to get the most personal and pleasurable parts of the lives of others under some sort of "control", or at least try to get the interracial couple to pay attention to them by means of public insults or even impromptu public cross-examinations. Controlling others and making others miserable might be the only sources of pleasure in their lives. They will settle for disrupting an interracial couple's enjoyment of their day, cutting you down a few notches to something closer to their own low level of enjoyment of life, and thus getting interracial couples to keep them "company" in their dissatisfaction.

"Thou suffering thing, Know that thy sorrow is my ecstasy That thy love's loss is my hate's profiting!"
Thomas Hardy
"Hap"

They've given up trying to enjoy their own lives, so they try to prevent others from enjoying life. They don't want the sun to shine on them, they want to stop others from enjoying the sunshine. If they don't have the nerve to say anything out loud, they will settle for using a nasty expression to try to stare down the interracial couple and make them feel bad for a few minutes. Their reaction to interracial couples is just a twisted form of sour grapes, like an old maid sneering at a woman in an enjoyable sexual relationship. They put down what they can't have, and want victims to cater to their deficits. The scarlet letter they point out in others is simply a mirror reflection of the scarlet letter of their own neuroses.

Fourth, you find anger at the world and about life in general. They think that life owes them something. The good things of life have passed them by, and they are resentful. They have loser self-images, in the sense of being impoverished backyard spectators sullenly watching a world full of affluent neighbors fly off to exotic foreign vacations. Thus, while you might think that their envy is focused on interracial couples, that is just the small slice of their behavior that you happen to see. The reality is that jealousy and envy steer and guide their overall approach to life. Were you to make the mistake of hanging out with such people, you would find that jealousy and envy are the prism through which they sneer at almost everybody and everything in life.

Fifth, they put forth unbelievable rationalizations about why they hate interracial couples. Rationalizations are outright lies designed to mask something they don't want to reveal about themselves. Sometimes you will hear religious rationalizations about why the races should not mix, proof that an idle mind is the devil's playground. Their gods are not your gods, and they need to learn to respect your freedom of religion and your freedom of association. On some occasions you might encounter a semi-literate with pseudo-scientific pretensions about race mixing masquerading as science, showing that a threadbare mind can also be the devil's playground. Again, these are just specious pretexts of convenience to try to get you under their control.

"Evil is wrought by want of Thought As well as want of Heart."
Thomas Hood
"The Lady's Dream"

Low-status people constantly seek scraps from the table of social status. Their idea of status is status as seen from the perspective of someone at the bottom of the heap looking upwards at those just above them on the ladder, meaning some sort of supervisor of flunkies. Low-status people are very imitative. They want to pretend to be boss, and look for situations where they can harangue someone, anyone, by setting themselves up as

175

the boss of a passing situation and positioning the other person as an underling. They want to control others as a substitute for what they do not have. They are the modern-day descendants of the witch-hunters of hundreds of years ago who would burn at the stake any person who dramatized their feelings of inadequacy and secret jealousies. Were witch-hunting to come back into style, the first to sign up would be those who see the scarlet letter everywhere except in themselves.

Low-status losers do things like this because they are typically at the bottom of some sort of authoritarian, hierarchical heap. They spend their lives obeying orders and getting permission to do almost everything. People at the bottom of authoritarian structures are big on conformity and rules for every situation in life, which shows that they lost, or maybe never acquired, the capacity to think for themselves. Conformity and obedience have brought them nothing, and they see life's rewards going to those who think for themselves. They thus become enraged with envy on seeing nonconformists enjoy themselves, and hate nonconformists who zoom ahead of them in most departments of life. This is envy. They never understand that in modern societies, it is those who think for themselves go places, not those who wait for others to tell them what to do. Intelligence and initiative are the traits in demand.

"The slave is always a tyrant, if he gets the chance to be one."
Harriet Beecher Stowe
Uncle Tom's Cabin

Low-status types are imitative creatures, and like to play at being boss outside their workplace. Their sole model for social status and self-esteem is the occupational hierarchy that their low-level job plugs them into, but they rarely have opportunities to be boss on the job. The result is that they try to pretend they have social status off the job by homing in on nonconformists whom they seek to berate or glare at as a means of "punishment." They are not psychological adults who can take on multiple roles, so they act out the limited roles they are capable of understanding on a limited, imitative level, meaning the role of flunky's boss. Interracial daters are the most visibly apparent of nonconformists by virtue of their color contrast, and thus destined to be hated on sight by the envious.

176

While several other mental forces are at work, one thing imitative, low-status types consciously do is imitate the boss by cracking down on anyone who steps out of line. They want you defer to them as some sort of superior being to whom you must justify your "aberrant" behavior. Misery loves company, and hates to see others "get away" with enjoying themselves without their "permission." These are disturbed people, and your best move is to put some distance between you and them as soon as possible. Nothing you can say will enlighten them or change them. They are beyond the point of reason.

Sixth, physical violence is quite rare, but does happen. Use your best judgment as to which people and neighborhoods to stay away from. If you see trouble coming, walk or run away if possible, defend yourself as necessary, and prosecute to the limit of the law. The suggestion of physical intimidation is much more common, however, and is most commonly used by Black men trying to act important.

Other Forms Of The Scarlet Letter

Sometimes you encounter Black couples who work together to stare at you or give you the cold shoulder as you walk by or go about your daily activities. Should you and your date sit down in a fast food restaurant, expect some Black couples to look at you, look at each other and just get up and move to another table, as far away as possible, all without saying a word. If you are standing on line at a checkout counter in a store with a White guy, you can sometimes expect cold and distant behavior from Black male sales clerks. This is how some Blacks express their disapproval of Black women who wear the scarlet letter that comes with dating White men.

Their viewpoint is that dating a White guy is a put-down of them, their dating choices and Blacks in general. If you are not with them, you are against them, and wear the scarlet letter their minds project onto you. They shun Black women who date Whites because they see such Black women as wearing the scarlet letter of associating with White men. Such views come naturally to those who think that people owe automatic allegiance to all others of their race by virtue of birth rather than by choice. This is the mentality of an isolated, besieged tribe that distrusts all outsiders. They want you to defer to their opinions because the sight of someone

177

expressing lifestyle choices reflecting values opposed to their own is seen as somehow invalidating their entire way of life. Such people have a neurotic insecurity problem, and apparently think their opinions rest on such foundationless sands that the sight of someone whose lifestyle choices are contrary to their own somehow invalidates them and their opinions.

Fortunately for you, such people are probably total strangers you have never crossed paths with before, and will very likely never cross paths with again, so their opinions and reactions don't really count. As long as they leave you alone (most will) don't dwell on them. Out of sight, out of mind. After a while, you just learn to tune out such people. You can't expect everyone, or anyone for that matter, to validate your dating choices, so don't waste your time waiting for it.

Now and then you will receive unpleasantly analogous treatment from frustrated, unattached White men and women. A White male who has probably not been in a relationship for a long time might burn with jealousy at seeing another White male enjoying what he is not. A deluded, unattached White woman might see a Black woman with a White man as the vanguard of an invading army on the verge of taking all White men away from all White women. As you descend the social scale, open hostility to public expression of whatever they don't like increases as a byproduct of the lack of social status and neuroses common among the trashier elements of cracker-barrel, trailer-trash society. The perception that you wear the scarlet letter of interracial dating is most often the misperception of people at the bottom of the social scale. Be aware, however, that there do exist more than a few middle-class and upper-class Whites with mental problems that they will want to project onto you.

Don't get the idea that most of the world is up in arms against you. The overwhelming majority of people you pass on the street couldn't care less if you're dating a White guy, and will do little beyond taking various types of casual glances. Some might have a vague notion of disapproval, but would never think of saying anything, and forget about you two minutes after passing you by. It's not a big deal for most people. The problem people are the ones you remember, not the thousands you pass on the street every day. The bad news is all you remember, not the overwhelming numbers of occasions when there was no news at all. When things go without a hitch, the lack of a disturbance usually leaves no impression in its wake, just another business-as-usual day. It's the rare bad news days that make the deepest and most lasting impressions by virtue of being so different.

Chapter Thirteen
The Scarlet Letter Of Interracial Dating, Part II

"Strangers looked curiously at the scarlet letter - and none ever failed to do so."
Nathaniel Hawthorne
The Scarlet Letter

The Psychology Of Dealing With Stares

"The encounter of assailing eyes"
William Shakespeare
Romeo And Juliet

Should you have been programmed early in life to take undue notice of the opinions and expectations of others, you may feel as if the stares that follow interracial couples everywhere are burning holes in the back of your head. This is a common problem. It's not the stares themselves so much as your sensitivity to them. It's what goes on in your head, both while you are being stared at, and afterwards, that is the real problem. In the final analysis, the ultimate issue is the psychological and social baggage you've picked up in life that stares elicit from within you. For most people, being stared at means that they think others think that there's something out of the ordinary, whether positive or negative, about you that merits the attention of others. In many public situations, being stared at automatically means that the thought "something is wrong or different about me" jumps into your head. The desire to avoid public social disapproval that stares reflect is behind the dislike of being stared at.

Stares are not bolts of lightning, and will not strike you dead, no matter how much lightning strikes within the minds of those staring at you. Some static in the air is about as bad as it gets, and the worst that static can do is make your hair stand up on end now and then. By grounding the discharges of psychological static electricity, you will conduct the shocks away from you and deprive them of having an effect on you. You become progressively desensitized to stares as a result of repeated experiences from which you eventually derive the rules that stick and stones may break your bones but stares will never hurt you unless you choose to let them hurt you. After a while, being stared at wears a groove in your mind and registers only on the fringe of your consciousness. A fear of social disapproval is partly a result of insecurity about acting differently, meaning a combination of inborn and learned needs for social ratification of your actions. Unless you're very insecure, there is no need to see yourself as someone who needs to justify her social interests and needs to others or live up to others' expectations.

The key is how you regard those who stare at you. Start reprogramming yourself to value your own tastes and opinions above those of others. There is no reason for psychological adults to assign any special importance to the stares and opinions of casual strangers on city streets. Think of strangers on the street as background foliage of no particular interest. You might even stare back at them. As for those few strangers who stare as a means of expressing disapproval or hostility, they don't count unless you choose to let them count. Ignore them and they will usually go away or at least fade from mind. Repeated exposures to stares eventually desensitizes you to being stared at. The trick is to not be so scared of being stared at in the first place that you are afraid to go out and walk against the tide. That's all there is to it.

If you are not used to being stared at almost everywhere you go, it admittedly can be a bit unnerving or disconcerting. Strange thoughts might go through your head, such as: "Uh-oh, they're looking at me because I've doing something wrong." In general, you will find that Whites are more likely to stare out of surprise or curiosity.

Blacks, usually meaning Black men, are more likely to stare as a means of expressing various shades of disapproval of Black women who wear the scarlet letter that goes with dating White men, though overt hostility is rare. For reasons best known to Black men, stare treatment is rarely administered by Black men to Black men who date White women, only to Black women with White men. Staring is simply a nonverbal form of expression of an person's opinion or reaction, making use of the eyes and facial muscles rather than the mouth.

While others have the right to their opinions, keep in mind that your opinions always take precedence over the opinions of others because they are your opinions and meet your needs for self-expression. Only you can

181

decide what opinions and tastes fit your needs. Should you have been brought up to always have undue regard or need for external approval, it may take some time and practice to flesh out your attitude that others need to learn to have a high regard for your right to express, and not interfere with, your dating choices.

Your dating choices are thus the actions you take to put your opinions into effect. Mentally classify the opinions others express as stares as something that you can take or leave as you wish. You should not be of the mindset that you need anyone's approval in the first place, least of all the approval of total strangers on the street. It's easy to tune them out if you're not looking for public approval in the first place. Focus on the guy you're with, not the peanut gallery. approval in the first place. Focus on the guy you're with, not the peanut gallery.

Snappy Comebacks

You have the choice of responding to stares by either ignoring them or staring back. Now and then one of the more articulate opponents of interracial relationships might try to harangue or cross-examine you. Do not engage in any sort of back-and-forth exchange. That only encourages them. People you don't want to deal with don't count, period, and you don't owe them anything, least of all an explanation that might waste a minute of your very precious time. Your only purpose in saying anything at all to them is to warn them off, or to intimidate them enough, to make them go away and stay out of both sight and mind. Just keep walking and demand that they go away and stay out of both sight and mind. Just keep walking and demand that they go away. Focus on the person you're with, not the peanut gallery. Potentially useful responses include:

*Three's a crowd.
*I don't want you around.
*Jealous, aren't you?
*Not interested.
*No thanks.
*Shut up.
*Get lost.
*Go away.

"My life is for itself and not for a spectacle."
Ralph Waldo Emerson
Self-Reliance

How Parents Try To Break Up Interracial Relationships

"What fools these mortals be!"
William Shakespeare
A Midsummer Night's Dream

Even liberal White parents may be petrified with shock on meeting their son's Black girlfriend, no two ways about it. For that matter, should he ever meet your parents, you can expect similar dance maneuvers from them. While overt racism has decreased among middle-class Whites, problems still happen. Some White parents have no problem living in integrated neighborhoods, but when it comes to integrating the family -forget it! Integration stops at the front porch.

Many, though hardly all, White parents take a neutral position on interracial dating, partly out of an unspoken hope that he will lose interest or "outgrow" it. Most will not voice overt opposition, thinking that such encourages him to redouble his efforts and intensify what they suppose to be a rebellious attitude. Interestingly enough, from the parents' point of view, the fact that their son is involved with a Black woman is not seen as the real problem. For that matter, should the two of you have personalities poles apart, they won't get too worked up about the relationship, believing it unlikely to become serious.

Where socially conservative White parents see a problem is in the possibility that the relationship might get serious, and lead to biracial grandchildren. For all too many Whites, "Biracial" equals "Black", and "Black" equals what they see on television news: poor, uneducated, possibly criminal and very, very different. Media-derived stereotypes rush in to fill informational vacuums. The more you have in common with him, the less socially conservative parents will care for you and the relationship, and the harder they will work at breaking it up.

183

"Few parents now-a-days pay any regard to what their children say to them. The old-fashioned respect for the young is fast dying out."
Oscar Wilde
The Importance Of Being Earnest

Should you have a high income or an advanced degree, that tends to ameliorate their outlook on you, because having such characteristics slots you into a somewhat different category than the Blacks they see on television news, though parental anxieties often take a long time to fade entirely. Parents are social products of their backgrounds, experiences and idiosyncrasies, and most middle-class White parents come from backgrounds where few Blacks were around when they were coming up the line. Parents of any persuasion, be it racial, ethnic, political, religious, intellectual, and so on, have decades of immersion in being members of their persuasion, and are in the grip of the inertia that such immersion produces. They fear the unknown.

To some extent, they may view interracial dating as a rejection of their whole way of life by their offspring. Rejection of their way of life equals nonconformity, and nonconformity is just one step away from seeing their son wearing the scarlet letter. And if their son wears the scarlet letter, the parents, by association, are themselves just one step away from also wearing the scarlet letter in the eyes of the neighbors. Parents tend to be set in their ways, and the exhilarating novelty their son enjoys may seem more disruptive than novel to them, as well as making them feel that he thinks their views on life are obsolete. Note that the perceived disruption occurs entirely on the parents' side, not the son's side. People of any persuasion tend to automatically invest themselves with an assumed, but nonexistent, tribal or territorial right to control others whom they perceive as being of the same social type as themselves. Families are really small tribes, and tribes are often narrow-minded and insular, seeing nothing to be gained from change that dilutes the group's control over individual members. The greatest degree of territorial control is perceived as existing over their offspring and other relatives, adult or otherwise.

Some parents take exception to their offspring becoming attached to anyone with whom they can not identify. Identification here means being able to mentally place one's self in the place of the person in question, and is probably related in some way to territorial instincts. Thus, a White guy's mother can not mentally place herself in the Black women's relationship with her son and thus objects to the relationship for the same reason a Black father can not mentally put himself in the place of the White guy involved with his daughter. A Black woman is alien social territory for White parents, and if a son from their territory wanders into alien social territory for keeps, that reduces, or might even eliminate, their control over him.

The more neurotic the parents, the more obsessed they are with control and keeping their offspring within social territory limits acceptable to the parents. Note the focus on the parents' needs, not the son's needs. Similarities to familiar social territory reassures parents, and breaks with tradition upset them, their lip-service protests to the effect that their offspring are free to do whatever they want with their lives notwithstanding. To some degree, all parents want to identify with their offspring's choice of companion. What such parents do not understand is that their offspring have lives of their own to live, which necessarily excludes letting anybody else control the most intimate parts of their lives. You're not really living your own life if someone else makes the big decisions. Don't worship the wishes of your ancestors, living or dead, or you'll get into the unfortunate habit of living your life for third parties with no compensating benefits coming to you in return.

"He who lets the world, or his own portion of it, choose his plan of life for him, has no need of any other faculty than the ape-like one of imitation."
John Stuart Mill
On Liberty

Some parents wage war against interracial relationships using overt or covert guerrilla warfare tactics. Redneck parents might use the iron fist approach: "stop seeing her - or else," implying withdrawal of financial support if he is in college. Should the son be self-supporting, iron fist tactics fly like a lead balloon. Most middle-class parents prefer to swathe the iron fist in the velvet glove of softball propaganda, and suggestions of retaliation or disenfranchisement are an absolute last resort. In such cases, they might try protracted discussions during unusually amiable, sumptuous weekend banquets where they concede "she's a very nice girl", but "she's really not right for you" and "all we really want is to see you happy." Parents always assume that they know what makes their offspring happy, ignoring that their offspring have had many years of enlightening life experiences that enable them to make well-informed personal decisions in favor of interracial relationships. Such lines of patter are just the White version of arguments that some Blacks use to discourage interracial relationships between Black women and White men. You would not hear parents say such things were the woman White. Black parents similarly would not bring up certain things in reference to their daughter being involved with a Black man, but such matters seem to be the first thing on their minds when she gets involved with a White guy. The parental need to be able to identify with the companionship choices of their offspring do not obligate their offspring to prune down their lives to meet parental expectations of social control. Some social roles are not worth learning to take on, such as the role of victim.

In the final analysis, such parental objections are just another way of saying that the parents think interracial relationships should be held to a higher standard than same-race relationships, and that they want their personal tastes and restrictions on social territory to take precedence over the opinions of the two parties most directly concerned. However, unless you actively cooperate with them, there is no way for them to run things. Victimization of this type requires the cooperation of the victims, and no cooperation means no victimization. Such parents want their offspring to take on a role that will allow some degree of victimization, in the sense of allowing a third party to make the big decisions, the ones that count. Some parents will actually use baby talk with adult offspring, the only way they can get them into a cooperative mode being to trick them into reverting to a childish role. You are doomed if you play along with such tricks. Think for yourself and live for yourself. Don't learn to play the role of victim for your parents' applause.

Everyone seems to have an opinion about interracial relationships that they want to share with you regardless of your level of interest in their opinions, and none of them care about your opinions, because they see it as a sociological issue, not a personal issue where those most directly involved are the only ones whose opinions count. This mentality of seeing interracial relationships as sociology permeates parental attitudes, possibly due to having seen them primarily in the context of the mass media. Having a sociological attitude means that the parents see an interracial relationship in terms of how it fails to meet group expectations for approval, rather than how it meets the needs of the two people most directly concerned.

"In all unbalanced minds, the classification is idolized."
Ralph Waldo Emerson
"Self-Reliance"

The parental need for social approval reflects the fear that having a son or daughter who chooses to wear the scarlet letter of interracial dating is something that will rub off on the parents by association. That is their problem and their concern, not yours. You should never set up your life to suit other people's opinions, and least of all should you set up your life to reflect a concern for the impact of your personal opinions and life choices on relatives. Note that the only people whose opinions do not seem to matter in this equation are the two people actually in the interracial relationship. Oddly enough, few people seems to think there is anything wrong with opposing interracial relationships, as if it is somehow natural to do so, for reasons that will be discussed in a later chapter.

As a last resort, exasperated White and Black parents sometimes bring up the oldest objection of all - "what about the children?" -meaning they assume that you share their assumption that you need to justify your reproductive choices to them, something parents would never have the nerve to try with two people of the same race. Answering such questions is strictly for neurotics who feel a need to cater to other people's expectations in every part of their lives. Don't cater to their assumptions and expectations. It's easy to see that the only thing on their minds is notions about how your choices fail to fit into other people's preexisting mental categories. Only neurotics obsessed with the need to seek external group approval would bring up such a thing. In fact, what they are really driving at is that they do not want their offspring doing anything that the parents might have trouble justifying to others, such as your total disregard for group approval. Should the situation get to that point, tell them that you never need to explain or justify your reproductive choices to anyone, particularly your parents, and that this rule of yours is something ill-mannered people need to learn about fast. The world is full of people who respect your personal territory only when you draw a line in the sand, and parents often like to operate under the very mistaken assumption that they can determine the ground rules for the lives of their offspring. None of

187

their arbitrary limitations are binding on you unless you voluntarily choose to allow them to become binding on you.

Should the two of you still be on speaking terms with your or his parents by that point, one follow-up you can make is that you like the idea of biracial children, and people who don't like that better stay out of your way. You'll never convince others to change their biases, so let them get used to yours. You have an unlimited right to hold opinions that others don't care for and live your life by your own standards. Let them get used to you. Members of any sort of racial group, religious group, family group or ideology have a vested interest in maintaining the group identity status quo of conformist solidarity that reduces your freedom of choice, and use subterfuge and manipulation to keep things the way they think it should be. You can't win a game where the only possible outcome is for you to trim down your life to suit others' expectations. Most parents probably think they mean well when they do these things, but probably have too much experience thinking and living in particular ways to really empathize with "wayward" children right off the bat. They might change, or they might not. The concerns of his or your parents about wearing the scarlet letter of interracial dating, or marriage, nevertheless remain their concern, not yours. If you structure your life around satisfying others first, you will find your own needs and concerns never get satisfied, because other people will always have endless demands to make of you. If you let others get away with treating you as a thing, there are those who will deliberately go out of their way to treat you that way.

Is He Or She Afraid To Be Seen With A Black Or White Person?

Some White men want to date Black women, but don't want to be seen in public with a Black woman. The same goes for some Black women. Such people are the modern-day counterpart of the hypocritical lover of the woman who wore the scarlet letter, but who did not want to be publicly identified as her lover. Dump those who do this. Such people are either grossly immature or so completely susceptible to the need for external approval that the thought that they might have to walk down the street wearing the scarlet letter of interracial dating nonconformity overloads their circuits. Don't become their "out-of-sight" girlfriend or boyfriend, unless all you're looking for is furtive sex and a short-term relationship. The other side of the coin is that it is not unknown for some people to not want to be seen socializing with people of another race due to the fear of social disapproval. The root of such behavior is the belief that those who date interracially wear a scarlet letter that identifies them as illicit nonconformists. If you don't think there is anything wrong with interracial dating, you won't feel you are wearing a scarlet letter, won't care about what others think of your nonconformity and will have no problem going out with a person of another race in most areas.

Exceptions should be made for those new to interracial dating, meaning people like you. Edge into coping with public reaction. Should you both live in the suburbs, and neither of you have dated interracially before, the two of you might want to get together on neutral territory somewhere in the downtown the first few times and edge into becoming acclimated to public reaction. It takes a while to learn how to tune out the rest of the world. Both of you may be a bit nervous, and understandably so, possibly even ready to bolt if any sort of vaguely-defined trouble arises. While a Black woman might be worried about stares and such, a White male who has not dated interracially before is thinking about something quite different. Some White men think there is a real possibility that certain types of Black men might see red at the sight of the scarlet letter of Black female-White relationships, and express their opinion by taking a swing at White men seen dating Black women. This supposition is statistically unlikely to become true, but it is a very real possibility in the minds of some White males. Trouble, in the sense of physical confrontation, is very unlikely to show up on the agenda except in rough neighborhoods.

People from sheltered backgrounds are likely to become disconcerted when first stared at everywhere they go. After going out two or three times and finding out there is really nothing to be worried about, there is no reason not to visit each other's neighborhoods, unless one of you either has something to hide. The primary exception to this rule would be where one of you either lives with close-minded parents or in an unusually close-minded neighborhood. Should either of you live with parents, unless they are unusually open-minded, you might expect volatility of the type you can neither ignore nor walk away from. In such situations, you have to make your own decisions. When you live in your parents' house, you have to play by their rules and live with their opinions, even if you are otherwise considered an independent adult. The only solution to a rough

189

neighborhood is to put some distance between the neighborhood and your relationship.

Meeting Friends

In meeting friends, after an initial moment of silence or surprise, you can expect the conversations to flow in many directions and cover many topics - except race. Whites rarely discuss race and racial topics with Blacks. One reason is that they may suspect you of being a closet militant waiting to jump on them if they say "the wrong thing." Middle-class Whites will generally try to avoid dancing close to the fire until after they ascertain whether they might get singed. So they will dance around the obvious issues that are both on their minds and right in front of their noses. They will edge into racial topics very slowly, see how you react, and back off should you seem hot under the collar, regardless of whether you have valid cause for being so.

A more common problem will be when they have no idea how to talk about your relationship with a White guy. A few particularly nervous types may be unable to say anything to you, though not for the reason you might think. They are not afraid of you. When they see a Black woman and a White man together, all they can think of is one thing. That thing is red-hot interracial sex. Having a White male acquaintance paired off with a Black woman may be so completely alien to their experiences that their thoughts just keep going along the edge of a sexual mental volcano. No matter how intellectual and middle-class a Black woman is, if she's involved with a White guy, you can be sure that the subject of interracial sex is lurking somewhere close to the surface of the minds of those middle-class Whites she talks with, even if they keep the lid on the pot while engaged in polite conversation. The idea of the scarlet letter of interracial sexuality will keep looping around in their minds even if they never come out and say it.

Even intellectual Whites do this. The reason is always the same. Should they know very little about a subject, what little they do know expands to fill every available inch of mental space. Since all they are likely to know about Black female-White male couples is that they rarely see such couples, such relationships have an illicit, forbidden connotation to them. By association, illicitness means that something of a sexual nature is

190

probably going on. Thus, even a nonsexual relationship becomes automatically equated with red-hot interracial sex. Some will try to push these ideas to the back of their minds, but you can be sure that it is bubbling somewhere in their heads. This is why some of his friends will act a bit strange around you.

Looking back these things from some point in the future, all of this may seem a little strange after you have actually been involved in an interracial relationship or two and found no shortage of other things to think about besides interracial sex. But, back before you had actually become involved with White males, your mind was probably just as fevered on the issue. If you think you are beyond such things, consider what goes through the minds of many Black women on seeing a Black man involved with a White woman. The answer is the words "interracial sex" in big red letters. It's not rational, but it happens. Take it one step further: can you push the idea of interracial sex completely out of your mind when you see a mixed couple? How far below the surface of your consciousness is it?

"It is not society that kindles strange longings or invents new pleasures, it is superior individuals."
Edward Alsworth Ross
Social Control

Chapter Fourteen
Understanding The Opposition
To Interracial Relationships, Part I

"Perplexed and ruffled by life's strategy?"
Elizabeth Barrett Browning
Sonnets From The Portugese

The Nature Of The Puzzle

When you date interracially, bizarre, seemingly incomprehensible behavior pops up around you on a regular basis. People stare at you wherever you go. Some acquaintances might become skittish in talking with you, acting as if dancing on the edge of a volcano. Black and White parents alike often go out of their way to sabotage the interracial relationships of their offspring.

Total strangers feel free to walk up to you and tell you that they do not approve of your choice of companions. You might even have the rare misfortune to run into a disturbed individual for whom seeing an interracial couple unlocks the psychological floodgates for public exhibitions of psychosexual problems usually encountered only in intensive psychoanalysis. Even those who date interracially themselves sometimes engage in mild versions of peculiar reflexive behaviors, as in unconsciously staring at other interracial couples.

Most mysterious of all, though few will admit it, is that some who date interracially feel a fleeting, inexplicable, but real, sense of guilt or shame about what they are doing, despite their sense of reason telling them their actions are in the right. They have an inexplicable feeling that what they are doing is somehow wrong, but can not define just why they feel it is wrong. Even those only contemplating the possibility of getting into an interracial relationship share some measure of this feeling, feelings which are probably a major factor in keeping large numbers of Black women and White men from making contact with each other in the first place.

These peculiar forms of behavior are not uniquely characteristic of Black female-White male relationships. Strangely similar forms of social disapproval can be found in cultures and societies where interracial or intercultural relationships are frowned on, either officially or unofficially, suggesting that such behavior derives from a psychological wellspring common to all people. There are subterranean psychological interconnections between these forms of behavior, and race turns out to be only a secondary factor in the overall equation, being only one visible tip of a largely submerged psychological iceberg.

The Framework Of The Puzzle

The answer lies in our peculiarly human heredity. Assume that generations reproduce themselves every twenty years or so. Our first primate ancestors with some vaguely human traits came on the scene about twenty million years ago, or a million generations ago. Slightly more advanced semi-human creatures with some capacity for making use of fire, and using antelope bones as hunting weapons, appeared about a half a million years ago, or twenty-five thousand generations ago. A very early version of true humans existed in Africa about two hundred thousand years ago, or ten thousand generations ago.

Ten thousand years ago, or five hundred generations ago, the first known agricultural societies came into being. Last, but not least, we began living in modern technological societies about two hundred years ago, only ten generations ago. Thus, over ninety-nine percent of our history and evolution transpired when our ancestors were in the hunter-gatherer state of evolution, wherein our human and pre-human ancestors lived by hunting and trapping animals, and gathering, or foraging, fruits, nuts, berries, vegetables and the like. Modern technological societies such as we now live in are a very recent development in our long evolutionary history.

Our remote ancestors gradually became human by means of the very, very slow process of evolution, whereby accidental mutations, such as the capacity for making and using stone axes as hunting weapons, slowly became widespread traits in the human and pre-human populations by virtue of giving a survival edge to those with such capacities. Thousands of generations were required for even minor physical and mental traits to develop and become established in our genetic code. Once our species gained a trait, it was similarly very, very slow to lose it. Thus, we all carry

193

around inside of us numerous rarely-activated traits, instincts and capacities that are vestigial carryovers from prior phases of human and pre-human evolution. Such carryover traits were useful in the Stone Age, but less useful now due to differences between the environments where those traits first evolved and our present environment. We continue to retain these traits because there has been no reason for us to shed them. Some such traits are relevant to interracial dating.

"A man hath no preeminence above a beast."
Ecclesiastes, 3:19
King James Bible

We have undergone surprisingly little, if any, biological change in developing modern societies during the last few thousand years. This is confirmed by comparing people from modern industrialized societies with people from the few remaining hunter-gatherer cultures in isolated parts of the world. There are no genetically-based mental or physical differences between us and them, only cumulative acquired cultural differences. We are all born with the capacities necessary to live as hunter-gatherers because those traits became locked in our genetic code over the course of millions of year that our human and pre-human ancestors lived as hunters-gatherers. Were you to be dropped into the hunter-gatherer world of two hundred thousand years ago, you would be on essentially the same footing as anyone else, assuming you had the personal database of acquired information about hunting and gathering survival techniques such societies require.

The human mind is like a computer in the sense of coming onto the scene with certain instinctual software programs already installed at birth. We are not born with blank-slate minds. Instincts are essentially predispositions to exhibit certain types of genetically programmed behavior, given certain eliciting stimuli. Let the environment press the right sensory stimuli buttons and your instinctual programs start running. You have a choice about whether you allow these instinctual programs run as they are, or whether you wish to modify their forms of expression to meet the needs your personal requirements. For example, while the sexual instinct is a universal human trait, the particular ways we express our sexual instinct vary widely both among cultures and individuals.

We usually think of our evolution into modern human beings in terms of the outwardly visible results of evolution, such as an upright posture and having an opposable thumb for using and making tools. While these are important parts of the evolutionary equation, they are actually minor parts of the larger picture. Most of our evolutionary development was not visible to the eye because it went on out of sight, meaning in the neural arrangements of the human brain.

We are born with dozens, and possibly hundreds, of instincts, such as the instincts for speech, language acquisition and tool-making, all carried over from our evolutionary past. Consider the example of language and speech acquisition. Human babies are born with a capacity for language acquisition, and usually learn the basics of a language by age two or three. These capacities for language must have met some sort of need at some point in our evolutionary past, or else they would not have become widespread. It can not be emphasized too strongly that whatever instincts we are born with in the present day, they served some sort of very real need during the millions of years of the pre-human and human Stone Age. Most important are our inborn instinctual social capacities.

"No other mammal.....shows so large an array [of instincts]."
William James
The Principles Of Psychology

Human beings are the only primates that cooperate to hunt and gather food in groups, plan their hunting and gathering in groups, and bring their food back to share with groups. Given that finding food was the key element of human survival during the millions of years of the Stone Age, it is not surprising that those who survived that era developed a number of inborn instinctual capacities, or cognitive modules, that fine-tuned their adaptation to Stone Age tribal social environment of other human beings with whom they interacted around the clock in hunting, gathering and sharing food. The evolution of the human mind was thus shaped to a large degree by the demands of living in a Stone Age social environment of small tribes, clans and other similar types of social groups for millions of years.

Evolutionary Adaptations To Other People

Early humans and pre-humans had no choice about cooperating with each other to live and work together in groups. Individual humans would have had a very tough time hunting anything except the smallest meat animals, and would have had an even tougher time defending themselves against predators such as wolves and lions, being easy prey due to lacking the claws and fangs sported by many other animal species. Working together made the big difference. Early humans cooperated as tribal groups who used stones, sharpened sticks and nets to hunt and trap meat animals during the day, and took turns defending their tribal camps against the predators during the night. They could seek out new fruit and vegetable patches in unknown territory by bringing armed protection with them. Our adaptation to hunting and gathering in cooperative groups was a thus the key initial element of our twenty million years of evolution, and eventually led to us developing additional adaptive refinements of our minds and bodies related to living and working in cooperative groups. It encouraged the development of selective adaptations that improved the efficiency of food collection activities, tribal defense activities and general social interaction with other members of the tribe. We are social animals because it was in our survival interest to become social animals.

After the initial adaptation to hunting and gathering in groups was made at some unknown point in the distant past, various other fine-tuned adaptations that improved group food-collection efficiency slowly worked their way into our genetic code. Speech is a prime example. Speech allows members of a tribe to better communicate with each other about plans to hunt in new territories, build hunting weapons, discuss where the best nut and berry patches might be, and so on. If speech allows for better planning for hunting and gathering, and results in more food being brought in, speech is a genetic trait likely to spread throughout the human species, because those who can speak find more food, and are thus more likely on average to survive and reproduce than those who find less food because the absence of the power of speech results in less food being collected. Thus, our ability to speak, and to understand the speech of others, is simply a genetic carryover from the Stone Age hunter-gatherer environment where it facilitated survival. Some carryover instincts have a direct relevance to interracial relationships, as will be seen below.

Our social evolution did not begin, or end, with evolving the capacity for speech. We retain modified forms of various pre-human instincts because those traits increased our chances of survival. We also piled up a long list of new, strictly-human adaptations of the mind. The human mind is a jerry-built structure filled to the brim with numerous adaptations retained because they happened to be useful somewhere along the line. Some such traits serve little purpose in our present-day environment, but we retain these traits because they are etched in our genetic code.

Men are born with a predisposition to enjoy physical aggression. That trait was useful in hunting meat animals on the African savanna for millions of years. Aggressive men were likely to be motivated by the good feeling they got from expressing aggression and go out every day to find and kill meat animals. Expressing aggression when hunting made them feel good, which motivated them to go out and seek food, which operated to ensure physical survival in the Stone Age environment where starvation and being eaten by carnivorous animals were very real possibilities. All men retain this aggressive instinct solely because it was a key survival trait in the Stone Age, and only those with the trait caught enough food to survive long enough to reproduce. "The destruction of prey and human rivals must have been among the most important of man's primitive functions." William James The Principles Of Psychology

Should aggression not be expressed in hunting, it does not just go away. Remember, it was a key survival trait for millions of years, an instinct thoroughly integrated into the woof and warp of human nature. If not expressed, it builds up internal psychological steam pressure until it is expressed in some modified form besides hunting, such as hitting a punching bag at a gym, or sublimated into some other form, such as on-the-job competition.

We retain many instinctual traits like this until the requirements of living in a new environment forces us to shed them or develop new ones, a process that can take thousands of generations. Among the many group instincts and social capacities carried over from the Stone Age, some have a surprisingly direct relevance to modern-day interracial dating.

Instincts As Group Survival Mechanisms

Survival in a cooperative group context meant evolving specialized mental capacities that make functional sense only when looked at in the context of small groups of a few hundred people, one of which is territoriality. Most types of birds, mammals and primates have some sort of territorial instinct, and human beings are no exception. Having a territorial instinct aids survival in two major ways. It operates to make you defend your territory against outsiders or predators seeking to steal food or reduce the limited supply of food available in your territory. Territoriality pushes you to repel outsiders who might bring in communicable diseases. The territorial instinct thus makes perfect survival sense in the context of tribal hunter-gatherer territories in the Stone Age where our species evolved and in which we spent almost all of our history.

Territoriality can be expressed as either individual or group behavior. When hunter-gatherer territory was under attack by predatory animals or another tribe, simply being physically close to others in an agitated group operated to make individuals lose their individual inhibitions and regress to instinctual group defense behavior that involves thinking and acting as a unit with the other mob-like tribe members. The tribal defense instinct forces us to regress to a primitive state of mind by blotting out rational thoughts. The group becomes an irrational, uninhibited, aggressive, collective entity that engaged in violently agitated behavior to drive invaders or predators away. Apes and our other primate relatives exhibit similar forms of instinctual, aggressive group defense behavior when they perceive their territory, meaning their sources of food and personal security, as being threatened. This sort of instinctual behavior must have been absolutely crucial to our survival long ago for it to have become woven into our genetic code. We act differently when in groups because it was in our survival interest to do so in the environment wherein our species evolved.

Another example of instinctual, irrational group behavior is the sort of mob panic encountered at disasters such as fires and floods. This is the human form of the stampede behavior exhibited by almost every sort of animal in dangerous situations such as forest fires. It is a form of instinctual flight-from-danger behavior combined with a measure of aggression and the herd instinct. We are genetically predisposed to display

198

such behavior when exposed to particular types of stimuli, such as being in a fire, wherein our instinctual programming kicks in, often overriding our rational faculties in the short run. Note that this behavior kicks in most often and most strongly in some sort of group context, further delineating its instinctual group-survival nature, as opposed to rational, individualistic behavior. We thus act in peculiar ways when influenced by groups solely because we were genetically programmed to do so during the millions of years our ancestors lived in the Stone Age.

"The most striking peculiarity presented by a psychological crowd is..... [that the] individuals that compose it, however like or unlike their mode of life, their occupations, their character, or their intelligence, the fact that they have been transformed into a crowd puts them in possession of a sort of collective mind which makes them feel, think and act in a manner quite different from that in which each individual of them would feel, think and act were [she] in a state of isolation."
Gustave Le Bon
The Crowd

Our instincts can sometimes be tricked into expressing themselves by modern-day stimuli that resemble Stone Age stimuli. One modern analogy to tribal defensive behavior is a street gang defending its turf. When the territory defined by a gang as its social territory is perceived to be under attack or invasion, even should the buildings and land within that territory actually be owned by other parties, the gang members become a single collective mob-like entity.

The members shed their individual inhibitions in aggressively repelling invaders. This is quite similar to hunter-gatherer tribal group reactions to territorial invasions by other tribes or dangerous animals. Just being in the presence of a group operates to pressures us to become less individualistic and more conformity-minded, as anyone who has been the subject of peer pressure knows. Being around a group of other people makes us more susceptible to exhibit various sorts of group behavior guided by Stone Age instincts.

Different Types Of Instincts

Birds, insects and other forms of life are born with instinctual capacities for extremely rigid, programmed forms of behavior, such as building a bird's nest. The instincts guiding such inflexible forms of behavior are known as closed instincts, meaning that the instincts are closed off to environmental influences. As we ascend the evolutionary ladder to species with larger, more complex brains, such as human beings, instincts become less rigid and more latitude is allowed to the forms in which the instincts are expressed. Behavior becomes less programmed and more flexible. When the form of expression of an instinct is open to modification by the culture, environment, or individual initiative, it is known as an open instinct, one open to outside influences.

Language is an example of an open instinct. Human beings are born with instincts for language acquisition and speech, but acquire the language of the particular culture they happen to be born into, and not some sort of inborn, instinctual language, such as the songs sung by birds. We have a content-dependent instinct to acquire a language of some sort, but not any particular language. Were this not the case, we would all speak the same inborn, instinctual language. Most human instincts are open instincts, and can be expressed in many different forms, or even extinguished through education and cultural conditioning, as when male aggressive instincts are dampened through education, parental programming or living in an environment which discourages violence through punishment. Language, sexual behavior, aggression and territoriality are open instincts whose forms of expression can vary widely.

The Conformity Instinct

"The virtue in most request is conformity."
Ralph Waldo Emerson
Self-Reliance

Social conformity is an open instinct which modifies our behavior in reaction to the expectations of, and social pressures from, those around us. This instinct probably met certain limited survival needs during the Stone Age. The conformity instinct pushes individuals to do what the group expects them to do, not what rational analysis might tell them is in their individual self-interest. Remember that Stone Age people lived in tribes. Men had to work together in planning and going on a hunt, and women had to work together in foraging for food. Sometimes, as when engaged in hunting dangerous animals, the act of being in a group induced individuals to shed their individual caution and regress to instinctual, primal group mind status, similar to what happens to an individual in a bloodthirsty mob. This aided the group in catching and killing animals, even though particular individuals might die in the process. It most likely taps into the same hidden instinct that drives mob behavior, in the sense that mob members feel invincible as a group and thus disregard considerations of personal safety when in a mob. It is a survival adaptation to the Stone Age environment, the implicit purpose of which is to perpetuate the group or the species, though not necessarily the individual. Conformity thus actually served a survival purpose at one point in our early evolution Without the conformity instinct, it probably would have been quite difficult to get individual tribe members to work towards a common goal.

"Even in what people do for pleasure, conformity is the first thing they think of; they like in crowds; they exercise only among things commonly done; peculiarity of taste, eccentricity of conduct, are equally shunned with crimes."
John Stuart Mill
On Liberty

How Individuals Change In Groups

"An individual in a crowd resembles primitive beings."
Gustave Le Bon
The Crowd

Although an individual might die taking risks in regressing to a de-individualized state of mind when in a tribal defense mob, tribes whose members were instinctually predisposed to take risks that benefited the group were more likely to survive than those with members not so inclined. While some individuals died while engaged in tribal defense and catching meat animals, the genetically-related, inbred tribe members who benefited from the food collected as a result of a tribe member's sacrifice would later reproduce offspring likely to have that trait. Thus, the conformity instinct enhanced tribal group survival and spread throughout

201

the human race. Conformity is a pre-human trait at the opposite end of the intellectual spectrum from rational thinking, which makes use of the more recently-evolved analytical and rational parts of the human mind.

The world is full of people who use various pretexts to lead others into situations where certain types of stimuli, such as simply being physically surrounded by others, are likely to activate instinctual mechanisms that make individuals easier to manipulate. Cults of every shape and variety do this all the time, knowing that when you are surrounded by a group, an almost automatic, contagious sort of disinhibiting, mentally regressive de-individualization of the personality spreads from one person to another. Being pressured by a group to not date interracially is another example.

"For nonconformity the world whips you with its displeasure."
Ralph Waldo Emerson
Self-Reliance

Get a group of people physically close together and emotionally worked up about something, and they become prone to shed their acquired civilized veneer and reveal the instinctual state of mind beneath. This is the cause of the mob behavior encountered when sports fans storm the playing field. Being surrounded by like-minded, agitated mob members encourages the emergence of a form of the mob behavior probably quite similar to the tribal territorial defense response during the Stone Age. It gives us a look backwards into time at how our semi-human ancestors behaved on a regular basis. They would not have developed such a trait unless there was some sort of very real need for it on a regular basis back in the Stone Age.

Instinctual imitation and suggestibility are tied to each other and the group instinct. We are born with an instinctual capacity for imitation, which operates to make learning language and basic motor skills easy early in life. Instinctual suggestibility makes us readily susceptible to being propagandized or led along as part of a group, but suggestibility has no room for rational analysis, leaving us wide open to suggestion by incorrect, fraudulent and improper ideas. We want to satisfy others' expectations, meaning we scale down our individual preferences to meet the lowest common denominator of behavior which satisfies all group members. Instincts such as these come associated with strangely intense emotions as part and parcel of their mental circuitry as a means of ensuring energetic response to the demands of survival. Instincts are thus nothing more or less than survival mechanisms that happened to be useful in the ancient world, pre-human training wheels for survival. Some instincts useful back then are quite counterproductive in the context of modern society.

Chapter Fifteen
Understanding The Opposition
To Interracial Relationships, Part II

"When we have eliminated the impossible, whatever remains, however improbable, must be the truth."
Arthur Conan Doyle
"The Sign Of Four"

Why We Are Susceptible To Anti-Interracial Social Pressures

"I have often wondered how it is that.....so much more respect have we to what our neighbors think of us than to what we shall think of ourselves."
Marcus Aurelius
The Meditations Of Marcus Aurelius

Our genetically-transmitted social instincts predispose us to be psychologically receptive to conform to social pressures exerted by others by means of speech, gestures and facial expressions, to say nothing of the threat of physical force. Fear of disapproval of nonconformity was a useful instinct in the Stone Age, a sort of an instinctual early-warning sign that you needed to change your behavior if you wanted to get along with the others in the tribe. In primitive environments, this made a sort of sense, given that people often died of starvation or exposure before the age of thirty.

There was little perceived need for nonconformists, meaning those too lazy to hunt or gather with the rest of the tribe. In a world where there was literally no change in the external environment for millions of years at a time, conformity to hunting and gathering traditions was the most likely way to survive, at however low a level.

Several archaic Stone Age open social instincts, either individually or in tandem, are at the root of various sorts of modern-day opposition to interracial dating. Remember that open instincts can be modified by both cultures and individuals. As a general rule, the less intelligent, civilized and rational people are, the more likely they are to revert to unmodified instinctual behavior when personal frustrations build, simply because there

204

is nothing else in their minds to modify the gut instincts which served survival purposes in the uncivilized eras, but which are now completely mismatched with the requirements of living in an industrialized society. Certain forms of opposition to interracial behavior are actually forms of expression of particular types of instinctual behavior. If there is no rational way to explain peculiar types of anti-interracial behavior, the operating principle is that some sort of misdirected or inappropriate instinctual behavior is at the bottom of it until proven otherwise. The irrationally powerful emotions often expressed against interracial dating are typical symptoms of instinctual behavior, showing that something other than a rational mind is at work behind the scenes.

Taking On Roles

We are instinctually able to take on different social roles because those roles are simply modern-day versions of roles common in the hunter-gatherer world, roles such as worker, spouse/mate, parent, child and so on. The capacity for taking on large numbers of different roles is etched into our genetic code, because twenty million years of evolution adapted us to become able to take on these roles to better facilitate life in the Stone Age. The general types of roles are constant, only the contexts within which we take them on have changed. These roles are biologically determined and limited by the genetic nature of human beings. We do not have the capacity to take on the roles animals take on within the social contexts of interaction with members of their own species, and they do not have the capacity to take on the roles that only human beings can take on. Only human beings have the mental flexibility and neural circuitry to take on roles evolved for specialized forms of interactions with other human beings.

Biology is destiny only for lower animals incapable of independent, self-directed, rational thought. Human beings who refuse to think for themselves thus give themselves no choice but to be pushed and dragged along through life by instinctual programming, precisely because refusing to think for yourself leaves nothing else to fall back on but pre-human Stone Age instincts.

The Group Identification Instinct

We are born with the need to identify ourselves with one or more groups. The particular group with which we identify is an acquired trait, meaning we learn to identify with a particular race, country, religion and the like. Identifying yourself with a tribe, or other group, is an open instinct, and subject to cultural or individual modification. Since being in a tribe was the key to survival in the Stone Age, it is not surprising we should have evolved this inborn need to identify with some larger group.

We are born with a need for group affiliations. We learn to become individuals, but some people never develop a real sense of differentiated individuality. They instead choose to imitate what they see other members of the group, or groups, with which they identify doing as the easy way out of deciding what is proper and consistent with how they identify themselves. This applies to both thought and action. It is not hard to see the parallels between this and Stone Age tribal conformity, because both draw on the same primitive instinct. People do this for different reasons. A few don't have enough brainpower to make individual decisions, and find it easier to go through life imitating others. Many more such people enjoy the instinctually good feeling they get from conforming, regardless of the rationally measurable ill effects of conformity, such as smoking because everybody else is smoking. This is a variation of the conformity-oriented herd animal instinct.

"Emulation is the very nerve of human society."
William James
Talk To Teachers on Psychology

As civilized societies developed, the definition of group affiliations expanded to include members of one's racial group, ethnic group, or nation, rather than being limited to one's local tribe or clan. We are usually socialized to identify ourselves with large units of social organization, such as a nation, early in life by parents and schools. You remain free to modify how you express your group identification instinct and loyalty to whatever social grouping you wish: a race, a political party, a nation, a special interest group, a social class and so on. For example, you might be born in one country but later decide to become a citizen of another country. You might be born into a particular religion but later convert to another religion. We are free to make choices about which particular groups we affiliate with on the basis of a mixture of rational and emotional considerations.

Still others scale themselves down to the lowest common denominator of group behavior because they were socialized to do so, probably due to not having been exposed to very many other alternatives to conformity. Such people are usually at the bottom of the socio-economic scale, and often have a bitter attitude towards those who have done well by virtue of thinking for themselves. They seek status by means of blind conformity to their social reference group, and become enraged when conformity produces no gain in status.

Nothing gets a conformist more enraged than seeing people who don't blindly obey the customs and traditions common at the bottom of the social scale enjoying themselves. Seeing nonconformists enjoying themselves engenders envy by virtue of providing living proof of the invalidity of the rules conformists live by, but from which their long-held conformist habits make it impossible to extricate themselves. Seeing nonconformists ignore their displeasure gets them even more enraged.

The less people have going for themselves as individuals, the more eager they are to believe that identifying or associating themselves with some sort of larger group or category gives them access to an undefined form of superiority not available to individuals not so well connected. Group identification becomes a substitute for individual merit. Placing themselves into such a category makes them good-by-association, a common form of defective reasoning among the weak-minded. Their wishful thinking might be based on membership in a racial group, nationality, or any dimension other than individual merit or achievement.

To some extent, group identification also gives them a sort of psychological permission to tap into that particular group's territorial feelings, as in the case of Black men who consider Black women as a group to be their exclusive social territory. Low-status White males feel a similar territorial instinct with regard to White women. Catering to social reference group expectations is their substitute for individualism, a bad role that freezes them out of other roles, precisely because conformity is an adolescent role that prevents one from taking on adult roles, no different than a street gang member who thinks he is important solely because of his gang affiliations and nothing else.

"Men, it has been well said, think in herds; it will be seen that they go mad in herds, while they only recover their senses slowly, and one by one."
Charles Mackay
Extraordinary Popular Delusions And The Madness Of Crowds

Not very surprisingly, those big on group identification as their primary means of personal identity tend to be poorly educated and unable, or unwilling, to engage in logical and abstract thinking. The greater the degree to which people classify themselves primarily in terms of group membership, the less adapted they are for life in a complex, industrialized society, where thinking for yourself is the trait in demand, not instinctual conformity. People who work at avoiding the burden of thinking find their capacity for independent thought atrophies, or maybe never develops in the first place, and defining themselves primarily in terms of group membership is a common symptom.

Being human requires thinking for yourself, not looking to others to see what they expect of you or what people like yourself usually do. A Black woman who thinks for herself is on the psychological defensive when surrounded by group-oriented people, because instinctual conformity mechanisms start kicking in when we are physically near other people, and make us susceptible to conformist pressures. They will work endlessly to pressure you to conform to their ideas of what Black women should be like.

Group pressures against interracial relationships are often fueled by thinly-disguised neurotic envy or jealousy. If they don't have it, or can't achieve it, or just plain want to control you, they don't want you to have it either. Defend your personal interests by avoiding situations where you can be pressured in a group context. Being aware that group pressures can influence you to go against your best interests is the first step in avoiding victimization by the many forms of groupthink.

"

Ethnocentrism is.....[where] one's own group is the center of everything, and all others are scaled and rated with reference to it."
William Graham Sumner
Folkways

Should something sound irrational, it probably is irrational, and remains irrational until proven otherwise. The explicit or implicit expectation that you scale down your dating behavior and relationships to suit the expectations of family, friends or total strangers with nothing offered in return is the herd animal instinct in action. Such forms of conformity are not rationally explicable because they are not rational forms of behavior in the first place. Since we do not live in the Stone Age, and no longer go on hunting and gathering expeditions with tribe members, this conformity instinct impedes both social progress and the realization of individual happiness with no compensating benefits. Fortunately, the instinct to conform is an open instinct, and subject to modification by rational thought and analysis, also known as thinking for yourself. Don't let personal decisions be irrationally swayed by group pressures, and don't let yourself do irrational things just because others expect you to follow the dictates of the herd.

Why We Feel Guilty About Not Conforming

You might feel a twinge of shame or guilt when you first go out in public to date interracially. This is common, but has no particular long-term significance once you understand the reason for this reaction. There is less to it than meets the eye. It is simply a reflexive manifestation of the conformity instinct. When we fail to conform to group expectations, or what we imagine others' expectations to be, we feel a sense of shame or guilt because this is part and parcel of the instinct. We are pre-programmed to be sensitive to what others think and the various social pressures they communicate in verbal and nonverbal forms in efforts to get us to conform.

Our susceptibility to conformity pressures probably aided our survival before we became truly human by forcing us to engage in cooperative food-seeking behavior. Part of the fail-safe mechanism for enforcing conformity against individuals who refused to immediately bow to community pressures was an internally-generated sense of shame or guilt

209

about not conforming. Feeling this guilt or shame about your nonconformity gave you an extra push to conform to tribal social pressures. Guilt and shame served the function of enforcing conformity and making group survival more likely in the Stone Age. Since the tribe was probably capable of violence against members who refuse to help hunt or gather food, this aspect of the instinct also had some individual survival value in the sense of alerting you to the possibility of physical danger from others and forcing you to change your behavior to save yourself. Since few of us are in any danger of starvation should we not want to help the tribe spear some saber-tooth tigers for dinner, the conformity instinct comes down to just another carryover from the Stone Age.

Conformity is not always a bad thing, as when we conform to social standards to not to kill our fellow human beings for entertainment. But, if no rational explanation is offered for conforming, it is almost always some sort of double standard in action, meaning something bad for the individual being asked to conform while providing hidden benefits to those others asking for conformity. The benefit might be only some weird sort of psychic satisfaction in bringing more herd animals into the herd. Blindly following tradition is not a rational reason for doing anything, since traditions that serve positive purposes can provide ample and observable justification for their existence. Demand proof of those who want to influence you.

"The danger which threatens human nature is not the excess, but the deficiency, of personal impulses and preferences."
John Stuart Mill
On Liberty

Instincts usually come with some sort of strong positive or negative emotions attached as a means of ensuring compliance. The conformity instinct is a form of Stone Age biological programming designed to perpetuate the human race, often at the expense of the individual's personal interests. While thinking of conformity as having value is a bit alarming in terms of modern thinking about individual freedoms, always keep in mind that this is a pre-human instinct now susceptible to being overridden by rational thought. You can override your instincts with both rational thought as well as positive emotional experiences that reduce the attraction of certain types of instinctual programming. After dating interracially you will associate interracial dating with positive experiences and positive states of mind, and this instinctual sense of shame will fade by virtue of being overwhelmed, and eventually extinguished, by the pleasures associated with rationally chosen behavior. However, the less rational the individual, the more likely they are to let themselves be carried along by the tide of their conformist instincts instead of the rational, human parts of their minds. Rational thinking creates choices, instincts limit them.

"Nothing is so contagious as example."
La Rochefoucauld
Maxims

Stares

Stares are a form of social pressure we are instinctually programmed to notice. It is easy to imagine a tribe of meat hunters ready to go out hunting for the day only to find that some tribe members prefer to sleep late, or even not want to go hunting at all. The others stare at them, possibly with a hint of potential violence lurking behind their stares and accompanying facial expressions. The stares activate the late sleepers' instincts to conform as well as their individual self-preservation instinct to avoid being on the receiving end of aggression, and soon all of the tribe members are on their feet and ready to go hunting. The irrational sense of guilt, shame and nervousness that result from being stared at are so common that it must have some sort of instinctual basis. Even those whose daily routines involve having others look at them, such as actors, never completely lose every vestige of their instinctual nervous response to being stared at. However, by understanding the nature of the instinct and learning to tune out the stares by not looking at those staring at you, stares lose much of their social pressure value.

People stare at interracial couples because mixed-race couples are not something seen as often as same-race couples. Like it or not, we are all fair game for curiosity when we go out in public. Curiosity does not necessarily mean hostility, just a mild state of alertness. But, just why do we feel a need to stare at anything new or different in the first place? As hunter-gatherers, it was to our advantage to have a visual sense that

211

immediately sent a warning notice to our minds, including our flight-from-danger instinct, that something different, possibly a predatory lion or predatory humans, was moving around out there. A sense of curiosity about new and different things was also was useful in the sense that curiosity might lead one to explore for new sources of food. Any sort of visual difference, contrast or level of novelty above a certain threshold level can activate this alert signal. Most people have no particular interest in interracial couples, so their minds slip back to standby status after sending out a low-level curiosity alert signal.

Prolonged, intentional staring is a mild form of aggression, meaning showing one's disapproval and potential readiness for aggression, even if no show of aggression ever actually materializes. Prolonged staring, or gaze behavior, is also a means of asserting one's social status or territorial feelings. The hoped-for result is almost always to engender a feeling of intimidation in those being stared at, but usually without overt violence. Intimidators often feel that they have achieved their aim if they detect signs of nervousness in the interracial couple, allowing them to think they "taught them a lesson," exercising their territorial and aggressive impulses without much legal danger to themselves.

Angry, prolonged staring is what envious, frustrated, low-status, instinctually-driven people do. A group, or small mob, of like-minded people feels strength in their numbers, and are often bolder about expressing anti-interracial behavior than single individual, because simply being in a group operates to regress them to less-inhibited, primitive group-mind status. Normal people do not need to engage in such behavior, because normal people already have some measure of status, such as holding a job, being educated, enjoying their leisure time, and so on, which dampens such feelings regarding status competition. Race is simply a pretext of convenience here for what comes down to a struggle for short-term status by means of putting down others. In the mind of a low-status loser, intimidating others is the only means available for asserting that they are not losers, because being able to control or influence others' behavior is a sort of proof they are not losers. This is intertwined with status competition. Men compete with other men for status, competition meaning they have the leverage to impact their social environment. Status is a means of attracting women, and at the bottom of the social scale, where money, education and good jobs are nowhere to be found,

212

aggression, fraud and street smarts are the only currency available to those men who choose to live by the premises of street corner society. Prolonged staring is part and parcel of this mindset. They feel that being able to intimidate others is proof they have status while also providing some outlet for satisfaction for their aggressive and territorial instincts.

The Instinctual Roots Of Racism

Prolonged hateful staring and related forms of mildly aggressive anti-interracial behavior are manifestations of psychological problems related to status competition, aggression, territoriality, the sex drive and similar instinctual factors. Race is simply a form of easy identification imagery.

Thus, Black racists hate Whites because the sight of any White person is associated with previous bad experiences with Whites, not anything that any particular person has done. White racists hate Blacks because White racists come from the bottom of the social scale where the sight of any Black person is associated with thoughts about propping up their own low social status by attacking those they think belong lower on the social ladder than themselves. If they think that members of some other group are automatically lower on the social scale than themselves, they will feel free to intimidate them at will. Black and White racists thus have more in common than you might think at first glance, both being venomous snakes differing only in details of their psychological snakeskins. Both types look for victims to target. In their minds, the ability to intimidate others is a sign of social status. Losers lead lives dominated by the one-note role of being losers who spend their time trying to prove they are not losers.

"A devil born, on whose nature Nurture can never stick."
William Shakespeare
The Tempest

Those at the bottom of any social scale don't like the feeling they get from being at the bottom of the social scale. They will work overtime to put down other groups as a means of demonstrating to themselves that some other group is beneath them. Race provides visual imagery of physical differences that constitute a supposed basis for discrimination, but which actually reflects only the simplified thought processes of a mob mind. Mob minds are quite illogical, and the perceived association of any one

213

thing with any other one thing can act as a flash point for an explosion of frustration. Extremely frustrated isolated individuals can take on some characteristics of an enraged mob at the sight of sufficiently inflammatory stimuli associated with status competition, territoriality and the like.

"Isolated individuals may acquire at certain moments, and under the influence of certain violent emotions.....the characteristics of a psychological crowd."
Gustave Le Bon
The Crowd

Interracial dating breaks down social and racial territorial barriers in the sense that simplistic, color-coded identification no longer serves as an automatic marker of who is, or is not, in certain slots in the social hierarchy or in certain kinds of exclusive racial territory. Interracial dating dissolves social barriers, and that notion enrages certain types of people who have gotten into the habit of looking down on members of some other readily-identifiable group as carved in stone rather than a product of psychosexual turmoil. They oppose interracial dating because it runs contrary to their overall insecure outlook on life and leaves them with nobody to look down on below themselves. Interracial relationships enrage those who have no source of status or means of dampening their envy besides control of others and anger based on hierarchical racial divisions.

Seeing Black women as the companions of White men destroys the mental foundation of their social universe, precisely because they can't make it go away. The very existence of interracial relationships invalidates both their beliefs and self-opinions grounded on being able to look down on those of other races as inferior or evil. They get enraged because the only thing that gives them status is the supposed importance and validity of their personal opinions, coupled with an occasional resort to violence to put their opinions into action. Interracial relationships say that those involved take no note of their opinions. Non-adults incapable of taking on adult roles often expect the entire world to revolve around their opinions of everything and anything, a common symptom of mental instability.

"There are many who consider [it] as an injury to themselves any conduct which they have a distaste for, and resent it as an outrage to their feelings."
John Stuart Mill
On Liberty

This is not logical, but Stone Age instincts can not be expected to operate logically. Thus, the sight of a Black woman with a White man enrages frustrated people because it is a glaring example of their envy and frustrations come to life. Low-status, frustrated men have minds on the edge. Almost anything that makes them think of what frustrates them, such as lack of money, education or a job with which to attract women, the most common means of measuring male status in our society, enrages their passions to the boiling point. The lower on the scale the individual, the fewer inhibitions they have against their instincts erupting in broad daylight when frustrations build and nothing can relieve them except violence. Race is a secondary factor in the equation, because what is really at issue is psychosexual disorders.

Race is just an easy means of identifying a target or focal point for their frustrations. If some means of dampening instinctual behavior is not available, violence erupts as a means of status competition, and involves letting out aggressive impulses and individual frustrations at the object that engendered their frustrations in the first place.

Chapter Sixteen
Understanding The Opposition
To Interracial Relationships, Part III

"Cannot we escape some of those hideous ancestral intolerances and cruelties?"
William James
Talk To Teachers On Psychology

Lynch Mob Psychology

"A crowd which slowly slaughters a defenseless victim displays a very cowardly ferocity.....very closely related to that of the huntsmen who gather in dozens for the pleasure of taking part in the pursuit and killing of a luckless stag by their hounds."
Gustave Le Bon
The Crowd

It's easy to see the unsettling parallels between a sadistic lynch mob and the sort of uncivilized tribal hunting mob behavior that went on every day during the Stone Age. The primary difference is motivational. Stone Age hunters went hunting to find food. Given that they used very crude hunting instruments, such as stones, sharpened sticks and hunting nets for millions of years of human and pre-human history, it usually took a long time to kill large meat animals such as lions, mammoths and stags. They needed something pleasurable to keep them engaged in that activity.

Hunters experienced a sort of primal, animalistic satisfaction in killing a meat animal through slow mutilation, a strong emotion that made animal-killing aggression more likely to be expressed because feeling good gave them an extra motivational kick to kill their food. Since hunting was crucial to human survival for almost all of our history, it is not surprising that men developed such an instinct. Sadism is an instinctual emotion that operated to reinforce protracted animal-killing behavior and aided human survival making the collection of a food meat more likely. Men who enjoy killing animals are more likely to seek out and catch meat.

216

We rarely need to catch and kill our dinner these days, but this sadistic, carnivorous instinct remains buried within us. Civilized people can override the instinct to kill and feel satisfaction in killing and mutilation because they channel this instinct into alternative forms such as aggressive sports. Frustrated, uneducated people burning with resentments about their lot in life are less likely to be able to, or even to want to, repress their Stone Age instincts. They don't get much satisfaction out of what civilized societies offer low-status people, so they unconsciously look for opportunities to let their instincts explode. They are so low on the social scale as individuals that they can find psychological satisfaction only in group-oriented violence, as in lynch mobs and street gangs. Note that such groups often kill their victims slowly and actually enjoy mutilating them and watching them die, underscoring the instinctual pre-human basis of such sadistic behavior. They shed their individual inhibitions most readily in lynch mobs and revert to a form of instinctually aggressive killing behavior quite similar to what went on every day hundreds of thousands of years ago both in hunting meat animals and in inter-tribal warfare.

Lynch mobs take a bizarre pleasure in slowly mutilating and killing their victims, something probably quite similar to what went through the minds of our Stone Age ancestors in hunting meat animals and slowly killing them with stones and sharpened sticks. Those at the bottom of the social scale are desperate to feel that they are not really at the bottom, and they prove this by treating members of some readily-identifiable group, meaning identifiable on the basis of simple skin color imagery, as the objects of their hunt. Lynchings were most frequent in the Deep South during times of low cotton prices. Whites at the bottom of the economic ladder felt helpless when wages were cut or jobs vanished from beneath them, so they tried to prove to themselves that they were not really completely powerless by imposing their will on another group. Racial differences let them focus their frustrations about their low social status on clearly-identifiable human scapegoat targets, little different than hunters and hounds after a red fox. Their psyches are infested with snakes of the mind.

"We find means to cure folly, but none to reclaim a distorted mind."
La Rochefoucauld
Maxims

Alcohol and drugs produce an artificial simulation of the group mind/tribal mob experience of the type found in hunting groups in killing their prey, producing an irrationally uninhibited, unintelligent, violently emotional state of mind. It is thus no accident that alcohol and drugs are often associated with violent criminal behavior, because they turn off the rational parts of the mind. People who can't cut it as individuals feel important only when narcotized or as a part of a mob, which allows their instincts and frustrations to explode, free from rational and physical constraints. A crowd of drunks has a great deal in common with a pre-human tribal mob of animal hunters, precisely because the rational parts of their minds are turned off. Certain types of people seek out alcohol and drugs precisely because it allows them to turn off the rational parts of their minds and take the restraints off their simmering pre-human instincts.

"When the higher brain functions are in abeyance, as happens in imbecility or dementia..... instincts sometimes show their presence in truly brutish ways."
William James
Talk To Teachers on Psychology

The Various Forms Of Territoriality

Human beings are territorial animals. Our territorial instinct is an open instinct, and is thus open to social conditioning to take on various forms. For example, since few of us now live by hunting and gathering, our territorial instinct no longer takes on the form of defending a geographic hunting territory, but rather forms such as thinking of our country as our territory, as during a war, or of our home as our castle. Whether you identify your tribal hunting territory, your home or your country as your territory, whenever you perceive that territory as being under attack, your territorial instincts awaken and get expressed as some form of aggression against invaders.

Many people do not own homes or have a physically measurable personal territory. In such cases, they are prone to become psychologically insecure due to having no territory to call their own as a means of expressing their territorial instinct. We get such feelings when we have little opportunity to express our instincts in some form or other, whether socially sanctioned or not. The lack of opportunities to express an instinct often leads to frustrations that bubble over into inappropriate areas of life.

Since our territorial instinct is an open instinct subject to cultural or individual modifications of form and means of expression, the territorial instinct can take on the form of social territory instead of geographic territory. That means a social class, race, religion or some other form of perceived group become "your" social "territory," regardless of whether your group of choice is tied to any particular geographic territory. Thus, some people with no other psychological territory to call their own decide their race is their social territory. Both Blacks and Whites do this, and this happens most often with males of the species. Men compete with other men for status, and status is the primary means of attracting women. When men mix the territorial instinct with social concerns, that intertwines territoriality with status competition. Feeling a bond with members of some group also operates to focus aggressive impulses against those outside that group, and focuses even more hostility, verbal or physical, against those perceived to be "invading" the group's supposed "territory."

Social And Racial Territory

Many instincts are unquenchable and seek alternative outlets and opportunities for expression. Aggressive impulses can be diverted to alternative channels of expression, such as one's job, or violent sports such as boxing. Territorial impulses similarly can be diverted into various unconventional channels that make sense only in terms of an open instinct seeking opportunities for expression when driven by individual frustrations.

"Ethnocentrism leads a people to exaggerate and intensify everything .....which differentiates them from others."
William Graham Sumner
Folkways

Certain types of incomprehensible behavior start making a weird sort of sense if you think of race as social territory. First of all, men are visually oriented, thinking in terms of what they see rather than the meaning of what they see. If others look like you, they become your territory, whether those others are interested in being part of your territory or not. This

219

makes no sense in terms of modern society, but does make sense in terms of frustrated hunter-gatherer instincts looking for opportunities for expression in a modern context. This focus on simple imagery is a key characteristic of a frustrated mob, which becomes agitated at the sight of something that evokes memories of, or associations with, unpleasant emotions, such as competition for women, even if the members of the interracial couple happen to be total strangers. Thus, when a Black man harasses a Black woman dating a White man, neither of whom he knows personally, that behavior is motivated in large part by distorted territorial feelings pushed into expression by feelings of frustration, status competition, the sex instinct and territoriality.

Instinctual drives, however misdirected or misguided, usually have a lot of emotional energy from deep within to back them up. Powerful emotions are often found as part and parcel of forcing into expression those instincts related to survival and reproduction. It's not hard to see why insecure, low-status men of any race might think along the lines of considering women of their own race as being their social territory, which also explains why they act with such incomprehensible hostility in defending their supposed "territory. " The more mentally unstable or low-status the individual, the more likely they are to see others as territory, and the more likely they are to revert to some sort of race-oriented, tribalistic behavior. Interracial couples are perceived by neurotics to be interfering with or frustrating the expression of their sex drives by "taking" part of their "territory."

Men are the ones who most often apply social pressures against interracial dating to women of their own race, but they almost never do so against men of their own race. Such men consider women of their own race to be their social territory, but do not extend this concept of social and racial territory to include men of their own race. This is additional proof that this is a specialized form of male-on-male status competition for women, mixed in with racial territoriality. The aim is to narrow the field of men available to women of their own race through manipulation and intimidation. Were their opposition to interracial dating of a purely rational nature, opposition would take the form of complete opposition to interracial dating, meaning the prohibitions would apply against both Black men and Black women. No such thing happens, of course.

Certain types of Black men stake out Black women as their social territory, and actually think Black women as a group are the territory of Black men as a group. Since there are far more Black women than Black men, there is no rational reason for Black men to fight with each other about Black men dating interracially, because when Black men date interracially, that only operates to further reduce competition among the remaining Black men for the pool of Black women. Race is simply a pretext of convenience for trying to get Black women to accept limitations on their search for men with status. The last thing certain types of Black men want is to open the floodgates to a pool of White male competitors several times larger the pool of Black males. A tribe that has traditionally staked out a particular territory as their hunting and socializing territory seeks to exclude other nearby tribes from dropping in to have a look around and poach on "their" territory. White women who become agitated on seeing a White male with a Black woman are expressing the same sort of irrational instinct. They don't want competition.

Why We Distrust People Who Look Different

Xenophobia, the automatic fear and distrust of strangers, is one form of expression of the Stone Age territorial instinct. For millions of years, it made sense to distrust strangers. Since a given territory, or piece of land, could support only a fixed number of humans, or pre-humans, newcomers were usually likely to be bad news, stopping by for the purpose of encroaching on the limited supply of food in your tribal territory, stealing your food outright, and maybe bringing along a communicable disease with them in the bargain. Distrust of strangers made sense back then for reasons readily understandable in the context of the limited food supply available during the Stone Age.

There were very few people in the world back then, maybe one person per square mile, and people did not have the means to travel very far to meet prospective mates. Tribes tended to be inbred. So, everyone in a clan or tribe was probably related to some degree to everybody else, were likely to have some degree of physical similarity making them readily recognizable to each other, and might even have had a distinctive tribal scent. Appearance was a shorthand form of visual identification which said many things about you on sight. Thus, as soon as you saw someone who looked different and unfamiliar, you knew them on sight as a stranger

221

and a potential threat to your food supply. Anyone from outside the tribe thus automatically became targets for aggression.

One modern-day example of this would be an isolated small town where everybody is related to everybody else. They automatically distrust all outsiders, sometimes running them out of town for coming in and disturbing their way of life, meaning some form of conformist groupthink or semi-tribalistic behavior. People tend to distrust strangers due to some form of this instinct, though cultural conditioning can make them focus their distrust on particular types of readily-identifiable strangers, such as those of another race or color.

Given that you identify outsiders as potentially dangerous, you bond with group insiders (however the group might be defined) and the strength of that bond operates to focus aggression against those not sharing that bond, meaning outsiders of whatever sort. Race is a physically observable similarity that can be the basis for a bond among those sharing that physical similarity, and conversely focus aggression against those of other races.

Xenophobia is yet another form of instinctual behavior that made sense in the context of the ancient world and which makes a lot less sense in the present day. In the context of the modern cosmopolitan world, it is hard to understand why people would take an automatic dislike to strangers simply because they are different, but such behavior makes perfect sense in terms of the purpose it served in the environment where most of our evolution transpired. Should people not be socialized early in life to produce contrary culturally programmed behavior, they tend to fall into some version of this instinctual programming by default, such as distrusting people who look different than those they grew up with. Race is simply a targeting mechanism for visual identification of color-coded "enemies," or at least what pre-human Stone Age territorial instincts would have identified as enemies, the human version of waving a red flag at a bull.

"By the mere fact that he forms a part of an organized crowd, a man descends several rungs in the ladder of civilization.....in a crowd, he is a barbarian - that is, a creature acting by instinct."
Gustave Le Bon
The Crowd: A Study Of The Popular Mind

Customs And Traditions

If you look closely at most customs and traditions, the only reason they continue to be practiced is because we imitate others who practice them. Such is the inertia of conformity. Should you be told that traditions are not to be questioned, that usually means there is no rational reason for sticking with them, and only the suggestion of some sort of intimidation keeps it in place. When this happens, there is often some person or group that benefits from forcing others to practice customs and traditions that provide no known benefits. This sounds quite similar to certain types of instinctual programming.

Traditions are the social analogs of biological instincts: you are programmed to follow both until you decide to analyze and question the functions and purposes they are supposed to serve, at which point you might find both to be hollow shells continuing to roll forward only by sheer inertia, and easy to override using your rational faculties. Traditions are hidden forms of social circuitry laid down to serve the needs of social groups, and instincts are hidden forms of biological-psychological circuitry laid down to help the species. Notice that both focus on the needs of the group, not the needs of individuals. Once you lay down new circuitry specifically designed to more efficiently meet your individual needs, you will be better able to override both instincts and traditions as warranted by your rational analysis of the situation. There is no reason to let Stone Age instincts rule your life when rational thought allows you a wider range of opportunities for pleasure and breadth of vision. Both instincts and traditions are training wheels of different sorts, and we all eventually outgrow our training wheels and move beyond the cries of those who demand that we stay with them in the sandbox forever.

The predisposition to carry on traditions is an instinct. We are apparently predisposed to cultural inertia simply because we evolved to fit into a Stone Age world where change was probably quite uncommon and there

223

was probably a tradition or custom for almost every situation. Maintaining irrational customs and traditions makes sense only in terms of genetic programming for life in a slow-changing Stone Age society. An inborn predisposition to follow tradition probably also eased one's entry into the slow-changing social structures of Stone Age tribal societies that changed little for millions of years at a time.

Mating Customs And Traditions

In the ancient world, grown children probably stayed close by both sets of parents to hunt and gather food. During the millions of years before the laws of marriage developed, most people probably mated with distant relatives from elsewhere within a tribe that spread out for many miles around. In addition, keep in mind that the nature of everyday life changed very little for millions of years. Anything untraditional probably faced quite an uphill battle in obtaining social acceptance, including mate selection. Another consideration was, if one did not conform to group expectations, life was probably nasty, brutish and short for those kicked out of a tribe and trying to survive on their own. Conformity to social pressures for mating only with certain types of people approved by one's parents and the tribe increased the likelihood of maintaining the status quo for tribal social status arrangements. This probably involved practices along the lines of maintaining the social status of the senior meat hunters' families by encouraging the offspring of those at the top of the local status hierarchies to intermarry only with others of like social status, thus keeping their social status within a limited group.

Parents like to influence their children's dating and mating choices because that is what tribalistic-minded parents did for millions of years. White and Black parents often prefer to have their offspring date and mate with members of their own race because that meets conformist parents' needs for telling others in their local status hierarchy about such things. While this is how it was in the Stone Age, there is no reason or need for it to be like this in the present day. Interpersonal relationships work best when they meet the self-determined inner needs of the individuals in question, not the externally-determined needs of third parties who think conformity to tradition and social pressures is the answer to every social situation.

Families are small tribes, and ill-socialized tribes simple-mindedly repel those perceived as outsiders, using simple-minded definitions of exclusion, such as physical differences, to define territorial invasion. Race provides an easy means of visual identification of strangers, and the more poorly people have been socialized, the more likely this anti-stranger instinct is to flare up in inappropriate contexts. Tribes of any kind automatically assume the worst about outsiders, because a territorial-minded group instinctually does just that. Always remember that a group mind is a simple-minded thing, not simply a collection of individuals, and treats both individual members of the group, as well as members of other groups, as things of a lesser order of importance than maintenance of the group's sense of lowest-common-denominator conformist solidarity.

People were socially pressured by the tribe as whole to mate with others who looked like themselves, and to avoid outsiders, who were to be distrusted on sight as potential food thieves. There was also the force of observable example they saw about them to push them in that direction, in addition to the lack of opportunity to seek mates from outside their sparsely-settled tribal territory. Individual choice is now an increasingly more important factor in mate selection in industrialized societies where numerous potential mates are available and one's parents and other tribe members can not exert social pressures on those geographically, psychologically and financially independent of their community or social reference group of birth. Becoming civilized has meant increasing latitude for individual choice in preference to family or tribal pressures to conform to traditions and others' expectations.

The stronger the bond among members of any racial group, the more that bond precludes real intimacy with individual members of other racial groups. Blacks and Whites with a strong degree of personal identification with their racial reference group are unlikely candidates for meaningful interracial relationships, because their bonding and intense identification with their own race precludes bonding with members of other races and often involves simmering hostility against other races and other groups. This is a classic example of irrational, instinctual tribalistic-territorial behavior. It has no rational basis precisely because instincts are pre-human forms of biological programming for the long-gone environment in which our species evolved. Thus, when Black or White families, or even strangers on the street, oppose interracial relationships, it is their pre-

225

human Stone Age instincts speaking, not the suppressed human parts of their minds.

Interracial relationships elicit xenophobic hostility from families and other social groups espousing instinctually xenophobic definitions of acceptable behavior for group members, and these instincts lead them to pressure family or social group members to conform to group expectations, as when parents oppose interracial relationships on the part of their offspring. This is no different than a tribe of meat-hunters that does not allow individual hunters to wander off and join other tribes. It does so simply because any group fears a reduction in numbers, and fears a reduction for no reason beyond the instinctual need for a large group to fight for the tribe's territory.

Xenophobia and territoriality are behind families' opposition to interracial relationships. In seeing physically different people with members of their family, the sight of the unknown activates the xenophobic reaction associated with the tribalistic territoriality instinct. Associating with physically different "outsiders" is seen as reducing group control over individual members of the group.

Groups are by their very nature predisposed to think and act in terms such as the control and conformity of the members of the group, especially among the uneducated, who have little beyond instinctual predispositions to draw on. The predisposition to conform to group pressures and expectations is inborn, and operates automatically unless the individual is socialized to do otherwise. The particular objects of xenophobia and territoriality are learned. Some distrust those from other countries, others distrust those of other religions and others distrust those of other races. All of these are manifestations of our Stone Age xenophobia instinct.

Conformist group thinking makes group members close ranks and circle the wagons when anything that might reduce the group's control over individual behavior comes into view, a version of the herd animal instinct. Groups automatically close ranks and react with xenophobic distrust to outsiders perceived to be invading their social or physical territory solely because such tribalistic thinking patterns and territorial defense behavior became embedded in our genetic code over the course of millions of years. The less educated and rational those in families or other groups are, the more likely they are to revert to instinctual xenophobic reactions to interracial relationships by members of "their" family or racial group because these xenophobic, tribalistic-territorial and conformist instincts automatically operate in this manner. Those who can't think rationally always want to control those who think and live independently.

"We call everything instinct which we find in ourselves and for which we cannot trace any rational foundation."
John Stuart Mill
The Subjection Of Women

Using Your Head To Bypass Counterproductive Instincts

Understanding that the bizarre compulsions and inhibitions regarding interracial relationships are simply the tug of Stone Age instinctual programming is the first step towards programming ourselves to meet our own needs rather than catering to the tribalistic expectations of other people and groups. We no more need to obey the tug of the Stone Age instinct for conformity than we need to sleep on cave floors and hunt saber-tooth tigers for dinner.

Practicing rational, independent thinking can become a habit that overrides the conformity instinct. We unplug ourselves from the instinctual tug of group expectations for conformity by actively and habitually practicing internally-generated rational behavior that goes against the grain of instinctual behavior. The more independent our mental lives, the better we can socially evolve beyond the instinct to seek social approval and program ourselves for purposes of our own choosing.

Group expectations and social territoriality are archaic, instinctual forms of Stone Age group social control. We feel the pressure to conform because that predisposition to be sensitive to social pressures to cooperate and conform is built into our biology. Our social and individual neural pathways have yet to fully evolve away from forms and patterns fine-tuned to the needs of our Stone Age evolutionary environment. However, we do have the means to override and modify our instincts.

Our rational faculties provide us with the means of escape from victimization by our instincts. All it requires is thinking for yourself.

227

Thinking is what makes us really human, in the sense of having free will and not being enslaved to instinctual conformity to group expectations. You override your instincts by using your mental muscles. The more you exercise your mental muscles, the bigger they get, the more experienced you get at using them in different situations and the more easily you can beat back, or completely neutralize, counterproductive instinctual responses to the modern world.

The more we rely on undiluted instincts, the less human we are. Instincts do serve certain limited purposes in the present day, but almost always need to be guided by our rational faculties.

This is why we spend our early years becoming socialized to divert and modify our sexual instincts, aggressive instincts and territorial instincts into socially acceptable forms, rather than just let them boil out of us without restraint, as was the case for our remote ancestors. Our history of becoming civilized human beings is the history of development of individual thought and individual choice in the context of organized societies, meaning using our rational faculties to create choices unavailable to purely instinctual individuals.

We become individuals only by shaking off the dehumanizing influence of the full moon of conformity. Thus, when you have a bad feeling about the prospect of dating interracially, what you really feel are the vestiges of your inborn Stone Age instinct to conform to the group expectations of your particular social tribe, one version of the herd animal instinct. Let the daylight of reason shine on the instinctual urges you feel, and you'll find less to them than meets the eye. You no more need to obey the tug of instinctual conformity than you need to wear bearskins, make stone axes, hunt saber-tooth tigers or sport the other trademarks of the Stone Age. Turning off your mind is the road to ruin.

How To Change

"How many persons are bold enough to run counter to the fashion?"
Gustave Le Bon
The Crowd

Unplug yourself from the instinctual tug of group expectations for conformity by actively practicing independent behavior that goes against the grain of instinctual behavior. You override your genetically-programmed predispositions simply by getting into the habit of overriding them. After going your own way for a while, the instinctual urge to conform just fades away, an appropriate fate for a pre-human Stone Age instinct. You don't have to obey your instincts just because you were born with them. Your life will improve when you move beyond the instinctual need for group approval. You'll stop defining yourself in terms of living up to other's expectations and start living up to your own. There's no reason to live up to others' expectations, such as your mother expecting you to marry a Black man, unless you have decided that doing so meets your personal definition of your needs. There's nothing special or worthwhile about other people's expectations that cannot bear rational examination and scrutiny. Expectations can be insidious things, but that happens only when you overvalue them in the first place. Should others' expectations have any value whatsoever, get them into the open for close-up scrutiny.

Education And Independent Thought

"Children are taught to fear and obey; the avarice, pride or timidity of parents teaches children economy, arrogance or submission. They are also encouraged to be imitators, a course to which they are already too much inclined. No one thinks of making them original, courageous, independent."
Vauvenargues
Reflections And Maxims

Anti-interracial behavior is instinctual behavior with little or no basis in rationality, but a strong basis in instinctual territorial and aggressive behavior. The other side of the coin is that, because interracial dating goes against the grain of a long list of instinctual practices, the more educated you are and the more you think for yourself, the more likely you are to become interracially involved when the right person comes along, precisely because you are less likely to be held back by the instinct to look to others for permission to get on with your life. People who think for themselves don't let Stone Age tribalism interfere with their lives. For that matter, all human progress is the history of moving beyond instinctual programming.

229

It should come as no surprise that as a Black woman's level of education increases, the greater her likelihood of becoming interracially involved when the right sort of guy comes along. The more intensively you use your mind on a day-by-day basis, the more practice you get at overriding group conformity expectations and family social programming, precisely because your daily routine involves flexing your mental muscles. Education also enhances your likelihood of being around other Black women who are themselves likely to date interracially. This increases the chances of positive psychological reinforcement for interracial activities, showing that group psychology is not always a bad thing if directed in rationally chosen channels. Of course, education also increases the statistical probability of you crossing paths with potentially compatible White males both in school and in jobs where educated White males congregate.

Be aware, however, that being educated does not automatically translate into one becoming a rational individual. We all know highly educated people without a functioning brain cell in their heads. Here and there you also find people with little formal education whose thought processes are head and shoulders above those with a great deal of formal education. The key difference is whether or not someone actually uses their mind. Anyone can think for themselves if they work at it, regardless of their level of formal education, but education generally operates to make it more likely by virtue of giving individuals more raw materials to work with in moving beyond instinctual behavior. An educated person who does not engage in rational conduct has simply gone through the motions.

"Ignorance is not lack of intelligence, nor knowledge proof of genius."
Vauvenargues
Reflections And Maxims

Individual And Social Rewards

Being human means having an active internal mental life. As you become more internally oriented, the external-behavior orientation of group expectations fades. This not only means the expectations of your current social group affiliations, but also the legacy of your past group affiliations, such as families, relatives and schooling. There is nothing sacred about what you were taught by others in the past except that it has acquired an inertia of its own by virtue of having been lodged in the back of your mind for many years, like a long-dead fossil embedded in sedimentary deposits.

Interracial dating is no place for conformists unable to tune out social pressures to conform. It requires shedding the instinct to meet conformist role expectations that get in the way without providing compensating benefits. It requires adopting an internally-generated framework for dealing with life and having an internal mental life. You should never feel that you need a group's permission to become interracially involved. It simply does not concern them in any way. Don't let other people or groups program you to serve their purposes. You have better things to do with your life than live up to other people's expectations for your private life or even be bothered listening to them. Such people are part of the problem, not the solution.

One common form of this group mentality is the notion that you "owe" Black men your time simply because they are Black and you are Black. What it really means is that those telling you "owe" Black men your time want you to turn off your rational mind and do what others expect you to do instead of what is best for you. If a particular Black man is worth your time as an individual, that is okay. But if he does not meet your needs as an individual, and says you have no choice in the matter, meaning he demands that you associate with him for no other reason than him being Black, that is a bad idea from start to finish. Note that the emphasis in such simplistic reasoning is not on your individual needs or what the other individual offers you, but rather on your mutual racial group membership being presented as the basis for a demand for automatic conformity and limitation of your freedom of association with nothing offered in return. People who offer little as individuals fall back on group membership as their pretext of convenience for manipulation. In other words, group membership is the only thing that counts, and your individual preferences, tastes and distinctions mean nothing to them. Catering to others' expectation that you conform will leave your life a hollow shell with nothing to show for catering to them. You have an unlimited right to pick and choose who you associate with using your own standards of reference. Turning off the rational part of your mind when someone tells you to turn on your herd animal instinct is the road to ruin. Your personal tastes in men always take precedence over the expectations of others. Don't let conformists impose on you.

231

"The group force is.....employed to enforce the obligations of devotion to group interests. It follows that judgments are precluded and criticism is silenced."
William Graham Sumner
Folkways

New Types Of Group Identification

After tuning out the conformity instinct and sealing yourself off from counterproductive people and influences that divert your energies away from personal fulfillment, what do you do? Interracial relationships do not require isolating yourself from society as a whole, just pushing disruptive influences off to the side. Maybe you feel the need to be part of some sort of larger group or society. We enjoy the society of our fellow creatures. This is to be expected, since the social instinct comes with being human. What do you do?

Should you feel a need for some sort of group affiliation and social support for your supposed nonconformity, channel your open instinct for group affiliation towards the interracial community. Interracial relationships, marriage and children have become common enough that a variety of organizations, lobbying groups, support groups and the like have emerged, and will probably continue to pop up as archaic cultural barriers and traditions continue to fall by the wayside. Instead of feeling like an outsider, affiliating yourself with others in similar life situations can plug you into an inclusionary community feeling. Self-help and support groups make use of the group instinct in a positive way to reinforce positive behavioral patterns by associating them with the emotional energies of instinctual drives. A sense of being in a community of like-minded people is not bad in and of itself, but rather becomes bad only when the demands and expectations of the group become a substitute for using your head. There is no reason to break all ties with your race of birth, either. Just pick and choose who you associate with. Program yourself for your own purposes and needs, not what others say they should be.

"We think very few people sensible except those who are of our opinion."
La Rochefoucauld
Maxims

Chapter Seventeen
Racism On The Street

"Distrust all in whom the impulse to punish is powerful."
Friedrich Nietzsche
Thus Spake Zarathustra

Harassment On The Street

"The vulgarity of many a nature spurts up suddenly like dirty water."
Friedrich Nietzsche
Beyond Good And Evil

While there are an endless number of ways that racist Black men, and the somewhat smaller numbers of racist Black women, are capable of expressing their opposition to seeing a White man involved with a Black woman, several common manifestations of Black racism soon become all too familiar to White men and Black women who are interracially involved.

Walk-By racism occurs when Black men, usually in a group, walk by a White man involved with a Black woman and deliberately make loud public outbursts consisting of a mixture of sexual and racial sneers. This is most common among gangs of Black men, less common with individuals. This treatment is rarely directed at Black men involved with White women.

Eyes-Only Racism occurs where one or more Blacks maintain a fixed direct stare at a Black woman seen to be involved with a White man. This staring usually involves rigidly hostile facial expressions directed at White male-Black female couples. This treatment is rarely directed at Black men involved with White women.

Stand-Up racism occurs when Black couples, individuals, groups or gangs spot a White man with a Black woman in a situation such as a restaurant, look at each other, say nothing, deliberately stand up and all walk out at the same time on the interracial couple. This treatment is rarely directed at Black men involved with White women.

Expectoration racism occurs when a Black man sees a Black woman with a White male within fifty feet of him and responds with a long, drawn-out clearing of the throat followed by him deliberately spitting the contents of his mouth onto the ground in the direction of the interracial couple. This treatment is rarely directed at Black men involved with White women.

Eye-Rolling Racism involves Black men deliberately rolling their eyeballs in the juvenile manner of high school dropout cut-ups when they see a Black woman with a White man. This treatment is rarely directed at Black men involved with White women.

Laughing-Hyena racism consists of Black racists deliberately laughing in an unusually loud, artificial and prolonged manner upon seeing a Black woman with a White man. This treatment is rarely directed at Black men involved with White women.

Ears-Only racism is when a Black racist feels compelled by the sight of a Black woman dating a White man to ask one of the member so the couple to step away from the other so that the Black male in question can deliberately whisper an insult or threat in their ear. This treatment is rarely directed at Black men involved with White women.

Tribalistic racism is the most common form of Black racism. Upon seeing a Black woman involved with a White man, the response is to deliberately tell her to stick with Black men, stay away from White men and other examples of instinctually tribalistic beliefs to the effect that Black women as a group "should" date and mate only with other Blacks for no reason beyond the Black men being of the subjective opinion that such is the way that Black men "expect" Black women to behave. They show no regard for any individual Black woman's opinions and preferences as to how she prefers to conduct her life. This treatment is rarely directed at Black men involved with White women.

Violent racism occurs when Black racists, usually males, use any form of physical violence in an attempt to disrupt a relationship between a White man and a Black woman. Their behavior is a form of criminal activity known as a hate crime that you are free to talk about with anybody at any time, including prosecutors. This treatment is rarely directed at Black men involved with White women.

White men who date Black women are automatically seen as trespassing on the Black man's social "territory," meaning whatever the gang consensus of the moment defines as being their "territory." Black racists define Black women as their tribal property and behave as if that bizarre notion were true. This is why Black male racists feel free to walk up to Black women they see dating White men and tell them that they can't stand to see a Black woman with a White man. Black women, of course, do not see themselves as being the tribal property of Black men in general.

Identification With The Aggressor

"There are the terrible ones who carry about in themselves the beast of prey."
Friedrich Nietzsche
Thus Spake Zarathustra

Identification with the aggressor is a psychological activity somebody, male or female, choosing to mentally put themselves in the place of someone who engages in unprovoked aggression against one or more other people.

As regards interracial relationships between White men and Black women, the vast majority of aggressors who express opposition to such relationships inevitably turn out to be Black men. The reason is that Black men are typically unable to identify, or mentally put themselves in the place of, the White man involved with a Black woman. They see the existence of that interracial relationship as an invasion of "their" personal social territory, meaning territory which the tribalistic-minded Black male racist aggressors define as any Black woman they feel like regarding as being included in their social territory. Such aggressors may express their aggression verbally, use gestures and body language, and, on rare occasions, will make their aggression known in a physically violent manner. Those who identify with the aggressors typically stay on the sidelines and cheer them on, but as time goes on may see fit to become personally and physically involved in perpetrating Black racism, especially if they think that they can get away with avoiding getting caught and being punished.

235

"Tyrant-longings disguise themselves."
Friedrich Nietzsche
Thus Spake Zarathustra

When a Black woman who opposes interracial relationships sees some other Black woman with a White man, she is psychologically unable to identify with the Black woman in that interracial relationship precisely because she sees that other Black woman involved in an interracial relationship that she would not choose to get into herself. The usual procedure in such cases is to make her displeasure known to the "offending" Black woman, usually using facial expression, gestures, body language and directed speech.

Another common form of Black racism is for Black women who oppose interracial relationships to attempt to get the Black woman seen in an interracial relationship away from the White man she is involved with and tell her, with no witnesses present, that she is disloyal to her race, that she needs to do her part to keep the race pure, that associating with Whites is contrary to the interests of the Black race and other forms of blatant racism rooted in tribalistic instincts.

"One must renounce the bad taste of wishing to agree with many people."
Friedrich Nietzsche
Beyond Good And Evil

Black women who promulgate racism do so because they sympathize with the sort of racist Black men who try to disrupt such relationships, support their behavior and identify with the Black men's attempts to disrupt interracial relationships for purely racist reasons. They have no sympathy for, or identification with, either the White man or the Black woman in an interracial relationship who have chosen to engage in behavior that is disapproved of by Black racists.

They disapprove of interracial behavior because disapproval is the group consensus among those she does identify with, meaning Black racists who want to keep the races separated in ways that benefit Black racists and those who identify with Black racists. Black women who oppose interracial relationships thus identify with the aggressor, and the aggressor is usually, but not always, the sort of Black male racist who confronts Black women seen to be involved with White men.

"Creeds are believed, not because they are rational, but because they are repeated."
Oscar Wilde
The Critic As Artist

Now and then you will encounter a White racist. If you ever meet such a person, you will immediately get the feeling that there is something wrong with them in the psychological and sexual senses of the word. They often act like, and may actually be, hysterical old maids of both sexes. Most White racists who feel compelled to express public opposition to relationships between White men and Black women do so due to pent-up neurotic sexual jealousy. What they are worked up about is that they do not like to see others enjoying themselves in ways that they themselves are not eligible to engage in. If they can't have it, they don't want you to have it either. People who, for one reason or another, do not enjoy their own lives try to psychologically compensate by trying to control or disrupt the lives of others for completely bogus reasons, because they do not like to see others having more than they do themselves.

"Many of them have suffered too much so they want to make others suffer."
Friedrich Nietzsche
Thus Spake Zarathustra

They infer that a White male involved with a Black woman has an enjoyable sex life, they do not like to see that happen, so they attempt to disrupt such relationships because it reminds them of what they do not have themselves, like a street beggar who does not like looking at someone who displays visible signs of affluence. They cannot identify with the White male in an interracial relationship, and the reason that they cannot do so is that they cannot identify with anyone who seems to be enjoying themselves, so they do what they can to disrupt that person's enjoyment of life, however momentarily.

"I live above them. Therefore they take a dislike to me."
Friedrich Nietzsche
Thus Spake Zarathustra

Oddly enough, White racists will sometimes identify with Black aggressors, because they are sexually jealous people who become psychologically disturbed by the sight of interracial couples enjoying themselves, and thus will identify with, and express support for, anyone, including a Black racist, who attempts to disrupt interracial relationships that disrupt their uneasy psychological repose.

"Whoever is dissatisfied with himself is always ready to revenge himself therefore; we others will be his victims."
Friedrich Nietzsche
The Gay Science

Psychological Identification

"Science [is] the slaying of a beautiful hypothesis by an ugly fact."
Thomas Henry Huxley
Collected Essays

Some people refuse to accept that others can freely engage in interracial relationships as they wish. The underlying problem is that, in the depths of their subconscious minds, they cannot psychologically identify with the member of the same sex as themselves who is in that relationship. Lack of identification here means that they are unable to identify with one of the people in the relationship, in the sense of being unable to mentally put themselves in that person's place, due to real or perceived social, psychological or physical differences, race being the dimension of difference in this case.

In the case of a Black father who might see his daughter dating a White man, the father is unable to identify, or mentally put himself in the place of, the White man involved with his daughter. The lack of physical similarities leads to his uneasiness with the existence of the relationship. In this case, the lack of physical similarities leads to the lack of vicarious identification, but the absence of almost any characteristic can produce

238

lack of identification – racial differences, psychological differences, social class differences, financial differences, educational differences, and so on.

Lack of identification can erupt on the street. Anybody who has been in an interracial relationship of any kind will eventually encounter hostile stares, whispers, outright public verbal opposition, and, on rare occasions, physical hostility. When an interracial couple hears someone behind them say, quite matter-of-factly, and at a volume deliberately intended to be heard by the interracial couple, that they don't think people of different races should be together, that sort of sentiment originates in the speaker's inability to mentally put himself or herself in the place of one of the people in that interracial relationship. The reason they talk like that is that, because they would not personally consider getting into an interracial relationship, it follows that they do not believe that anybody else should do so either.

This is simply a spur-of-the moment subjective opinion that those involved in interracial relationships are free to ignore, or interrupt, as they wish. You do not give up your right to interrupt and drown out the public pronouncements of others when you engage in interracial relationships.

Black men almost never publicly criticize other Black men for dating White women. The primary reason for this is that Black men are quite capable of identifying with, meaning vicariously putting themselves in the place of, some other Black man who is seen to be involved with a White woman, because this is something that a sizeable proportion of Black men either have engaged in, are currently engaged in or are seeking to become engaged in at some point in the future.

It is true that on rare occasions some Black men will privately criticize other Black men for being involved with White women, but it is unbelievably rare for such criticism to take the form of a public confrontation. Black men as a group have always felt quite free, however, to publicly confront and criticize any Black woman they see with a White man, because Black men as a group have long been of the opinion that Black women as a group are the Black man's private standby equipment, off-limits to all but Black men. Their behavior says it all.

When Black men see a Black woman with a White man, they are unable to psychologically identify with the White man, meaning that they are unable to mentally put themselves in the place of the man in the relationship. Psychologically speaking, it is as if the proprietor of a small town store suddenly found one of the relatives of one of his long-term captive audience customers suddenly patronizing, and socializing with, the manager of the new store in town. He doesn't like competition one bit, because there is nothing that he can possibly gain from change, especially if he is unused to competition and does not feel like doing the dirty work of actually competing.

"In thy presence they feel themselves small, and their baseness gleameth and gloweth against thee."
Friedrich Nietzsche
Thus Spake Zarathustra

There is little that he can do, however, but rant, rave and propagandize against anyone in his captive-audience town patronizing the new store in town, regardless of whether not doing so meets their self-determined needs better than does his own store. He does not like the fact that the manager of the new store in town can do exactly as the proprietor of the older store does.

Competition between men for women is a permanent fact of life, and those who can't take the heat should get out of the kitchen. Telling lies is a form of competition, because it is an attempt to disrupt the competitive abilities of the competition by trying to pull the rug out from under them. Lies only work, however, when somebody believes them. When nobody believes their lies, the liars can only pick up their marbles and go home empty-handed.

"The free spirit is the enemy of fetters."
Friedrich Nietzsche
Thus Spake Zarathustra

Street Confrontations

"The less men reason the more wicked they are."
Paul Henri Thiry D'Holbach
Good Sense

Don't waste your time attempting to talk rationally about interracial relationships with anybody, Black or White, who appears hot under the collar about such matters. If somebody you don't know is yelling, looks like his eyes are going to pop out, is clenching his fists, and sees fit to tell you what he thinks of a White man dating a Black woman (such people are usually male) try to exit the scene. Your chance of coming out on top in such confrontations is about the same as your chances of winning an argument with a hurricane. Do what you can to get away while being as resistant and uncooperative as possible.

When someone becomes agitated by the sight of an interracial couple, what is really going on is that the irrational, instinctual part of the mind is drowning out the rational parts of the mind. For whatever reason, that person's instincts are kicking into high gear, and you cannot tell what such people might become capable of, such as taking a swing at you for no reason beyond the fact that a White man is in close proximity to a Black woman.

"All things being equal, the simplest solution tends to be the best one."
William Of Ockham
Occam's Razor

When people are caught in the grip of their instincts, they do things that they routinely deny later on. For example, when there is a fire in a building, people will trample others to get out of the building while held in the mental grip of their flight-from-danger instinct, and later on will deny that they did anything reprehensible, not that their lack of professed recollection should inhibit you in the slightest from prosecuting them.

Black women are told in many ways and on many occasions, starting early in life, to back off from all thoughts of involvement with White men. Contrast this with the pleasant and obliging treatment, overt and tacit, that the Black community offers to Black men who date and marry White

241

women – a perfect example of an irrationally racist double standard involving making endless excuses for Black men who cross the color line while explicitly or implicitly condoning confrontations against Black women who engage in the same behavior. When Black racists rattle their chains in public, their fellow travelers never seem to want to acknowledge that someone is rattling their chains in public, but that does not oblige you to defer to them or agree with them.

Competition Between Men

"Society admits no right, either legal or moral, in the disappointed competitors."
John Stuart Mill
On Liberty

Men compete with other men for women. The man who was physically strongest or toughest may have been the one the woman went with back in ancient times, but in the modern world, that is not the case. Men compete these days in largely nonphysical ways. Men work in offices completing reports and work in factories adjusting machines to improve production efficiency, with very little muscle power involved in either case.

Modern competition between men these days is largely mental rather than physical, except in atypical situations such as barroom brawls and back-alley fistfights. Most importantly of all, competitions between men for women are decided within the minds of women, and not in the physical-world sense of a victor emerging from the competition of armies on the battlefield.

"The means utilized by an exploiting class are the lifeless tools of cold-blooded policy, shaped by cunning."
Edward Alsworth Ross
Social Control

Women decide which men they want to spend time with partially based on their evaluation of a man's social status, which usually comes down to whether or not he gets regular paychecks. Employment status determines how well a man will be compensated financially, and compensation in the form of money is our society's primary measurement of a man's social status. While it is true that a small number of men are highly regarded by nonfinancial criteria such as artistic ability, most of the time it is the case that most single women are looking for single men who will bring the bacon home.

Not too many Black women want to be the sole breadwinner, either while dating or after tying the knot. Men who disagree with this are free to disagree, and women are free to disagree by walking away from men with whom they disagree. Women are thus the final arbiters of a man's desirability with respect to themselves, just as men are the final arbiters of a woman's desirability with respect to themselves. Women, of course, compete fanatically with other women for male attention, and can be just as competitive as men, though female-on-female competition takes on very different forms than male-on-male competition. Women do not delude themselves about what men want, but men often delude themselves about what they think women should be looking for in men.

White men are free to outclass any number of other men in terms of your social status, and status competition is a means of competition between men for women. That specifically means that you can toot your own horn as much as you want when talking with a Black woman about their education, income, social class, personality and other aspects of their behavior and lifestyle.

" 'I dislike him.'
- Why? -
'I am not a match for him.'
Did anyone ever answer so?
Friedrich Nietzsche
Beyond Good And Evil

Not All Black Racists Are Actually Racists

Some supposed Black racists are not really racists in the dyed-in-the-wool sense of the word of being racists who really believe in bogus racial theories. Their public acts of supposed racism are actually things they do in certain situations in an attempt to structure their personal social universes to provide themselves with social benefits, which usually involves persuading Black women of their acquaintance to avoid socializing with Whites.

"The Negro overseer is always more tyrannical than the White one."
Harriet Beecher Stowe
Uncle Tom's Cabin

If they can lie and thereby persuade Black women to ignore White men as social possibilities, that reduces the amount of competition that Black men, including themselves, have to face when competing for the attentions of Black women. Lies about interracial relationships to the effect that White men are not "supposed" to get involved with Black women are lies told for the purpose of attempting to control thoughts and behavior in a manner that benefit Black racists by steering White men and Black women away from each other.

"A lie is wrong, because its effect is to mislead..... [and] is evidence of that want of power to compass our ends by straightforward means."
John Stuart Mill
Bentham

The supposed racism that such Black men espouse is simply a garden-variety form of fraud routinely used by con men who want to manipulate others into providing them with favors. The precondition for perpetrating such fraud is to persuade their targets to stop thinking critically. When potential victims think critically and push back, frauds have nowhere to go and exit empty-handed. Their bogus rationalizations for double standards for Black men and Black women are simply run-of-the-mill lies of the sort routinely churned out by frauds unaccustomed to being challenged or laughed at.

Such frauds are in the position of the proprietor of a small, dusty, out-of-the-way general store with a limited selection of merchandise whose sole competitors are similar proprietors. The customers have no place to go if they do not like the merchandise being offered. Suddenly, one day they find that a new shopping mall filled with different sorts of stores offering different selections of merchandise has moved into "their" backyard territory.

"When war is declared truth is the first victim."
Baron Arthur Ponsonby
Falsehood in Wartime

Naturally, they immediately begin to propagandize their long-time captive-audience customers to stay on "their own" side of the street because they do not want anyone finding out whether the grass is indeed greener on the other side of the color line. The last thing they want is for Black women to shop around and compare. Truth, critical analysis and the best interests of other people go out the window when someone perceives their personal interests to be at stake.

"Hypocrisy is, in fact, the thing we must expect whenever men are ranked and organized for moral guidance and get honor or pay out of it."
Edward Alsworth Ross
Social Control

Chapter Eighteen
Motivating Yourself

"If you have built castles in the air, your work need not be lost; that is where they should be. Now put the foundations under them."
Henry David Thoreau
Walden

Getting Beyond Laziness And Inertia

"The mind attaches itself from indolence and from constancy to whatever is easy and agreeable to it."
La Rochefoucauld
Maxims

You develop good and bad habits alike by practicing them. Laziness is a bad habit we have all battled with, and one which will impede your efforts to date interracially. Interracial dating happens when you make it happen, rather than when you wait for it to "just happen" without effort on your part. Laziness makes interracial dating less likely to happen of its own accord because too many countervailing social pressures are going on that work against it. The more motivated you are, the more likely you are to proactively engage in activities that make interracial relationships happen. You have to make it happen. Nobody else will do it for you.

Laziness and inertia have three common causes. First is a desire for inactivity due to everyday wear and tear on your mind and body. In this case, you are just plain worn out, and what looks like laziness is actually a good thing. Should your job require you to wake up early, take an early-morning train to get to work downtown, put up with an obnoxious supervisor, work overtime and come home to a microwaved late-night dinner, anybody would be tired keeping up a routine like that. It's hard to rewire yourself for interracial dating when your circuits are already melted down to slag after a long day's work. What looks like laziness here is actually an automatic psychological shutdown mechanism that prevents further erosion of your psyche. We evolved in a Stone Age environment where the norm was a few hours of activity per day, things such as hunting animals, gathering food, eating food and social activities. In prehistoric societies, leisure time periods of twelve or more hours a day were enforced by the rising and setting of the sun. You had no choice about prolonged recuperative inactivity back then. Our minds and bodies are not really well-adapted to the prolonged demands on our time and mental energies that our present workday environments make on us.

"Give thyself time to learn something new and good, and cease to be whirled around."
Marcus Aurelius
The Meditations Of Marcus Aurelius

Feeling burnt out is due in large part to overloading yourself with excessive physical and mental activities. Should you already be bogged down with responsibilities, don't take on something new and expect to get it right. Wait until the weekend. Jumping into something new when burnt out will leave you even more overwhelmed and frustrated than before. Don't try to develop new habits when burnt out or under major stress, or all you will be able to think about is your stress symptoms, not whatever you want to start doing. Failing to budget in chunks of time for relaxation predestines your efforts to failure, and interracial dating issues will be relegated to the mental sidelines. Be sure to budget free time or quiet time for developing new habits and trying out new things. Even machines are scheduled for down time for maintenance and repairs, and most people have lower stress tolerances than the machines they use at home and work every day.

The second most common cause of laziness and inertia is the lack of a sufficiently enticing carrot with which to lead yourself on. The prospect of a real romance can get you going and keep you plugging along. Should you have had few positive experiences with men, you probably have little idea of what a real relationship is all about, and thus feel little incentive to push onwards. You need something enticing to lure you onwards and get you off your rear. Slowly developing a mental picture of a positive interracial relationship is one possible source of motivational attraction you can use to lead yourself on.

"Some unusual stimulus fills them with emotional excitement, or some unusual idea of necessity induces them to make an extra effort of will."
William James
Essays On Faith And Morals

You can best motivate yourself to develop a high level of interest in interracial dating by vividly imagining something exciting about it, such as such as fantasies about the prospect of romance or at least the idea of a positive relationship. Anticipating good things to come reinforces your focus on your goal. Wanting it makes you lead yourself on, drawn by the prospect of positive experiences to come. Enticing yourself into developing subconscious enthusiasm about the idea of interracial dating increases your level of motivation to pursue what you are enthused about. When you want something to happen, you work to make it happen. Linking the idea of an interracial relationship with a primal drive such as your sexual instinct increases your energy level for pursuit of that goal by enabling you to tap into the hidden motivational energies associated with instincts.

The third most common cause of laziness and inertia is having a moderately comfortable lifestyle that induces you to just sit on whatever little you've already got and stop pressing onwards. Maybe you meet a guy every few weeks for regular installments of a no-commitment relationship. Maybe you come home every night, sit in a big comfortable chair, watch television and lose yourself in your favorite programs and your many comfortable fantasies. Fantasies, whether internally-generated or garnered from television, can make you feel just happy enough to not want to reach out elsewhere for something better.

You may have invested your psychological energies in a routine that brings you small, but guaranteed, measures of comfort such that you do not want to take a chance on disrupting it for something new and different that is not guaranteed to pay off, and which might hurt your feelings in the process. Holding on to the penny you have today sounds safer than working to get a dollar tomorrow. The problem is that avoiding unhappiness is not the same as being happy. Again, having a romantic goal of some sort in mind is the best way to lure yourself away from your favorite prime time soap operas to seek out the real thing.

248

"Many people lose a great deal of time by laziness; they loll and yawn in a great chair, tell themselves that they have not time to begin anything then."
Philip Stanhope, Earl of Chesterfield
Letters To His Son

Even should your habits of laziness be embedded in granite, given a large enough psychological sledgehammer, you can chisel your way through almost anything. Chip your way through your habits of laziness, piece by piece, not all at once. First, let the general idea of interracial dating sink into your mind and spread out to associate with other things in your mind. Second, slowly get into the habit of taking small actions that involve seeking out interracial dating, a little bit at a time. Don't try to go from zero to cruising speed overnight, since that is probably too ambitious a target for you to hit during your favorite show's commercial break. What sort of things should you do? Any little thing that does not involve sitting in front of a television every night. At first, do only little things that minimize the discomfort inherent in making a total break with the past. Maybe hang around a local coffee shop one night per week at first, then two nights per week the following week. Read a newspaper with personal ads while on the bus or train home. Start writing a personal ad after your favorite television show is over. While some few people can shed their habits of laziness cold turkey, most need to gradually draw away from their old habits while slowly acquiring new ones that offer the prospect of more stimulation or excitement than the old habits.

"New habits can be launched....on the condition of there being new stimuli and new excitements."
William James
Talk To Teachers On Psychology

Window Shopping And The Checkout Counter

Some Black women get into the rut of organizing their lives around not being involved with anyone. There's a related rut into which you can fall: "getting ready" for an interracial relationship. If you're not careful to kick yourself into action, "getting ready" can become a way of life in itself, a substitute for taking the small, but real, steps necessary to get into an interracial relationship. You continually put off taking action until some

249

undefined point in the future when you will be "ready" to stop "getting ready" and get on with it. Many such people become permanently frozen at the "getting ready" stage and never move any further, like professional students who hang around colleges taking "just a few more courses." Sooner or later, you have to bridge the gap from thinking about it to getting on with it.

When you go into a store, you do not expect to find exactly what you want the instant you walk in. You look around, ask questions and try on some clothing. You might need to visit other shopping centers and stores elsewhere to find what you want. You will never find what you really want by window shopping and thinking it over by yourself. Finding a compatible White guy in the interracial relationships marketplace is no different.

Talking with White guys is the real dividing line between interracial window shopping and the interracial checkout counter. Not talking with guys means no relationships develop. Regardless of whether you cross paths with them in a laundromat, at work, in a store, in a museum, in church, through a personal ad, on the street or through a friend, at some point you absolutely must to talk with them or nothing will ever develop. Even should you meet a guy through a matchmaker, you still have to talk with him, if only to say "I do" at the altar. Talking means getting your hands dirty, and putting up with more than a few guys who are not right for you. Some will be married, engaged, gay, playing games or not particularly interested in you. That goes with the territory of being single and on the prowl.

"You must sit down" says Love,
"and taste My meat."
So I did sit and eat.
George Herbert
"Love"

For example, you might go to the local laundromat every week when you know that there's usually a number of unattached White males washing their socks under the pretext of gathering information about White males, but avoid making eye contact with them, week after week, and sit all the while at the far end of the laundromat, visibly engrossed in a romance novel while wearing radio headphones to advertise that you do not want to tune into anyone who might notice you. That is window shopping. At some point you must stop window shopping and go to the checkout counter, or at least walk around the store to peruse what's available. Don't miss the boat.

Proactively Coping With Depression

"Those who do not observe the movements of their own minds must of necessity be unhappy."
Marcus Aurelius
The Meditations Of Marcus Aurelius

Everybody feels down now and then. Depression is a natural reaction to bad circumstances or a bad life situation. Sometimes you can feel hit pretty hard by events such as being dumped by someone, or a string of bad events, such as being used and thrown away by several men in a row. Things like that would depress anybody. Feeling bad for a day, or a week, after a breakup or rejection is natural reaction to such situations. Take some time out. Your depressed thoughts will eventually wear a groove in the mind, become stale, you will stop thinking those thoughts and you will emerge from your funk. After a few days, you'll feel it's time to go out on the prowl again and look for some positive experiences to overlay your depressed feelings and recharge your batteries. Your batteries will not recharge when you wallow in the mud. The right guy is out there somewhere, and wallowing in depression will not bring him any closer.

Depression reduces your level of motivation by virtue of being a powerful, if negative, emotion that decreases your interest in activities other than experiencing depression. You can accelerate the speed of your departure from a spell of depression by deliberately exposing yourself to positive experiences to overlay the mental watermark of depression. Even better, actively seek out other things to dwell on besides the many sad tales of your life. Taking the passive approach and waiting for positive people and events to come your way of their own accord, with no active intervention on your part, means things will take longer to improve, because you waste time waiting for things to come your way by chance, as opposed to getting out and making things happen.

Books And Music

"Why music was ordained! Was it not to refresh the mind."
William Shakespeare
The Taming Of The Shrew

You can accelerate your departure from a state of depression by introducing new, positive influences into your life to induce positive states of mind. Books and music are simulated experiences, in the sense that reading or listening to music is like injecting your mind with some measure of the states of mind of the writers of books and composers of music. Exposure to a book or music induces a mental simulation of that writer's or composer's experience or vision, creating sympathetic vibrations in your own mind. Books and music are thus pipelines into an endless variety of other individuals' minds, a selection among which you are bound to find some offering at least partial answers to improving your own state of mind and adding value to your life.

Music stirs the emotions, and is particularly important for transmitting positive states of mind. While books can pass along various sorts of useful information and improve one's rational understanding of life, music conveys something closer to a real emotional experience than books usually provide, because music uses a different language to find its way to a different part of our minds than books. Listen to music and composers that have something positive to say about life.

While it is true that life is sometimes a book with many sad chapters, that does not obligate you to take up any of those burdens on your shoulders. No matter how much misery is out there, you are free to ignore the misery and pick and choose what you allow into your mind. You are not obligated to take on a quota of misery, and you are least of all obligated to spend your money on books or music that might reinforce your bad feelings. Don't listen to music that puts down Black women or says that our lives are predestined to be a vale of tears, and don't read books that run contrary to your aims and aspirations.

"Music be the food of love."
William Shakespeare
What You Will

There's so much positive music and so many positive books out there that there is no reason to allow yourself be infected by anything negative. Negative books and music pass along only minuses, with no pluses or advantages offered to compensate for the damage they do. While any one book or piece of music will not make or break you, the cumulative effect of large numbers of little negative inputs year after year is to depress your outlook on life more than might have been the case without those influences. There's an endless variety of positive music out there, from Beethoven to the Beatles, and no need to waste even one second on rap music or any other form of music that induces depressed outlooks on life, negative states of mind, and negative opinions about women. You become what you think about all day, so pick and choose what you let into your mind.

Reading negative books makes it hard to put your depressed state of mind behind you. For example, should you just recently have gotten out of a bad relationship, reading books about divorces and the like reinforces your preexisting negative state of mind, rather than injecting new thoughts and new ideas into the closed loop of your depressing thoughts. If you have no idea what books might be worthwhile, one time-tested fallback option is the classic novels, plays and poetry available in libraries and as inexpensive reprints in bookstores.

There's something out there for almost every taste, from Shakespeare's comedies and sonnets, to Oscar Wilde's stage plays and Elizabeth Barrett Browning's love poems. Expose yourself to some of the best-expressed thoughts of the best writers and you will find that some of their ideas start to rub off on you. If it comes down to filling your mind with either the thoughts of rap music performers or those of the best poets, playwrights and composers of really good music, whose ideas would you allow to take up mental space and float around for years to come in the back of your mind?

"Stick to the best established books in every language; the celebrated poets, historians, orators, or philosophers."
Philip Stanhope, Earl of Chesterfield
Letters To His Son

Life Is What Your Everyday Thoughts Make It

"The thought is always prior to the fact."
Ralph Waldo Emerson
"History"

Whatever the specific nature of the thoughts that pass through your mind all day, in the final analysis they determine what sort of person you are and what sort of person you become. What you think about all day long continually shapes your future in a thousand unseen ways by virtue of those thoughts inserting themselves into your deepest realms of consciousness and thereafter guiding your thoughts and actions. Thoughts exert a cumulative influence on you by either pushing you to orient your life in the direction of those thoughts or holding you back from making changes in other directions. Thinking about something positive pulls your actions along in the direction of those thoughts, by virtue of creating hundreds of mental associations that pull, and subtly guide, your actions in the direction of your positive thoughts.

For example, dwelling on the positive aspects of interracial dating digs a channel in the mind for potential actions to flow in. Once you tune into the possibility of interracial dating, you automatically drift to thinking about matters such as places to go to make it happen. Thinking about it provides your subconscious with the catalyst for building a mental framework to attract relevant information and for taking action. Thoughts blaze the path in which actions follow, and thoughts about interracial dating are no exception.

Many of your thoughts on various subjects have been absorbed, unfiltered, from the external world. You can't consciously filter everything to which you are exposed. One example is the hundreds of advertisements on billboards, t-shirts, newspapers, television and radio you see and hear every day. You can't consciously dwell on all of that advertising and expect to have any psychological energy left over for other things.

Informational inputs come into your eyes and ears and get sent to your subconscious, which junks a lot of it, incorporates some relevant material and indiscriminately absorbs some random items. The end result is that, while you may actively think about selected subjects, you mentally incorporate a lot of second-hand information and opinions without debate or analysis. When something not of your choosing enters your mind, unintended consequences follow in their wake.

As a result, we take on some characteristics of the people and environments to which we are exposed. Living in a tough neighborhood can make you think that the world in general is a tough place, and you adapt yourself to fit into the world you think is around you. On the other hand, should you see the world as a place offering the potential for positive experiences, you are likely to focus your energies on seeking out positive experiences and adapting to live in a positive environment. It makes no difference what mental route you follow in getting to this point, whether your vision is accurate or inaccurate, or whether those thoughts were of internal or external origin. Whatever the nature of the thoughts that pass through your head, they determine the sort of person you are and will become. Your subconscious automatically fills in the blank spots in your view of the world and personality using the raw material that comes into your head every day.

You subconsciously piece together your self-image from your informational inputs and emerge with a level of motivation commensurate with your self-image. Should you think little of yourself, your mental framework of a poor self-image comes packaged with a low motivation level that operates to box you in by making it difficult to bring sufficient psychological energy to bear to change that self-image. A poor self-opinion forces you to trim yourself down to a low level of motivation consistent with a poor self-opinion. Falling into certain kinds of psychological ruts thus leaves you no motivational energy with which to make your escape.

Should you become a rolling stone gathering low self-regard in rolling through life, the negative motivational energy accumulated with that low self-regard becomes increasingly, and thoroughly, integrated into your personality and ever more difficult to shake off. You get too much experience and practice invested in staying as you already are to attempt change, like a hypochondriac whose entire lifestyle is organized around having supposed sicknesses. You wind up burning huge amounts of energy remaining consistent with your self-image and blocking urges and temptations that beckon you elsewhere. The depressing, inhibiting circumstances of your daily life leave you too drained to accumulate sufficient motivational energy to move on to better things. Hence, be careful about what you let into your head or you might develop a victim mentality. Don't define yourself in terms of your environment or other people's opinions and expectations. Screen out what you don't want.

Screen Out Psychological Garbage

"Such as are thy habitual thoughts, such also will be the character of thy mind, for the soul is dyed by the thoughts."
Marcus Aurelius
The Meditations Of Marcus Aurelius

Computer programmers say that feeding garbage into a computer as raw data results in garbage coming out the other end of the information processing system. The same principle applies to your mind, which works in a similarly predictable way: garbage in, garbage out. Feed endless negative information about yourself and life in general into your head all day, or allow your environment to feed it into your head, and endless negativism accumulate. Should all of the information that enters your head be negative, your subconscious will distill such negative inputs into a negative self-image. This will slow you down in dating interracially, because interracial dating requires going against the grain of a number of social customs, a difficult endeavor for those with low self-confidence.

Low self-regard reduces your enjoyment of life by making it less likely that you will seek out positive experiences such as interracial dating due to hesitation that such things are right for you and also makes you feel that you don't even deserve to enjoy life or have positive experiences come your way.

You are involuntarily exposed to many things that make you infer low self-regard. Maybe you have a boss who always tells you that you're stupid and should never do anything on your own without first getting the boss' permission. Maybe you are forced into daily contact with a relative with an ax to grind about not being able to get ahead because Whites in general conspire to keep Blacks down. The more you are exposed to things like this without countervailing influences, the more such junk gets pumped into your head and winds up being used as raw material for your self-regard, your confidence in your own judgment and your perceived freedom to seek satisfaction of your tastes.

Whatever your mind absorbs sets down roots in keeping with the mental framework for sorting and routing new information already in place. Should you think poorly of yourself, whatever positive inputs come in get classified as irrelevant to your preexisting mental framework, which deems you unworthy to think such thoughts. Conversely, should you think highly of yourself, your mind automatically disregards and filters out incoming negative ideas because they are difficult to integrate with preconceptions. Be it or good or bad, your self-opinion sets down roots and spreads out to encompass your entire personality, guiding you into lines of thought and action consistent with your self-opinion.

What do you do if nearly everything you are exposed to at home, on the job and in the neighborhood is bad news? There are two possibilities. First, screen out, avoid and seal yourself off from, as many negative inputs as possible. This includes people as well as books, magazines, newspapers, music and anything else that might slow you down. Don't mix poison into your food, and don't let psychological garbage into your mind. The world is full of losers who've given up on life and who put all of their energies into defending their personal status quo to the effect that life is hopeless, things won't change, and so on. Whatever the particular details of their monologues, they want to hook you into sharing their vision of life. Misery loves company, and the more miserable they are the more they want company to ratify the validity of their mindset. Examples might include a divorced relative who says, because she got divorced, that you should never trust any men. A fire-and-brimstone preacher who says that we should spend our lives apologizing for the sin of being born is another example of the kind of person who can steer you wrong.

The world is full of parasites who will drain every last erg of energy from you if you make the mistake of giving them an opening. Whatever the particular nature of their problems, they never have the right to impose those problems on you. Give them an inch, and they'll take a mile, so don't give them an opening in the first place. Your good manners should end where their bad manners begin, and imposing their problems on you is definitely bad manners. Even if you are successful in beating back their assaults on your time and psychological energies, fighting a war with them every day with such people can leave your warehouse of psychological energy empty. Save your energy for the things that count and people who count, not the cockroaches of the social environment.

Second, it is not enough to just screen out negative people and influences. You have to put something into take their place. You can't leave a blank spot in your mind for long, or else whatever sort of mental mortar happens to be floating around will slip in and your efforts will be to no avail. Negative things will start creeping back into your mind, because you are used to having some kind of self-image, good or bad, and not having one allows negative things to re-establish influence. By changing the overall pattern of what you allow into your life and your mind, you start tilting the balance in a different direction.

Problem people are best dealt with by excluding them from every possible part of your life, to the extent that your personal circumstances permit. Don't be ashamed to be judgmental. They have obviously passed judgment on you to the effect that they feel free to victimize you, impose on you and disrupt your life and thought processes. They want to divert you from the good things in life without offering anything to compensate you. Wherever and whenever possible, seal them off as if they were carriers of infectious diseases. You have an unlimited right to screen undesirable people and influences out of your life.

After The Dust Settles

"Thus I drink of life's great cup of wonder!"
Elizabeth Barrett Browning
Sonnets From The Portugese

It's easier to motivate yourself to do something new, like interracial dating, when it fits into the overall pattern of your life. It creates much less friction that way, and the less friction, the easier and more enjoyable it becomes. You have the energy to do positive things because you don't waste your energy combating negatives influences that you keep out of your path. Create a new pattern for your life that encourages interracial dating, or at least which excludes negative influences.

Life will look different after you push the assorted motivational barriers that block pursuit interracial relationships out of your life. The landscape will look different without the smog that once cluttered up your field of vision. You'll see things more clearly, and the road ahead will beckon you. Without the dead weight of negativism that once diverted your energies, you can jog along to wherever the interracial relationships rainbow leads you. While life offers no guarantees, at the very least, your vision of what life offers will be unimpeded by unwanted mental baggage and distractions, and you will feel free to close in on the opportunities life offers for seeking out positive feelings and people.

"Your heart's desires be with you."
William Shakespeare
As You Like It

Made in the USA
Monee, IL
20 September 2021